Memoirs of an Arabian Princess

By Emily Ruete,
born Sayyida Salme bint Said bin Sultan Al Bu Said,
Princess of Oman and Zanzibar

An Accurate Translation of Her Authentic Voice
from the 19th Century German
by Her Descendant, Andrea Emily Stumpf

The translated text contained in this publication comes from the first and second volumes of *Memoiren einer arabischen Prinzessin*, published by the Friedrich Luckhardt publishing company of Berlin, Germany, in 1886 under the authorship of Emily Ruete, originally known as Sayyida Salme bint Said bin Sultan Al Bu Said, Princess of Oman and Zanzibar. The translated text incorporates subsequent edits from her marked copy provided by her son, Rudolph Said-Ruete, to the Oriental Institute in Leiden in 1937. This collection was moved as a permanent loan to the Netherlands Institute for the Near East (NINO) in 1977 and became a part of the Leiden University Libraries in 2018.

www.sayyidasalme.com; www.emilyruete.com

ISBN 978-1-7323975-3-8
Library of Congress Control Number

To Martin M. Stumpf

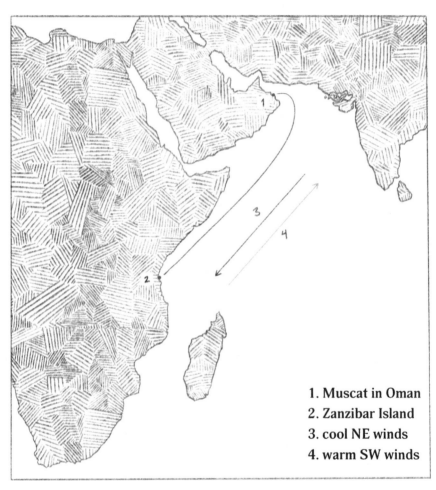

1. Muscat in Oman
2. Zanzibar Island
3. cool NE winds
4. warm SW winds

Indian Ocean monsoon trade winds

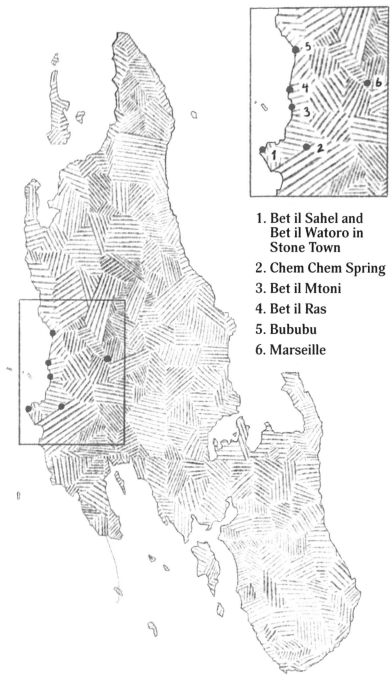

1. Bet il Sahel and
   Bet il Watoro in
   Stone Town
2. Chem Chem Spring
3. Bet il Mtoni
4. Bet il Ras
5. Bububu
6. Marseille

Zanzibar in the 19th century

CONTENTS

Introduction:

Memoirs of an Arabian Princess

— see the detailed table of contents on the facing page —

From the translator:

Memoirs of an Arabian Princess, translated from the original German:

ON CONTEXT AND CONTENT

Sayyida Salme—Princess Salme, Emily Ruete—surely knew, in her lifetime, that she was special. Born into the household and harem of the great Sayyid Said, venerated Sultan of Oman and ruler of Zanzibar, she grew up with the rank and privilege of royalty. But it was more than her station in life that made her stand out. Living forthrightly, she crossed color and culture lines, religious beliefs, country boundaries, and global hemispheres, all of which gave her exceptional insights and made her a remarkable resource.

To her great credit, she wrote about it and then decided to share it, her own story in her own words, written with care, perspective, and incisive commentary. She promised readers upfront that she would speak authentically, knowing they might not approve of all she had to say, but committing to accurate descriptions and frank observations, as best she could. In eloquent prose, she recounted her life growing up in Zanzibar as an unconventional daughter amidst scores of siblings and *sarari* (concubines), subject to all the rules and rituals of a Muslim household that became prone to political intrigue. And then she did the unthinkable, which set her on an extraordinary path from East to West.

When her *Memoiren einer arabischen Prinzessin* came out in Germany in 1886, she was—we believe—the first ever female Arab author of a commercially available book. The book immediately garnered great interest, was re-issued four times that year, and then quickly translated into English, with appearances in the United Kingdom and United States in 1888 to more popular acclaim. Today she remains an icon of inspiration.

Sayyida Salme crossed a first boundary early on when she secretly taught herself to write, something young girls were not supposed to do. But her literary significance begins with her mother Djilfidan, who had also outdone her contemporaries, the other *sarari* in the harem, by learning how to read. Sayyida Salme describes how her mother's unusually early entry into the harem at age seven or eight let her learn to read with the young princes and princesses, unlike the others who arrived mature enough to have no interest in school classes for youngsters. An enduring image for Sayyida Salme was her mother going from room to room, with books in hand, to read religious verses to the sick. What a wonderful image, words on a page as a salve for the ill, nurturing the body and soul in times of need.

Sayyida Salme was unique and unusual in many ways; indeed, special enough to still be among us today. Could she have imagined that her book and name would be so widely known all these many decades and generations later? Naturally, her *Memoirs* are a national treasure for Omanis and Zanzibaris, even many East Africans, whose cultures, conventions, and historical leaders are depicted in intimate detail. But the nineteenth-century story still fascinates and resonates far beyond those shores, even experiencing an uptick of interest in this post-modern age. Not only is her book still being read after more than 130 years, but it has generated a whole cottage industry of readily available reprints and reissues. Her detailed accounts are mined word-for-word and worldwide by scholars of history, sociology, anthropology, ethnography, semiotics, race relations, feminism, colonialism, Arab studies, African studies, and more.

Even her name signals something out of the ordinary. Born Salme, she later took the name Emily in a Christian baptism and Ruete in a Christian marriage, both on the same day. Thereafter she presented herself as Emily Ruete and signed the *Memoirs* Preface as "Emily Ruete, born Princess of Oman and Zanzibar." But she notably also placed her Arabic signature on the title page of her *Memoirs*, thus presenting her Arab self as the author. Over time, she kept both names close, one surely of necessity while living in Germany, the other intrinsic to her identity.

Beyond her double name that doubled her identity, we can see her in an array of other dualities. She was the consummate insider who became the observant outsider, the rare bird that flew the coop. She got caught in the currents of colonialism—first aided, then cornered, then jilted by the one power; useful, and then discarded by the other power. She changed her religion in good faith and remained a woman of great faith, even though she was condemned for giving up her Muslim faith. Split in two, she personified the bridge between East and West, but had to find strength in herself, as she lost her foothold on the one side and secured only weak moorings on the other. From young princess to young widow, she moved from a patriarchal dynasty to a patriarchal society—one box here, another box there—always finding her rights and agency curtailed. She was a pawn much of her life, driving her own destiny, but caught in the webs of other people and powers. And with that, she went from the height of privilege and prosperity to the edge of depression and poverty. Even so, she outlived every one of her many Sultanate siblings and lived vigorously to tell the tale.

The comparisons let Sayyida Salme see more clearly. Experiencing the West through the prism of the East, she perceived flaws and foibles of both Occident and Orient more directly. In this, she found a mission. Long before the technologies that now enable our extensive, pervasive, worldwide sharing, she sought to promote multicultural understanding. In her *Memoirs* lies a quest against disinformation, pushing back against caricatures and lockstep common wisdom. She was especially aware that her original culture and context were heavily shielded from the world. She also realized that cultures and customs tend to be self-validating when there is no awareness of alternatives.

Sayyida Salme handed us the intimate renderings of a most fantastical existence, one that reads like a fairy tale and a thriller, but in fact reflects a real life. And so, her story intrigues even as it engages. Her upbringing is out of this world, but still gives us mirrors and markers for our time. We see, for example, the unacceptable views of someone who grew up in a caste system and slave society, even as we continue our own struggles with questions of equality. Today's society has progressed, but there are still places where girls are not fully educated, and women cannot freely dress or vote; the list goes on. Then, too, Sayyida Salme reminds us that some challenges are nigh on eternal. There is no escaping hard choices when loving someone becomes a series of existential trade-offs, and we are all vulnerable to hard times when losing someone results in life-changing loss.

The value of Sayyida Salme's account lies in her dedication to fact, not fiction. She sought authenticity, not duplicity or publicity. She knew she was touching on sensitive subjects, but chose to speak her truth. As she wrote in the Afterword of her London edition from 1888, this was to be a "faithful recollection" and an "unvarnished reflection," which she saw as a way to contribute her share.

Against this backdrop, it is perhaps no wonder that I would step up, in my own small way, to offer a new translation, intended to replace prior inaccurate and archaic translations, so as to revive her true story as she told it. Could Sayyida Salme have imagined that a fourth-generation descendant would seek to restore and refresh her authentic voice? Could she have contemplated that her great-great-granddaughter, yet another continent over, would embark on a lifetime of lawyering, authoring, and love of language to prime herself for this project? I was born into German and English the way Sayyida Salme was born into privilege. Having both languages is a natural fit. Here, with this translation, I hope to make the most of it.

Sayyida Salme originally wrote these *Memoirs* for her children, but offered them to us all:

> *And so, too, may my book travel into the world and find many friends, as I have been so blessed to do. (*Memoirs, *page 1)*

The world was already getting smaller then. The importance of knowing and appreciating each other, across continents and cultures, was already on her mind. How now, that I can reach back into history to revive her revelatory voice, could she ever have suspected that these accurate and authentic *Memoirs* might be on your doorstep within two days, or (coming soon) immediately on your tablet! And in this way, may Sayyida Salme continue to find new friends throughout the world and into time.

Andrea E. Stumpf
October 2022

Memoiren

einer arabischen

Prinzessin

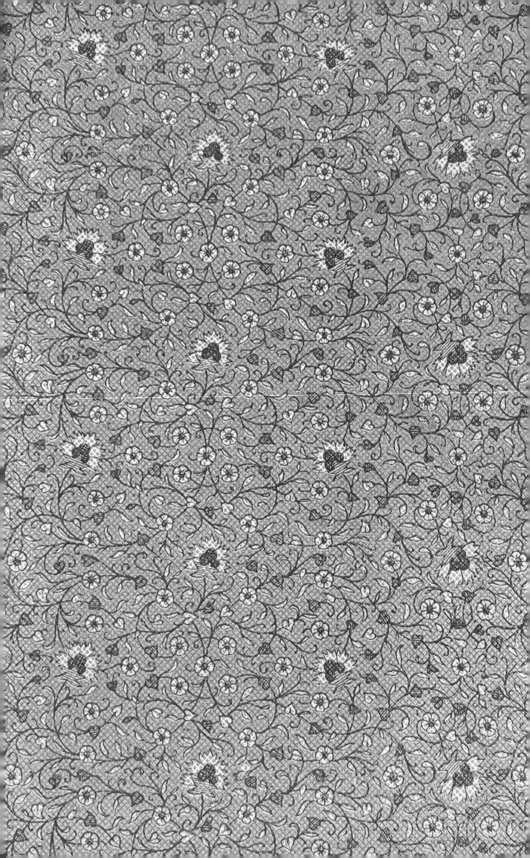

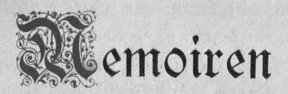

Memoiren

einer

arabischen Prinzessin.

—⟶ Erster Band. ⟵—

Dritte Auflage.

Berlin.

Verlag von Friedrich Luckhardt.

1886.

Memoirs of an
Arabian Princess

Volume 1

On the preceding pages, the end paper and title page are from an original edition of Volume 1 that belonged to either Rosa Troemer, the author's youngest daughter, or a member of her family. The bookplate on the previous page is from Emily Troemer, the author's granddaughter and the translator's grandmother.

All footnotes in the following pages were added by the translator.

PREFACE

————— · · —————

Nine years ago, I was inspired to recount some of my experiences for my children, who otherwise knew nothing about my past, except that I was Arab and came from Zanzibar. Physically and emotionally spent, I did not expect to last long enough to see them into adulthood to then tell them about my fateful journey and childhood memories. I therefore decided to write up my experiences and undertook the project with great love and dedication, knowing it was for my dear children, whose tenderness had comforted me during long and troubled years and whose deep empathy had sustained me through my trying times.

As such, my Memoirs were not originally written for the whole world, but as a testament of enduring love from a mother to her children. After much encouragement from others, I finally decided to have them published.

These pages were already completed years ago; only the last chapter was recently added. It describes the trip to Zanzibar, my old homeland, that my children and I were privileged to take last year. So, too, may my book travel into the world and find many friends, as I have been so blessed to do.

Berlin, May 1886
Emily Ruete
born Princess of Oman and Zanzibar

Bet il Mtoni

CHAPTER ONE

Bet il Mtoni

It was in Bet il Mtoni, our oldest palace on the island of Zanzibar, that I was born in 1844 and lived until the age of seven.

Bet il Mtoni lies on the sea, about eight kilometers from the city of Zanzibar, in a most lovely setting, completely hidden away in a grove of majestic coconut palms, mango trees, and other tropical giants. The name of my birthplace, "Mtoni House," is from the little river Mtoni, which comes from the interior several hours away and streams through the whole palace in numerous basin-like extensions before emptying directly behind the palace walls into the wonderful, well-trafficked sea channel that separates the island from the African mainland.

A single, expansive courtyard fills the space between the various buildings that make up Bet il Mtoni. With a hodgepodge of structures that was built over time to meet the needs, and countless hallways and corridors that would merely confuse the uninitiated, the place is more ugly than pretty.

The rooms in our palace are also too many to count. Their layout slips my memory, though I clearly recall the spacious baths at Bet il Mtoni. Half a dozen bathhouses, all in a row, lay on the far side of the courtyard, so far off that when it rained, these beloved resorts could be reached only with the help of an umbrella. Off to the side was what we called the "Persian" bath, which was in fact a stand-alone Turkish steam bath whose masterful design was unmatched on the island.

Each bathhouse contained two basins about four meters long and three meters wide. The water level was set to reach chest-high for adults.

These bathhouses and their refreshing baths were very popular with all the residents. Most of them spent many hours a day there, praying, sleeping, working, reading—or even eating and drinking. From four in the morning until midnight, the traffic here never stopped. Day and night, people could be seen heading in and out.

At the entrances of these identical bathhouses, there were elevated resting areas on both sides immediately to the right and left, covered with the finest colorful mats, with verses woven into them, on which to pray or simply rest. No one is allowed to wear shoes on these elevated places, since that would be considered unholy. Rugs and all other luxury items are also banned from these rooms. To pray, Muslims (Mohammedans) are supposed to wear special, completely clean outfits intended only for this purpose and, if possible, all in white. Of course, this rather inconvenient religious prescription is strictly observed by only the most pious.

Narrow colonnades separate these resting areas from the bathing basins, which lie fully exposed under open skies. Steps on two arched stone bridges lead upwards from the basins to other completely segregated rooms.

Every bathhouse had its own designated occupants, and woe to anyone who failed to strictly observe these distinctions! Bet il Mtoni had a pronounced caste system that was impeccably followed by everyone, from high to low.

VUE DE M'TONI, RÉSIDENCE DE CAMPAGNE DU SULTAN
prise de la pièce d'eau

Orange trees as tall as the largest cherry trees here[1] bloomed in dense rows across the full expanse of the bathhouses. As young children, we often enough sought protection and refuge amidst their branches from our very strict teacher.

People and animals mingled quite comfortably throughout the immense courtyard, without bothering each other in the least. Peacocks, gazelles, guinea fowls, flamingos, geese, ducks, and ostriches roamed freely and were petted and fed by young and old alike. It was always a great delight for us youngsters to collect the many eggs here and there, especially the big ostrich eggs, and deliver them to the head cook, who would then reward us for our efforts with various treats.

Two times a day, early morning and evening, eunuchs gave children five years and older riding lessons in the courtyard, while our little zoo inhabitants kept undisturbed about their business. Upon completing enough basic training, we each received our own mounts from the father.[2] The boys could choose their horses from the royal stables, while the girls got large, snow-white donkeys from Muscat, which were often more valuable than the regular horses. These beautiful creatures were, of course, provided with the complete trappings. Virtually all the bridles consisted of heavy silver chains and other accessories.

Riding is a favorite pastime in family houses like these, since there are neither plays nor concerts to provide entertainment. Competitive races were often organized out in the open, although they unfortunately rather frequently ended in mishaps. Such a race even came close to costing my own life. Riding with complete zeal, so as not to let my brother Hamdan overtake me, I failed to see a mighty, oddly bent palm tree that suddenly blocked my way. Not until the trunk was directly in front of my forehead did I register the unexpected obstacle. In sudden alarm, I threw myself backwards and, as if by a miracle, escaped the looming danger.

An oddity of Bet il Mtoni was its many staircases, with steps of unrivalled steepness fit for a Goliath. Most of them headed straight up, without room to pause, turn, or pass, and practically the only way to reach the top was to grab onto rather primitive handrails. The stairwell traffic was so lively that these railings were in constant need of repair. I still remember the morning that residents in our wing were shocked to discover both handrails of our stone stairs, which were already so daunting, had collapsed in the middle of

---

1   "Here" in this case means Germany, where the author was living at the time.
2   "The father" was Sayyid Said bin Sultan, the Sultan of Oman and ruler of Zanzibar from 1806 to 1856.

the night. I marvel to this day that no one was hurt on these stairs, despite the enormous traffic at all hours.

Statistics being unknown in Zanzibar, no one really knew how many people actually lived in Bet il Mtoni. Were I to hazard a guess, all in all, I do not think a thousand inhabitants would overstate the case. To understand this, it is important to remember that in the Orient[3] one must occupy an extraordinary number of hands to be considered wealthy and well-off. Our father's other palace in the city, Bet il Sahel, also known as the "Beach House," had no fewer residents.

My father, Sayyid Said, the Imam of Muscat and Sultan of Zanzibar, along with his principal wife, a distant relative, resided in the wing of Bet il Mtoni that lay closest to the sea. He spent only four days a week here in the countryside, with the rest of the week spent in his city palace, Bet il Sahel. The title "Imam" is a religious honor that is very rarely bestowed on a ruler. We owe this distinction originally to my great-grandfather, Ahmed. Since then, this title has become hereditary for the whole family, and we are all entitled to add it to our signatures.

As one of my father's younger children, I only ever knew him with his venerable, snow-white beard. Somewhat taller than average, he had in his countenance something extraordinarily winsome and endearing, and yet his appearance commanded the utmost respect. Despite reveling in war and conquest, he was exemplary for all of us as the head of the family and ruler of his people. Nothing mattered more to him than justice, and he made no distinction between his own son and a simple slave when addressing possible transgressions. Above all, he was the definition of humility before God the Almighty. He had no trumped-up pride, unlike so many others of rank. Modest and with few needs for himself, he was charitable and generous toward others. He also appreciated when the people around him were well-dressed, cheerful, and in good spirits. I never saw him angry with anyone or heard him berate them. He had a good sense of humor and loved to put on a good joke. And yet, he was a great authority figure for young and old. If there was one thing he did not like, it was wastefulness. —If an ordinary slave that had gained his respect over many years of loyal service got married, it was not unusual for him to get his horse saddled, so he could ride out completely on his own to extend his personal congratulations to the young couple. —He always called me the "Old One" for my love of cold milk soup (Arabic *farni*), a dish favored by many of our toothless seniors.

---

3   The author places Zanzibar in the Orient relative to Germany in the Occident, the East relative to the West, and the South to the North. As understood in the nineteenth century, these geographical terms were laden with cultural and religious differences that also spawned no shortage of clichés and stereotypes.

My mother, a Circassian by birth, was torn from her homeland already at a young age. She had been living peacefully with her father, mother, and two siblings on the family farm. Then war broke out, marauding bands rampaged across the land, and the whole family fled to an underground location, per my mother's description. She apparently meant a cellar, something we did not have in Zanzibar. A wild horde penetrated even this refuge. They struck down the father and mother, and then three Arnauts galloped off with the three siblings. The one with her older brother soon disappeared from view. The two others with my mother and her three-year-old sister, who could not stop crying for her mother, stayed together until nightfall when they, too, separated. My mother never heard anything more of her siblings.

My mother was still a child when she came into my father's possession, probably already at the tender age of seven or eight, since she lost her first tooth in our house. From the start, until maturity, she was paired as a playmate with two of my sisters[4] her age and raised and cared for the same as them. She also learned how to read with them, a skill that set her apart from those of her rank, many of whom had arrived at age sixteen to eighteen, if not older, and were naturally in no mood to join very young children on hard school mats. She was not that attractive, but tall and strong, with black eyes and black hair that reached to her knees. Gentle by nature, she derived her greatest pleasure from being able to help others and bring them joy. When someone got sick, she would be the first at their bedside and then care for them, as needed. I still see her before me, how she would go from one sick person to another, books in hand, to read them religious passages.

The father always had a special regard for her and never turned down her requests, which she usually made on behalf of others. He would regularly walk towards her when she came to him, a recognition that was very rare. With a good and pious disposition, she had a most self-effacing manner and was sincere and open in all things. Although not particularly gifted intellectually, she was very proficient in her needlework. She gave birth to only two children, namely a daughter who died at a very young age, in addition to myself. She was a tender, loving mother to me, although that never stopped her from punishing me vigorously when necessary.

She had many friends in Bet il Mtoni, which is not the norm in an Arab harem. Her faith in God could not have been more steadfast and solid. I still remember

---

4   The author refers to sisters and brothers who are, in fact, half-sisters and half-brothers, all sharing the same father, but with different *sarari* mothers. Since she was one of the youngest, it made sense that some of her siblings were the same age as her mother.

a fire that broke out on a moonlit night in and around the adjacent royal stables when I was perhaps no more than five years old, while the father and his retinue were in the city. When a false alarm rang through our house that it, too, was in immediate danger of being engulfed by the fire, my good mother had nothing more urgent to do than take me under one arm and her large, handwritten Kurân (that is how we pronounce the word) under the other and rush out into the open. Nothing else had any particular value for her in this hour of peril.

As best I can recall, my father had but two wives equal to his rank in my time. The other wives or *sarari (*singular *surie*),[5] which numbered seventy-five at his death, were all purchased by him over time. His principal wife, Azze bint Sef, a born princess of Oman, was the absolute mistress of the house. Although very small in stature and outwardly very plain, she exerted unbelievable power over my father, such that he always acceded to her demands. As far as the other women and their children, she was exceedingly imperious, arrogant, and demanding. Fortunately for us, she had no children of her own, whose tyranny would have been unbearable. All my father's children—not more than thirty-six at his death—came from his concubines. We were therefore all equal amongst ourselves and had no need to dwell on the color of our blood.

Bibi (Swahili for lady-in-charge) Azze, whom everyone had to address as "Highness" (Arabic *Sayyida*), was feared by young and old, high and low, and loved by no one. Even today I remember her vividly, how she walked past us so stiffly, rarely addressing anyone in a friendly tone. How very different from my dear old father! He had something kind to say to everyone, regardless of rank. My superior stepmother knew only too well how to exert her entitled status, and no one dared come too close, unless they were invited to do so. I never saw her without her entourage, except when she went with the father to the private bathhouse that was exclusively for them. All who encountered her in the house were overcome with the same respect that a recruit pays a General in Europe.

Although we all felt the pressure she exerted from above, it was not enough to undermine the overall quality of life for the residents of Bet il Mtoni. Custom required that all my siblings, young and old, visit her at the start of each day to wish her a good morning. But everyone was so ill-disposed toward her that only rarely did anyone arrive before breakfast was delivered to her chambers,

---

5   Although the original German *Frau* can mean both woman and wife, Professor Abdul Sheriff, the widely respected Zanzibari historian and visionary promoter of local museums and archives, has clarified that *sarari* are considered wives—as he puts it, "secondary slave wives"—in contrast to Western-styled concubines, who have no such status. A. Sheriff, "*Suria*: Concubine or Secondary Slave Wife?—The Case of Zanzibar in the Nineteenth Century," in G. Campbell and E. Elbourne, *Sex, Power, and Slavery* (2014).

thereby denying her the pleasure of receiving the wholesale submission she demanded.

My oldest siblings lived in Bet il Mtoni. Some of them, like Shecha and Zuene, could have been my grandmothers. The latter already had a son, Ali bin Suud, whom I knew only with a speckled beard. She was a widow and had sought refuge in her parental home after her husband's passing.

In our family circle, we did not, as many here assume, favor sons over daughters. I do not know of a single case where the father or mother wanted a son over a daughter, or advantaged him just because he was a son. Nothing of the sort. Even though the law gives preference to boys over their sisters and affords them significant advantages—for example, in matters of inheritance where the sons get twice as much as the daughters—all children are nevertheless equally loved and cared for. That a particular child, both there in the South and here, whether boy or girl, might be a favorite, even if not overtly, is natural and certainly also human. And so it was with our father, except that his favorite children were clearly not sons, but two of his daughters, Sharife and Chole. Once, when I was about nine years old, my very rambunctious brother Hamdan, who was about my age, shot an arrow into my side, which fortunately caused no great harm. When the father learned of the incident, he told me: "Salme, go and get Hamdan for me." I had hardly arrived with my brother when he was subjected to a stream of invectives for being so reckless, words he would long remember. On this score, then, people here are very ill informed. Of course, it depends everywhere on the children themselves, and it would surely be very unfair to treat inconsiderate ones the same as considerate ones, without any noticeable difference between the two. —

The nicest spot at Bet il Mtoni was the *bendjle*, an immense, round balcony near the sea, in front of the main house, where one could have comfortably put on a grand ball, had such a thing been known to us or customary. The whole area was like a giant carousel, since even the ceiling, like the rest of the structure, was round. The entire framework, floor, and bannisters, as well as the tentlike ceiling, were made of painted wood. My dear father would spend hours here, pacing back and forth, head bent down, deep in thought. He limped a little. A bullet from the war, lodged in his thigh and a frequent source of pain, hindered the gait of this strong man.

Many cane chairs stood along the perimeter of the airy *bendjle*, surely several dozen, in addition to a powerful telescope for general use. But beyond that, nothing more. The view from this lofty balcony was breathtakingly beautiful. Multiple times a day, the father, Azze bint Sef, and all his adult children would

9

VUE DE M'TONY.

come for their coffee. Anyone seeking an undisturbed word with the father would look nowhere else but here, where he was mostly alone at certain hours.

All year round, the warship *Il Rahmani* lay at anchor across from the *bendjle*, with the sole purpose of sounding the cannon for us to wake up during the month of fasting and to man the many rowboats we needed. Signal flags were hoisted on a tall mast under the *bendjle* to order a larger or smaller number of boats and sailors to the shore.

As far as cooking is concerned, Bet il Mtoni, as well as Bet il Sahel, offered Persian and Turkish cuisine in addition to Arab cuisine. Indeed, the greatest diversity of races lived together in the two houses, amply reflecting the full range of looks from the most enchanting beauties to the complete opposite. But we were permitted to wear only Arab attire, and Africans only Swahili attire. Whenever a new Circassian showed up in her wide skirts, or an Abyssinian arrived in her fantastic robes, she had three days to put all that aside and start wearing her assigned Arab clothing.

Much in the same way that a hat and pair of gloves are indispensable for every proper woman here, the same is true for us with—jewelry. Jewelry is such a necessary part of a woman's presentation that even beggar women wear it when they beg. The father had his special coffers in both houses in Zanzibar, as well as his palace in Muscat in the kingdom of Oman, which were richly filled with large Spanish gold coins, British guineas, and French Louis d'ors. But they were also, and in greater part, filled with all sorts of women's accessories, from the plainest piece to a diamond-studded crown, all acquired to give as gifts. Whenever the family took on a new member, be it through the purchase of a *surie* or the frequent birth of a prince or princess, the door of the coffer would be opened to select a gift for the new arrival according to rank and station. When a child was born, the father would wait to visit the mother and child on the seventh day and then take along jewelry as a gift for the baby. A newly arrived *surie* would also receive the requisite items of jewelry right after being acquired, at the same time the head eunuch assigned her servants.

Although the father loved utter simplicity for himself, he was very particular about his overall environment. None of us, neither his children nor the youngest eunuch, were ever allowed to appear before him in anything less than our full attire. We little girls wore our hair braided into many thin plaits (often up to twenty). The ends from both sides were diagonally tied together in the center, and a heavy gold piece, often set with gemstones, was hung from the middle down the back. This hairpiece usually took the form of a crescent moon with a star set inside. Or sometimes a gold coin with holy verses was hung from each individual plait, which was a much more becoming look than the other one. At bedtime, nothing at all was removed except these specific jewelry pieces, which servants tied on again the next morning. We girls also wore bangs, exactly as one does here now, until the time we had to start masking daily. One morning, I ran undetected to the father without waiting for this hair adornment, so as to get the French candies he handed out to us children regularly at the start of every day. But instead of getting this much-desired treat, I was promptly sent back out because of my unfinished appearance, and a servant had to return me *nolens volens* from whence I had come. Ever after, I always took great care to never again show myself to him without being fully prepared.

My sister Zeyane and my stepmother Medine were among my mother's most intimate friends. Zeyane, the daughter of an Abyssinian, was practically the same age as my mother, and they loved each other indescribably dearly. My stepmother Medine was likewise a Circassian. This grounded the friendship, since she, my mother, and also Sara, another one of my stepmothers, all came from one and the same region. Sara's two children were my brother Madjid and my sister Chadudj (the ch is pronounced like the guttural German in *noch*, *doch*, etc.). The brother was a good bit younger than the sister. My mother had an understanding with her friend Sara that if Sara were to die first, my mother would care for Madjid and Chadudj as their second mother, and vice versa. But when Sara died, Chadudj and Madjid were already older and no longer needed my mother's help as long as they still lived in the paternal house. For us, which is to say my extended family, it was customary for the boys to remain with their mothers in the paternal house, entirely bound to the house rules, for some time after their boyhood. Once a prince reached the age of about eighteen to twenty, sooner or later depending on his good or bad conduct, the father would declare him of age. Then he could count himself among the adults, an honor he would have been awaiting with great impatience, there as here. At this time, every prince would then receive his own house, servants, horses, and all the rest, in addition to a sufficient monthly allowance.

My brother Madjid had now reached this point. He deserved the honor more for his overall character than his age. Madjid was the embodiment of modesty, and his kind and friendly manner won the hearts of everyone he encountered everywhere. Not a week went by that he did not ride out to us from the city (since he, like his mother before him, lived in Bet il Sahel, rather than Bet il Mtoni). Despite being about twelve years my senior, he still played with me as though we were one and the same age.

Thus he came to us one day, happy and excited, to let my mother know that the father had just declared him of age, set him on his own two feet, and given him his own house. Then he urgently entreated my mother that we, she and I, should now move into his new home to live with him and his sister there forever. Chadudj echoed the request. In response to this rousing appeal, my mother cautioned that she could not fulfill this wish without the father's permission, but would discuss the matter with him and then share the result. For her part, she was quite willing to live with them, if that was what they wanted. Madjid, however, offered to talk to the father himself, to spare my mother the effort. The next morning he returned with news that the father, who happened to be staying at Bet il Sahel, had approved Madjid's request. And with that, our move was decided. After lengthy consultations, my mother and Madjid agreed that we would move a few days later, so he and Chadudj could first settle somewhat into their new home.

RUINED PALACE OF SYED SAAID BEN SULTAN AT MTONY.

CHAPTER TWO

Bet il Watoro

My mother found it hard to follow through with the upcoming move. She was attached to Bet il Mtoni with heart and soul, having lived there since childhood. Her separation from my stepsister Zejane and my stepmother Medine was especially difficult. Nor did she relish change. But, as she told me later herself, the feeling that she might be of use to the children of her deceased friend outweighed any personal misgivings.

No sooner did my mother's decision to move into the city become known than she was accosted everywhere she showed her face with calls of "Djilfidan (that is the name of my dear mother), are you so heartless as to leave us forever?" "Oh friends," she would answer, "it is not my will that I would leave you; it is fate that I should go."

I believe some readers may read the word "fate" and feel some pity towards me, or if nothing else, shrug their shoulders. But one must not forget that the author was a Muslim and raised this way. And I am of course telling the story of an Arab life, an Arab household, that is, a real Arab home, in which two concepts in particular were as yet unfamiliar: the word "chance" and materialism. A Muslim not only recognizes his God as his creator and keeper, but also feels the presence of the Lord at all times. He is certain that it is not his will, but the will of the Lord that comes to pass, in all things, large and small.

A few days went by as we got our things together. Then we awaited Madjid's return, since he wanted to manage our trip himself. Three siblings, two sisters and a brother, all about my age, had been my playmates in Bet il Mtoni. I was very sorry to leave them, especially little Ralub, who had become quite attached to me. On the other hand, I was elated by the prospect of saying good-bye to our new and inhumanely strict teacher forever. —

With the coming separation from our many friends and acquaintances, our large room became a beehive. Everyone brought farewell gifts according to their means and degree of attachment. People take this custom very seriously. All true Arabs insist on presenting gifts to their friends, even if they have virtually nothing to give. This even applies to Africans. I still recall a case in point from when I was very young. We had taken an outing from Bet il Mtoni to our plantations and were in the process of boarding our many boats for the trip home. Suddenly I felt a tug from behind and saw a little old African lady beckoning to me. She gave me something wrapped in banana leaves with the words: "This token is for you, *bibi jangu* (my mistress), for your departure; it is the first ripe harvest from in front of my house." I quickly opened the leaves and found a single, freshly-picked—corncob. I did not know this little old African lady at all, but it later turned out that she was an old protégée of my dear mother. —

Madjid finally arrived and informed my mother that the captain of the *Rahmani* had orders to send a cutter the next evening for both of us, plus another boat for our belongings and the people bringing us to the city.

My father happened to be in Bet il Mtoni on the day of our departure, so my mother took me to see him to say good-bye. We found him walking back and forth on the *bendjle*. Upon seeing us, he immediately came towards my mother. They were soon engrossed in a lively conversation about our trip. He ordered a eunuch standing on the side to bring some sweets and sharbet (fruit juice) for me, probably to redirect my endless questions. I was, of course, very excited and curious about our new home and generally about everything having to do with life in the city. Up to this point, if I recall correctly, I had been in the city only once before and then only briefly. That is why I did not know all my siblings, nor all my many stepmothers.

After that we went to the chambers of my venerable stepmother to take our leave from her as well. Azze bint Sef accorded us a standing farewell, honoring us in her own way, as she otherwise always stayed seated when receiving or dismissing. My mother and I were both allowed to take her delicate hand to our lips, before turning our backs on her forever.

Then we traipsed up and down many more stairs to shake hands with all our friends, but found barely half of them in their rooms. So my mother decided to say farewell to them altogether at the next regular prayer hour, where everyone would be in attendance.

At seven in the evening, our cutter, a large one reserved only for special occasions, docked under the *bendjle*. It was manned by fourteen sailors as oarsmen and adorned at the front and back with large, blood-red flags, our flag, which has no further insignia. A large baldachin, with side curtains to shelter the women and ward off potential rain, was draped above the back end of the ship, under which ten to twelve people could sit on silk cushions.

Old Djohar, one of my father's loyal eunuchs, came to tell us everything was ready. He and another eunuch had been ordered by the father, who was watching our departure from the *bendjle*, to accompany us on the trip. Djohar, as usual, took the helm. Our tearful friends followed us to the front door, and the call *wedâ, wedâ!* "farewell, farewell!" still rings in my ears to this day.

Our beach is relatively flat without a jetty. As a result, we had three different ways to get onto boats. One was to sit in an armchair and be carried out by sturdy slaves; another was to simply ride on their backs; or we could instead walk to the boat on a plank extended out from the dry sand. My mother used this last, more comfortable approach to get on board, supported on both sides by eunuchs walking next to her in the wet sand. Another eunuch carried me to the boat in his arms and deposited me at the helm next to my mother and old Djohar. A few colorful lanterns in our cutter, together with the shining stars, spread a truly magical shimmer. As our boat launched into motion, the fourteen oarsmen broke into the rhythm of a melancholy Arab song.

We took the usual route along the coast, while I, half lying on my mother, half resting on my cushions, soon dozed off. Suddenly I was startled from my sleep by a cacophony of voices calling my name. Greatly alarmed and still only half awake, I eventually realized that we had reached our destination, meaning I had slept my way through the whole trip. We stopped directly under the windows of Bet il Sahel, which were all lit up and filled with countless heads. All these spectators were my stepsiblings and their mothers, mostly as of yet unknown to me. Many of the siblings were younger and no less curious to meet me than I was to meet them. They were the ones, my mother explained, who had started calling my name from a distance, as soon as our boat had come into view.

We disembarked the same way we had embarked, and my young brothers gave me a more than rousing welcome. They bid us come with them, but my mother of course declined, as Chadudj, who was already standing at the window of her house, would have had to wait for us that much longer. I was terribly sad not to be able to join my young siblings right away, having looked forward to that for days, but I knew my mother well enough to know whatever she said and wanted was final. Despite her incomparable, selfless love for me, she was always and in all things very firm and resolute. She consoled me with the prospect of spending the whole day together at Bet il Sahel as soon as the father returned there.

And so we passed Bet il Sahel and continued on to Bet il Watoro, Madjid's house. It lay directly beside Bet il Sahel and had the same unobstructed view of the sea. Upon entering, we found my sister Chadudj waiting for us at the foot of the stairs. She gave us a very hearty welcome and then took us straight up to their rooms, where her favorite eunuch Eman soon arrived with all sorts of refreshments. Madjid was in the parlor with his friends, but came up when he heard we were there. Oh, how happy he was, our dear, noble Madjid, to welcome us into his home!

Our own room was of a moderate size and looked directly onto a mosque next door. It was set up like most Arab rooms and left nothing wanting. We needed only one room. Since dress changes happen in the bathroom, and nightwear is the same as our washable daywear, no separate rooms are needed as in Europe. For people both high and low, the bedroom is in the living room.

The rooms of those who are rich and high society tend to have the following arrangement: Persian carpets or the very finest, soft mats cover the floor. Whitewashed walls, of considerable width, feature correspondingly deep recesses from floor to ceiling that are divided into multiple compartments. Green painted, wooden boards further divide these compartments into a kind of shelving. Symmetrically arranged on these shelves are the very finest and most precious glass and porcelain objects. Nothing is too expensive for Arabs when it comes to decorating their shelves—finely polished glass, a nicely painted plate, a stylish pitcher, no matter the price tag. If it looks pretty, it will be bought.

Efforts are made to cover even the bare and narrow wall spaces between the compartments. They are inlaid with large mirrors that reach from the top of the divan, just slightly above floor level, all the way up to the ceiling. These mirrors are always custom-ordered by height and width from Europe. Muslims generally disapprove of pictures as imitations of divine creation, although they are more recently tolerated now and again. By contrast, clocks are much beloved, and houses often have extensive collections, sometimes placed above the mirrors, or in pairs on either side. —In the gentlemen's rooms, the walls are adorned with all sorts of valuable trophy weapons from Arabia, Persia, and Turkey, the kind of ornamentation with which every Arab man prefers to decorate his home, according to his rank and riches.

17

The great double bed made of what is known as rosewood and covered with wonderfully skilled carvings, a product of East Indian craftsmanship, stands in one corner. White gauze or tulle drapes the entire bed from above. Arab beds have very high legs. To access them more comfortably, one first steps onto a chair, or uses the hand of a chambermaid as a more natural step. The ample space beneath the bed is then often used as a sleep station by others as well, such as wet nurses of small children or caretakers of the sick.

Tables are quite rare and then only with people of the highest rank, in contrast to chairs, which abound in all sorts of styles and colors. Cabinets, wardrobes, and the like are also missing. We instead used a kind of coffer or case that usually had two or three drawers, plus a secret internal compartment for money and jewelry. Every room tended to have several of these very large chests, which were made of rosewood and beautifully adorned with thousands of tiny yellow brass nail heads.

Windows, and by day also doors, stay open all year round, the former closed up at most briefly now and again for rain. And that is why the phrase "there's a draft in the air" is never heard in those parts. —

I completely disliked our new apartment at the start. I missed my young siblings too much and then also found Bet il Watoro oppressively small and confined in comparison to the enormity of Bet il Mtoni. Am I now supposed to live here forever?, I incessantly asked myself those first days. Where do you want to sail your boats now? In a washtub? There was, of course, no little river like the Mtoni here, and water had to be brought in from a well outside the house. And when my dear, good mother, who would have preferred to give everything she owned to others, advised me to take those pretty sailboats that I loved so much and give them to my siblings in Bet il Mtoni, I initially wanted to hear nothing of it. In short, for the first time in my life, I felt very unhappy and bitterly sad.

My mother, on the other hand, immediately settled in and stayed busy all day long, organizing and arranging things with Chadudj, so that she also had no time for me. Good-hearted Madjid took care of me the most. The very next morning, he took me by the hand and showed me his whole house from top to bottom. But I could not find happiness in anything. I was indifferent to everything and implored my mother to return with me to Bet il Mtoni, to my dear siblings, very soon. Of course, there was no chance of that, all the more because she really was a great help to both of them.

Fortunately, I discovered that Madjid was a big animal lover, with a large collection of all sorts of live creatures in his house. Among them were masses of white rabbits, who left the house in a complete mess, to the dismay of Chadudj and my mother. He also kept a large number of fighting cocks from all over the world. I have never again seen such a huge collection, not even in a zoo.

In visiting his pets, I soon became Madjid's constant companion, as he let me join in all his passions with endless goodwill. Through his generosity, it did not take long for me to accumulate a troop of fighting cocks, which did wonders to ease my loneliness in Bet il Watoro. Almost daily, we would both stand in front of our matadors, which servants had to carry on and off. A cockfight can really be quite interesting. It keeps the spectators riveted, and the whole thing presents an entertaining, often highly comical, picture.

Later he also taught me how to fence with sword, dagger, and lance, and when we went to the countryside together, he showed me how to shoot with rifle and pistol. In short, he made me half an Amazon, to the great consternation of my dear mother, who wanted to know absolutely nothing of fencing or shooting. Of course, my interest in embroidery flagged by comparison. I much preferred handling all sorts of weapons to spending quiet hours on the bobbins making lace.

All these new activities, coupled with my total freedom—they had not yet found a new teacher for me—livened me up in short order, and I overcame my initial displeasure with "lonely" Bet il Watoro. Nor did my horseback riding suffer. Eunuch Mesrur had to follow Madjid's orders to continue my training.

My mother was unable to pay much attention to me, as she was kept very busy by Chadudj. So I became increasingly attached to an experienced Abyssinian by the name of Nuren, who also taught me some of her language. Of course, by now that is all forgotten. —

We stayed in regular contact with Bet il Mtoni. Whenever my mother went there with me, we were warmly received and cared for by our friends. Beyond that, our contact was limited to oral dispatches through our respective slaves. In the Orient, no one really enjoys composing letters, even those who have learned to write. Anyone of wealth and standing owns several slaves that can run hard and fast, who are used exclusively for this purpose. All these runners have to cover a good number of miles every day, but they are also especially well-treated and cared for. The very well-being of their owners depends on their honesty and discretion, knowing they will be relaying the most confidential of messages! It is not uncommon for a friendship to be destroyed forever because of an act of revenge by such a messenger. And yet, despite all this hardship, very few are motivated to learn to write and make themselves self-sufficient in life. Nowhere else does the phrase "just take it easy" mean as much as it does for us.

My sister Chadudj loved to entertain. Rarely did a weekday go by that the house was not full of guests from six in the morning until midnight. Guests that came for the day, and arrived as early as six, were received by house servants and ushered into a specific room for this purpose, to be subsequently greeted by the mistress of the house at more like eight or nine. Until then, women that had arrived early tended to use this room to resume their interrupted sleep. I will take the opportunity later in a separate chapter to report more fully on such visits by the ladies.

While it took no time for me to become attached to dear Madjid, I did not have the same success with Chadudj. As strict and imperious as she was, I never found it in me to love her fully. The contrast between her and noble Madjid was too great. I was not alone in this assessment. Anyone who knew the two siblings, also clearly knew which of the two was kinder. She could be especially cool, even off-putting, towards strangers, and thus managed to make even more enemies. Despite her reputation as a hostess, she strongly resisted anything new and unfamiliar and was always very unenthused when a European woman came calling, even if such visits lasted at most half to three quarters of an hour.

Beyond that, she was, by our standards, extremely prudent and practical. She almost never sat still, and, when she had nothing else to do, sewed and embroidered the clothes of her married slaves' children as diligently as her brother's fine shirts. Among these children were three of the sweetest boys, whose father served as our building foreman. Selim, Abdallah, and Tani, as they were called, were a few years younger than me, but soon became my daily playmates for lack of other children my age, until I got to know my other siblings at Bet il Sahel.

CHAPTER THREE

A Day at Bet il Sahel

The day I had been waiting for with indescribable longing finally came, the day I would join my mother and Chadudj to be at Bet il Sahel from dawn to dusk. It was on a Friday, the Islamic Sunday, when we left the house early at five thirty, draped in our big black silk shawls with broad golden borders (called *shele*). We did not have far to go, as our destination lay only about one hundred steps away.

The loyal, but insufferable, grey-headed warden gave us an unfriendly welcome. He grumpily declared that he had been standing on his weak legs already over an hour just to receive the visiting ladies. Called Said il Nubi, the crotchety doorman was, as his name indicated, one of the father's Nubian slaves. His white beard—the only way I can put this, since it is an Arab custom to keep a clean-shaven head—had aged honorably in our service. The father valued him greatly, especially after the time the father was about to undertake a rash deed in a justifiable rage, and Said interceded by knocking the unsheathed sword out of the father's hand, thereby sparing his master pangs of conscience for the rest of his life.

As young children, however, we were not yet aware of Said's meritorious service, and our considerable rambunctiousness often led us to play the naughtiest tricks on our gruff, loyal servant. We were especially focused on his enormous keys, and I believe there is no place in all of Bet il Sahel where we did not hide them at least once. Particularly my brother Djemshid had an uncanny ability to cause them to vanish completely, without even us, his accomplices, suspecting their hiding place.

21

Upon reaching the residential floor, we found the house and inhabitants already in full swing. Only the especially devout were still in their morning prayers and totally invisible to the outside world. No one would dare disturb these worshippers, not even if the house were in flames. Our dear father was one of them, and so we were obliged to wait for him. Like many others, we had chosen this day to visit because he was present, to the aggravation of old Said.

The women that arrived were not all our acquaintances, much less friends. On the contrary, many were complete strangers in our house and unfamiliar to us. They mostly came from Oman, our original native country, for the sole purpose of requesting material support from the father, which he almost never denied. Both our home country and our tribal kin there are very poor, and our own prosperity dates back only to our father's conquest of rich Zanzibar.

Even though Islamic law generally prohibits a woman from interacting with male strangers, it nonetheless allows for two exceptions: She may appear before both ruler and judge. Because thousands upon thousands of women have no idea how to write, and therefore cannot submit written pleas, such needy supplicants have little alternative but to make their requests in person, even if it means taking the short trip from Asia to Africa in stride. Gifts were allocated on the basis of rank and position, without interrogating the hundred things Europeans try to draw out of their poor petitioners. Everyone received what they needed and what there was to give. There it is generally assumed that no respectable person would call on outside assistance for the mere pleasure of begging, and in many cases that is surely correct.

Siblings I knew and did not know received me very warmly, above all my unforgettable, beloved sister Chole. Having until then focused all my childhood love exclusively on my dear mother, I now also began to idolize this ray of light in our house from the fullness of my heart. My sister Chole soon became my ideal; she was also admired by many others and the father's favorite child. Whoever judged her fairly and without jealousy had to admit that she was an extraordinarily rare beauty. And is there anyone who is entirely unaffected by beauty? Not in our house. Chole was without equal in our whole extended family, and her beauty was the stuff of legend. Although it is well-known that beautiful eyes are no rarity in the Orient, everyone called her *nidjm il subh*, meaning "morning star." To wit, an Arab tribal leader was taking part in a popular mock sword fight in front of our house, as was customary during festivals, when his gaze was drawn by some invisible power to a particular window, causing him to completely ignore both the blood coming out of his foot and any pain that it caused, until one of my brothers snapped him to attention. It was our Chole who stood at that window. When this Omani's gaze fell upon the window and became so transfixed by Chole's beauty, he had, without realizing it, stabbed his own foot with his sharp, iron-shod lance. — After this incident, poor blameless Chole had to endure many years of teasing from the brothers.

Although Bet il Sahel is much smaller than Bet il Mtoni, it also lies directly by the sea. Its bright and cheerful atmosphere rubs off on its residents. All the rooms in the house offer the most splendid views of the sea with its boats, a sight that is deeply engrained in my soul. All the doors on the upper floor (where the residences are located) open onto a long, wide, and open gallery. The gallery ceiling is carried by columns that reach all the way to the ground, and between them runs a tall guardrail, with many chairs along its length. The plentiful, colorful lanterns that hang from the ceiling set the house aglow with a magical shimmer when it gets dark.

Looking out over the railing, it would be hard to find a more colorful, lively, and noisy courtyard view. I was later reminded of this colorful commotion, albeit on a smaller scale, by the bustling market scenes in the operetta *The Beggar Student*.

Two large, completely freestanding stairs handle the traffic between the residential rooms on the second floor and the courtyard. An uninterrupted stream, traveling up and down, continues all day and night, at times so crowded at both ends that it can take several minutes just to wind one's way to the stairs themselves.

In one corner of the courtyard, large quantities of livestock are slaughtered and then skinned and cleaned in bulk, all just to feed our house, with every house here having to procure its own meat.

Off to the side, seated Africans are getting their heads shaved bald and bare. Next to them, numerous water carriers stretch out their tired, but likely also lounging, limbs and pay no heed to any calls for water, until one of the feared eunuchs comes over to remind them, at times a bit roughly, of their neglected duty. Upon spotting their strict supervisors, these men would often gallop off with their *mtungi* (water jugs) in such a rush that general laughter would ensue.

Not far from them, a dozen nannies are basking in the sun with their little ones and telling them all sorts of fables and stories.

The kitchen is situated in the open around one of the columns on the ground floor, where smoke merrily disperses upwards for lack of chimneys in these parts. Nearby, the greatest, sheer indescribable havoc is being wreaked. Untold numbers of kitchen staff are pitching endless quarrels and fights. Both male and female head cooks are uncommonly generous in distributing well-aimed slaps whenever their helpers are slower to react than they would like.

Here is where massive amounts of meat, always by the whole animal, would be cooked. Huge fish, so large they had to be carried by two stout Africans, could often be seen disappearing into the kitchen. Small fish were accepted only by the basket, and poultry only by the dozen. Flour, rice, and sugar, too, were counted only in bulk by the sack, and the butter, in liquid form from the north, especially from the island of Socotra, would be brought in by pitchers weighing about a hundred pounds. Only spices were measured at a different scale, namely by the *rattil* (a pound).

Almost more astonishing was the amount of fruit we consumed. Every day thirty to forty, even fifty porters came to the house bearing loads of fruit, in addition to the many small rowboats bringing deliveries from plantations abutting the sea. Without exaggeration, I would estimate the daily demand for fresh fruit at Bet il Sahel to equal the load of a two-axle railcar. Even so, there were days, like during the mango harvest, which we call *embe*, when we easily used up twice that amount. The massive transport of fruit was handled extremely carelessly. The slaves who had this task felt no compunction in letting the soft baskets filled with ripe fruit drop with all their might from their heads onto the ground, so that half of the contents ended up bruised and much was completely squashed.

The oranges of today mostly stay green on the outside, even when they are fully ripened. There are also two kinds of mandarins there, one the size of push buttons and the other like the usual Italian ones.

A long wall about two meters wide had been erected to protect the house from the sea. On the far side, a few of the best horses were tethered with long ropes every day at low tide, so they could roll around and frolic in the soft sand to their hearts' content. The father was extremely attached to the thoroughbred horses he had brought over from Oman. He visited them every day, and if one ever got sick, he would personally attend to its comfort in the stables. Indeed, here is an example of how gentle an Arab man can be with his favorite horse. My brother Madjid had a precious brown mare and wanted nothing more ardently than for it to have a foal. When the time came that his wish for "il Kehelle" (that was her name) was about to happen, he ordered the stable master to alert him immediately, whether day or night. And sure enough, one night in the wee hours between one and three, we were one and all roused abruptly from our beds for the happy event. The stable boy who had brought the glad tidings received a fifty-dollar reward from his overjoyed master. This is by no means an isolated case. The personal devotion to horses is said to be even more extreme in the Arabian interior.

When the prayer session ended and my father returned to his room, the three of us, my mother, Chadudj, and I, went to him. After a short while, he turned to me with his usual humor and asked: "Salme, tell me, how do you like it here? Do you want to return to Bet il Mtoni? Here, do they also serve your—milk soup?"

Between half past nine and ten, all my older brothers left their quarters to join the father for a communal breakfast. Not a single *surie* (purchased wife), not even the most favored, was ever allowed to eat with the father. Beyond us, his children and grandchildren, and then not before age seven, no one else sat at his table except his equal-status wife Azze bint Sef and his sister Aashe. The social stratification of people in the Orient is never more evident than at meals. Guests are treated with kindness and grace, often more so than their treatment by the upper ranks here in this country. At mealtimes, however, Oriental hosts courteously take their leave from their guests. This is such a deep-seated custom that no one takes personal offense.

The *sarari* have developed even further classifications amongst themselves. The pretty and pricey Circassians, who are quite aware of their own worth, do not want to eat with the coffee-brown Abyssinians. In this way, by some unwritten code, they all dine according to race. Of course, with the children, as noted above, this sorting by skin color has found little application.

Watching the activity at Bet il Sahel, I got the impression that people here were much happier and more playful than at Bet il Mtoni. Only later did I understand why. In Bet il Mtoni, Azze bint Sef ruled the day. She reigned over husband, stepchildren, and their mothers, in short, everything in her realm. Here by contrast, in Bet il Sahel, where Azze rarely appeared, everyone, my father included, felt totally free and could do whatever they pleased. There was no one to exert their authority, except the father, who could not have been kinder or milder. This feeling of being free and unencumbered makes people invigorated and inspired wherever they are in the world, whether they live in the North or the South. The father must have felt this as well. For years, he had not sent anyone permanently to Bet il Mtoni unless they had asked to stay there, even though the house still had ample space, and Bet il Sahel was filled to the brim. Bet il Sahel's overcrowding eventually became so dire that the father ingeniously had wooden pavilions built on the huge, aforementioned gallery to create more living space, and ultimately also needed to have a third house built, named Bet il Ras (Cape House). This one lay a few kilometers north of Bet il Mtoni, likewise by the sea, and was intended especially for the younger generation of Bet il Sahel.

Our gallery in Bet il Sahel would have presented ample material for any painter's brush. The continuous panorama of genre-pictures it offered was especially full of color and variety. Just the faces alone in the crowds that came and went presented complexions of at least eight to ten different shades, and an artist would have needed the most garish colors to faithfully reproduce all the colorful clothing. Equally pronounced was the noise from the gallery. Children of all ages scampered, quarreled, and skirmished in all corners. Mixed in were the sounds of loud calls and clapping hands, which the Orient uses in lieu of bells to summon the house help. And on top of all that came the clonking of women's wooden sandals, the *kabakib* (singular *kubkab*), pitched five to ten centimeters high and often very richly decorated with silver and gold.[6]

Our jumble of languages was especially delightful for the children. We were supposed to speak only Arabic, and that rule was strictly observed with the father. But the minute he turned his back on us, a kind of Babylonian bedlam took over. In addition to Arabic, there was a wholesale mix of Persian, Turkish, Circassian, Swahili, Nubian, and Abyssinian, not to mention all the various dialects.

And yet, no one was bothered by any of this noise, except an occasional sick person who might complain. Our dear father was entirely used to it and never showed any displeasure. —

On this day, all my adult sisters appeared on the gallery in their festive attire, partly because it was the Arab Sunday and partly to honor the father's visit. Our mothers came and stood in groups, where they conversed enthusiastically, laughing and joking in such high spirits that no one who did not know the context could have believed they were all wives of one and the same man. But from the stairs came the clanging of weapons carried by my many brothers and their sons, who also wanted to visit with the father and mostly, bar a few short interruptions, stayed with him the whole day.

Bet il Sahel was much more luxurious and extravagant than Bet il Mtoni. It also had many more of the beautiful and graceful Circassians than Bet il Mtoni, where my mother and her friend Medine were the only ones of this race. In fact, the great majority of the women in Bet il Sahel were Circassian, without

---

6   As can be seen on the frontispiece of the author, page xviii.

a doubt much more distinguished in appearance than Abyssinians, although exceptional beauties are often found in the latter group as well. These natural advantages gave rise to much envy and resentment. A Circassian blessed with a courtly manner would mostly, through no fault of her own, be shunned and even despised by the chocolate-colored Abyssinians, merely because she looked so regal.

Under these circumstances, it was unavoidable that a kind of ludicrous "racial hatred" occasionally also reared its head among us siblings. An Abyssinian is by nature, despite her various virtues, often hot-headed and quick-tempered. Once enflamed, her passion seldom knows any bounds, much less a sense of decorum. Our Abyssinian siblings typically called us Circassian children "cats" because a few of us were unlucky enough to have—blue eyes. They also referred to us derisively as "Your Highness," further proof of their anger that we had been born into this world with lighter skin. They naturally never forgave our father the fact that his chosen favorites, Sharife and Chole, were of the detested cat race. Both had Circassian mothers and Sharife even had blue eyes. —

In Bet il Mtoni, the oppressive reign of Azze bint Sef had made for a kind of monastic living, while in Bet il Watoro, I felt even lonelier, and so in Bet il Sahel, I loved its cheerful lifestyle all the more. I soon linked up with the siblings of my same age. Two nieces my age, Shembua and Farshu, my brother Chalid's only children, were also part of this inner circle. They were sent from their home to Bet il Sahel every morning and picked up again every evening, so they could study together with their aunts and uncles and then join us in our games. Chalid's mother, Churshit, a born Circassian, was a very striking personality. As someone with a mighty build, she also exhibited exceptional willpower coupled with a high degree of natural sagacity. I have never in my life seen another woman like her. It was said that when Chalid stepped in for the father during his absence, she did the governing, with her son but her instrument. She gave indispensable advice to the whole family, and her opinion carried great weight in decision making. Her two eyes watched and immediately absorbed everything just as sharply as the hundred eyes of Argus. When it came to matters of importance, she always maintained a type of Solomonic wisdom. As children, we found her disagreeable and pointedly tried to stay away from her. —

We were getting ready to return to Bet il Watoro that evening when, to my dismay, the father told my mother that I needed to resume my lessons and get back to reading. When my mother responded that we were still looking for a suitable teacher, he determined that I should, like my nieces, be brought to Bet il Sahel every morning and picked up every evening, so I could benefit from lessons with my siblings. This was very distressing news. I was much too wild to take any pleasure in sitting still, and besides, my last teacher had positively ruined my appetite for any learning. Only the thought that I could now spend every day, all day (except Fridays) with my siblings gave me some comfort, especially when my charming sister Chole assured my mother that she would take me under her wing and watch over me. And so she faithfully did, caring for me like a mother.

By contrast, my dear mother was very saddened to have to give me up six days a week. But she, too, had to live with the father's decision. Several times a day, though, she bid me to appear at a particular spot, so she could at least see me from Bet il Watoro and nod my way.

⁂

Frontispiece]   Portrait of Said bin Sultan

29

CHAPTER FOUR

Of Our Life in Bet il Watoro and Bet il Sahel

All I want to say about my new teacher is that I will forever owe thanks to the Almighty for also giving me such a faithful friend while I was still young! She was a strict, but fair teacher. I was often the only one with her, since my siblings disliked going into her dark sickroom and instead took advantage of her infirmity by staying away. I could not bear to see her, my poor, wretched teacher, ask something of me and then not fulfill her requests. Of course, my obedience brought me not only her satisfaction, but also much teasing from my absconded siblings, on top of the frequent beatings they made me endure.

I came to like Bet il Sahel more and more, where I could romp around far more than in Bet il Watoro. Nor did we forgo any chance to play a stupid prank. When it came to potential punishment, though, I usually fared the best, since my caretaker Chole was far too kindhearted to impose any consequences.

Here are just two examples of our pranking:

The house had a number of magnificent peacocks, including a very cantankerous one that had it out for us children. One day we were walking around, five of us, past the round dome of the Turkish bath that was connected to Bet il Sahel by one hanging bridge and to Bet il Tani, basically a side house of the first, by another. Suddenly this peacock raced toward my brother Djemshid in a foaming rage. Quick as a flash, we threw ourselves onto the beast and subdued it. Our anger, especially Djemshid's, was too great for us to simply let the animal go. We decided to exact gruesome revenge by plucking every one of his beautiful tail feathers. Oh, did that formerly feisty, color-spangled bird look pitiful now. We were lucky that the father happened to be in Bet il Mtoni just then, and the incident was fortunately hushed up by the time he returned.

In the meantime, two new Circassian women had joined us from Egypt, and it did not take long for us children to conclude that one of the two was rather arrogant and dismissive of us. That hurt our pride, so we tried to come up with an appropriate punishment. It was not easy to encounter her, since we never crossed paths and normally had nothing to do with her. That fed our grudge all the more, especially since she was but a few years older. It was in this spirit that we one day happened to walk past her room. Her door stood open as usual. The poor thing was sitting on an unusually frail Swahili bed, made of nothing more than a mat with four posts latched together by coconut rope, while belting out a merry national song. My sister Shewane was our ringleader this time. One look from her was all it took to secure our immediate, like-minded consensus. In no time, we had grabbed the bed ties, raised the bed with its inhabitant as high as we could, and then suddenly let it drop again, to this unsuspecting soul's great shock. It was a rather childish prank, but had the intended effect. Our victim was thereafter cured of her disregard for us. From then on she was kindness itself, and that was all we had wanted.

Full of mischief, I also played my own pranks. Once, shortly after moving to Bet il Watoro, I almost broke my neck. We had gone, as we often did, to enjoy some time at one of our many wonderful plantations. One morning, I managed to evade my chaperone and instantly climbed undetected up a tower-high coconut palm, agile as a cat, but without the *pingu*, the heavy cord that fastens to the feet, without which not even the most skilled climber would be persuaded to climb a palm. About midway up the tall trunk, in my total exuberance, I began to shout at unsuspecting passersby, loudly wishing them a very fine good morning.

What a fright! Immediately a whole throng of people gathered below me and pleaded that I carefully come down. Sending someone up would have been inadvisable. Climbers need both hands when scaling palm trees and cannot additionally carry a seven- or eight-year-old child. But I was having a great time up there. Not until my mother stood below me, desperately wringing her hands and promising me all sorts of treats, did I slowly slide down and land, happy and unharmed, back at the base. On this day, I was everyone's beloved child and received more than a few presents to mark my salvation, even though I had instead earned an exemplary punishment.

We put on pranks like this daily, and no punishment was enough to deter us from new ones. There were seven of us, three boys and four girls, and we kept the whole house in a perpetual state of upheaval. And we also unfortunately often enough left our poor mothers with a range of inconveniences.

Now and again my dear mother would keep me at home in Bet il Watoro in addition to Fridays, and kind-hearted Madjid eagerly used those occasions to spoil me. It was on such a day that he gave us a huge scare. The poor man suffered from frequent seizures, and for that reason he was only rarely, and basically never, left alone without immediate help nearby. Even when he was in the bath, my mother and Chadudj, who did not entirely trust the slaves, would take turns keeping watch at the door, exchanging a few words with him from time to time, to which he liked to jokingly respond "I'm still alive." One day Chadudj was pacing up and down in front of the door to the bath when she suddenly heard a dull thud inside. Scared to death, she rushed in with others and found her beloved brother lying on the raised prayer area in the midst of a truly awful seizure. It was his worst one ever. A messenger on horseback was dispatched immediately to Bet il Mtoni to fetch the father.

Out of general medical ignorance, we were always beholden to wretched quackery. Now, after having gotten to know the natural and sensible way that doctors handle things here, I fear that many of our dead may have fallen victim to the barbaric treatments more than the disease. Were it not for the unwavering, rock-solid belief in our "destiny," I am not sure we could have endured the oh! so many deaths in our family and all around us with such resignation!

Poor Madjid, who lay unconscious with these dreadful spasms for hours, had to spend the time on his bed inhaling air that would have harmed even a healthy person. Although we have a great, natural preference for fresh, open air, at the very moment someone gets sick, specifically, as in this case, the moment the devil comes under suspicion, the room is hermetically sealed to the outside and massively fumigated, along with the whole house, through and through.

An hour later, to everyone's amazement, our dear father arrived in a *mtumbi*, a small, one-person boat, and rushed with rapid steps into the house. My father's relationship to his children was truly patriarchal. He loved each and every one equally, just as we all venerated him. More than forty children called the old man their own, and yet he was deeply shaken by the illness of even one.

Visible tears ran down his cheeks, as he stood by Madjid's sick bed. "Oh Lord, oh Lord, spare me my son!" he prayed incessantly, and his plea was heard by the Highest. Madjid was spared.

Later my mother asked him why he had come in such a miserably little dinghy. "When the messenger brought me the news," he said, "there was not a single boat on shore. I had no time to wait for one to be signaled over. Even getting a horse saddled would have taken too long. Then I happened to see a fisherman in a *mtumbi* under the *bendjle*, headed out to sea. I grabbed my weapons, called him to me, and as he got out, I immediately jumped in and rowed over." Now one has to know that such a *mtumbi* is a wretched vessel, consisting only of a hollowed-out tree trunk, seldom holding more than one person, and propelled forward with a double-shovel, rather than oars. Narrow, pointed in front, and relatively short, it is no comparison to our so-called Greenlanders here.[7]

For Western sensibilities, it must also seem quite odd that a father, who is concerned about the life of his child and recklessly sets aside all protocol, would still find time to remember his weapons. But here, too, the saying applies: Other countries, other customs. Just as Europeans cannot comprehend the unbounded love that true Arabs have for their weapons, there is much in turn about the North that Arabs find incomprehensible.

And so I attended school in Bet il Sahel daily, returning every evening to my mother in Bet il Watoro. Once I had finally learned about a third of the Koran by heart, at about age nine, I was considered to have outgrown school. After that, I only got to Bet il Sahel on Fridays with my mother and Chadudj, when the father was there.

---

7   Large, reinforced whaling ships that sailed past Greenland and could push through ice in the Arctic Ocean.

CHAPTER FIVE

Relocating to Bet il Tani

We lived comfortably and peacefully together in Bet il Watoro for about two years. But times like these seldom last. The least expected, least anticipated events and circumstances are bound to come along. And thus it was for us as well. The disruption to our homelife could not have come from a dearer or kinder person. Aashe, a distant relative of ours, had only recently come to Zanzibar from our Omani homeland. It did not take long before she became Madjid's wife. We all loved her dearly and were glad for my brother's good fortune and happiness, save for his own sister Chadudj. It pains me deeply to admit that Chadudj treated Aashe utterly unfairly from beginning to end. The latter was, as mentioned, charming in every way, but still very young. Instead of being taught by Chadudj and respectfully mentored over time commensurate with her status, as it should have been, she was simply ignored by Chadudj, yes, even treated with hostility. Aashe should have become mistress of the house when she married Madjid, and yet, Chadudj lorded over poor, gentle Aashe so much that she often came to my mother, tears streaming down her face, to complain about the latest injustice.

My mother was caught between two fires, and her situation became increasingly fraught. Chadudj had no intention of giving up any of her perceived rights and continued to treat Aashe like an underage child. My mother tried in vain to impress upon Chadudj the proper rights and status of Madjid's wife. For naught did she ask her, for the love of Madjid, to refrain from anything that could cause him anger or annoyance. It was all to no avail. The once pleasant and happy conditions in Bet il Watoro deteriorated so much that my mother finally decided to leave the house she loved so dearly, to no longer bear witness to the perpetual strife.

Madjid and his wife would hear nothing of it, and especially Aashe, who even called my mother Umma (Mama), was inconsolable. Chadudj, by contrast, remained completely indifferent, which only strengthened my mother's resolve in her decision.

Eventually Aashe could no longer bear to live under Chadudj's rule and decided to divorce Madjid. The poor thing had, despite her youth, taken this bitter lesson so much to heart that she wanted nothing more to do with Zanzibar and its inhabitants. When the south winds started to blow, the ones that take our ships north, Aashe came to us to say good-bye. She wanted to go to Oman, to return to her old aunt near the capital Muscat. She was a poor orphan, with neither father, nor mother.

My mother and I had already left Bet il Watoro by then and moved to Bet il Tani. My sister Chole rejoiced, now that we lived in practically one and the same house. She had even obtained and furnished the new quarters for us.

With our houses already filled beyond capacity, individual rooms were very difficult to find. Sometimes rooms had to be shared by multiple residents, and not until someone died were room assignments rearranged. Over time, it became customary to console people with the prospect of someone's eventual death, much as with some of our asylums here. It was rather profane to watch how often one or the other person would take note of a neighbor's light coughing and immediately suspect the onset of a severe case of consumption,[8] thereupon conjuring up plans for a tasteful renovation of the soon-to-be-inherited space. Truly sinful thoughts, but the overcrowding was simply too great. We owed significant thanks to Chole that we got an attractive, spacious room in Bet il Tani right away, without first having to wait for someone to die.

After that, we seldom saw Chadudj. She felt offended by our departure and accused my mother of a lack of affection. How completely unjustified! My mother's sense of fairness simply could and would not allow her to watch such ugly treatment of a defenseless, inexperienced woman, especially because poor Aashe bore no fault other than having simply dared—to become Madjid's wife. Madjid, on the other hand, continued to visit us frequently and remained a good and loyal friend.

Bet il Tani stood right next to Bet il Sahel and was, as already mentioned, connected to the latter by a hanging bridge that stretched above the former joint Turkish bath that lay midway between the two houses. Only the

---

8   A medical condition whereby the body was "consumed" from within, usually a reference to tuberculosis, one of the major killers of the time.

remnants of Bet il Tani's original splendor were left. Many years ago, the upper floor of this palace had housed my father's second equally-ranked wife, a Persian princess, the delightfully charming Shesade. She was said to exalt in extravagance, but loved her stepchildren no less dearly. One hundred fifty horsemen, naturally all Persian, lived on the ground floor and made up her little entourage. She rode and hunted with them in broad daylight, which for Arab sensibilities went rather too far. For their physical training, Persian women enjoy a Spartanesque upbringing. They are free, much freer than Arab women, but also coarser in their thoughts and conduct.

Shesade's display of luxury was also said to have defied description. Her clothes (always worn in a Persian cut) were stitched with genuine pearls, literally from top to bottom. In the morning, when slaves rounded up a large number of fallen pearls during their morning cleaning of her chambers, the princess never wanted them back. She not only abused our father's coffers, but also overstepped some serious boundaries. She had married the dear father only for his rank and wealth, while her heart had long belonged to someone else, something she made no attempt to hide. Upon returning with her retinue one day from one of her outings, the father confronted her in open anger, and it was only the loyal Said il Nubi who singlehandedly kept him from committing a rash and ill-considered deed. Divorce was the only possible outcome after such a scene, and fortunately, Shesade had

not had any children. A number of years later, when my father led the Persian war and had enough good fortune to seize the fortress Bandar Abbas on the Persian Gulf, it is said that the lovely Shesade was spotted among the enemy troops, taking aim at members of our family.

Here, in the former house of this princess, I also began to teach myself to write, although in a very rudimentary fashion. Of course, I had to do this in secret, since women are never taught to write, nor may they let on if they can. I simply took the Koran as a guide and tried to replicate the letters faithfully on a kind of slate, using the bleached shoulder blade of a camel. It worked, and my courage grew. I needed but a few last pointers to

get it right. So I entrusted one of our so-called learned servants with the rare honor of becoming my writing teacher. When word got out, I was denounced in the strongest terms, but not much bothered. Oh, how grateful I have been over the years for a decision that enabled me, however imperfectly, to correspond directly with my loyal friends in my distant homeland!

CHAPTER SIX

Daily Life in Our House

How endlessly often have I been asked, "Tell me please, how can your people possibly live without ways to occupy their time?" In the course of a single evening, I was afforded the pleasure of addressing this same topic between six and eight times at a large gathering, and naturally found this line of questioning altogether appealing and stimulating in the repetition. Clearly, the question is justified from the perspective of a Northerner, who cannot bear to imagine a life without work, while holding the firm conviction that an Oriental woman does nothing more than dream her days away in the confines of a harem, at most briefly livening up with some luxury item every once in a while.

Natural conditions vary everywhere, and they contribute to our differing perspectives, traditions, and customs. Northerners have to work to survive and then work even more for the pleasures in life. Blessed Southerners have a entirely different lot. Yes, I repeat the word "blessed" yet again because the contentedness of a population is one of its significant, invaluable features. Arabs, who are so often caricatured in books as indolent, in fact have a great degree of contentedness, comparable perhaps only to the Chinese. By virtue of their natural surroundings, Southerners *can* work, but Northerners *must* work. Northerners tend to think highly of themselves and look with pride and disdain upon their opposites, a trait that does not seem very praiseworthy. But this easily overlooks how essential Northern diligence and Northern hard work are if hundreds of thousands are not to perish. A Northerner must work, and there is no point in turning that necessity into an excessive virtue. Are not Italians, Spaniards, and Portuguese also less industrious than Germans and

Englishmen? And why? Well, simply because the latter have much more winter than summer, and accordingly more of a fight for their survival. The cold brings with it so many thousands of needs and wants that the day often flies by like a short dream, with daily tasks that are so crucial for life, but as to whose meaning, even existence, the Southerner has no clue.

Everywhere one goes, luxury is the same. Anyone with the requisite funds and corresponding inclinations will find ample opportunity to give their passions free rein, whether they live in the North or the South. We can therefore set this aspect aside and instead focus only on the really essential needs of people here and there.

Whereas here even a newborn child needs a hundred things to protect its frail life against the rigors of the variable weather, a brown-skinned, Southern baby can basically just lie there with next to nothing on and doze uninterrupted in the warm breeze. Here, a two-year-old child absolutely needs, among other things, shoes, socks, pants, a dress, two skirts, mittens, an overcoat, a hat, a scarf, gaiters, a muff, and a fur cap, whether that child belongs to royalty or a tradesman—only the quality varies—but there as well, the wardrobe of every two-year-old son of a prince consists of only two items: a shirt and a little cap.

Should an Arab mother, who needs so precious little for herself and her child, work as much as a German housewife? She has no idea what it means to darn holey socks and mittens or undertake all of the countless activities that are needed for a German mother to provide continuous care for her child. In particular, she knows nothing of the one major chore in every European household: the big laundry. There, clothes are washed daily, dried in less than half an hour, pressed flat (not ironed), and set aside. She also has no tiresome curtains like the ones that block every ray of sunshine here, whose care and cleaning take so much time. And the amount of clothes an Oriental woman might tear, may she be the finest of ladies, is unbelievably minuscule. That is easily explained by the fact that people move around less there and do not go out much.

All this and much more contributes to making the life of Oriental women, virtually without distinction across positions, more comfortable and bearable. But it takes being there, and living there for a "longer" time, to learn about all this household minutiae. Tourists with their temporary stays, who cannot penetrate such detail and are likely to glean their information from hotel staff, cannot be relied upon to know. As for any European women who actually may have been admitted to a harem, whether in Constantinople or Cairo, they still have not seen a real harem, but just its outward shine, as it were, the sanitized showrooms that are already heavily influenced by Western decor.

Moreover, the magnificent climate is so enjoyable and beneficial that no one practically ever needs to worry about the next day. I am not disputing that people there are generally quite relaxed by nature. But one need only recall the July and August days of a hot European summer, and it becomes evident what effect a tropical sun can have on people.

By disposition, Arabs have little inclination toward industry. They care far more for the art of war and agriculture. Only the smallest percentage takes up an artisanal trade. Arabs also do not figure prominently among merchants and exhibit virtually no Semitic business hustle, although they have to barter extensively. With their modest lifestyles, they can easily make do with very little, and, as a rule, their focus is day-to-day, especially since they are always mindful that their time may come at any moment. This constant anticipation of their last hours limits the impulse to craft any plans for the coming future. Only rarely do they plant things they cannot harvest for their own needs. Anyone who does is considered a foolish farmer (see Luke 12).[9] I also recall a case where a rather aged minister leased his plantations out for many years. He was accordingly considered a godless person for disposing of his land well beyond his expected lifetime.

Oriental life thus proceeds calmly without much work, something I needed to highlight and justify before going into details about daily life in Arabic households. But I also have to emphasize that I am referring only to Omani and Zanzibari conditions, which differ in many respects from other Oriental countries.

To an extent, every Muslim's day is governed by prayers. They happen five times a day, and when properly conducted with everything that goes along with them, like the mandated ablutions and change of clothes, all told, they take up at least three hours.

Those in the ranking class are woken for the first prayer between four and five thirty every morning, after which they go back to sleep. Especially pious individuals, however, choose to add a prayer at sunrise. For ordinary folk, daily work starts with the first prayer.

In our house, with its hundreds of residents, fixed rules were elusive, since everyone could and did follow their own tastes and convenience. Only the two main meals and regularly recurring prayers forced the community to live according to a specific, more established order.

---

9   This biblical reference to Luke 12:16-21 reflects the author's Christian faith at the time she wrote her *Memoirs*.

39

Most of the residents therefore slept on until about eight o'clock, at which time women and girls were woken by female slaves with gentle and indescribably pleasant massaging, before bathing and dressing for the day. Islamic law stipulates that bathing and cleansing of the body be done only with flowing water. Since there was no river in Bet il Tani, as there was in Bet il Mtoni, we made use of large masonry or brass containers, positioned at a certain height with large spigots and sprinklers, which streamed water onto the body, while the bathing individuals wore wooden sandals and stood on marble surfaces with built-in drainage. Already the previous night, the attending female slave had laid everything out that was needed to get dressed, including bestrewing the outfit with jasmine and orange blossoms and perfuming it with amber and musk.

It takes having lived in the Tropics to truly understand how blissful a cold bath can feel for the whole body. Such a bath greatly freshens and strengthens, and the fine aromas that are so expertly assembled liven up the spirit in the most pleasant way.

After the hour it usually took to get ready, everyone presented themselves to the father to wish him a good morning and soon thereafter settled down to breakfast, the first of our two main meals. Because everything had already been put out in advance, before the drum roll called us to the table, our mealtime, even in all its abundance, took much less time than it does here.

Now the actual day begins, and it is of course spent in various ways. Men arm themselves before heading to the official gathering room. Women, who have no need to work, seat themselves at the windows to watch the bustling street, especially any noteworthy arrivals for the gathering, perhaps even to catch a private greeting known only to the recipient. This diversion is highly entertaining and variable. A lady might easily be disturbed, pushed out of her spot, or even slyly displaced by a concerned mother or aunt. —

Two or three hours can fly by like this, with no notice of the passing time. Meanwhile, men reciprocate each other's visits and relay their oral messages to ladies about evening plans. Demure and decent women, who have no taste for such behavior, retire on their own or in groups to their airy rooms and busy themselves with handiwork, where they embroider their masks, shirts, or pants with gold, or even the batiste shirts of their husbands, brothers, or sons with red or white silk that requires special skill, or make lace with silk and gold lametta. Others read novels, visit healthy or sick people in their residences, and take care of their various private affairs.

And then it is already one o'clock. The slaves come to announce the second prayer. Now the hot sun is at its peak, and everyone is glad to take time after praying to comfortably dream away some hours in cool and light attire on a lovely, soft mat, usually interwoven with holy verses. Between sleeping and chatting, and cakes and fruit to eat, this time, too, passes quickly.

At four o'clock, everyone conducts their third prayer and then throws on their more stylish afternoon attire. The father is once again sought out to wish him a good afternoon. The older siblings are allowed to call him "Father," while us young folk and our mothers address him only as "*Hbabi*" (Sir).

This was the liveliest time of the day for us. The main meal followed, when the whole, big family came together with the father for the second and last time.

At the end of the meal, the eunuchs carried European-style chairs into the open hall fronting the father's quarters, but naturally, only for the adults. The young children had to stand in deference to their elders, who likely receive more respect in the Orient than anywhere else. The sizeable family gathered around the usually rather earnest-looking father, while well-groomed, well-armed eunuchs stood in rank and file at a set distance along the gallery. Coffee was passed around, along with lots of the children's favorite fruit juice imported from southern France. A massive barrel organ played in the background, while conversations ranged. For an occasional change of pace, one of the large music boxes would play its melodies, or a blind Arab woman named Amra, who was gifted with a delightful voice, would be brought in to sing for us.

After about an hour and a half, the family split apart again, and everyone sought out activities and leisure according to their moods and inclinations. Betel chewing had a big part in this. As a Swahili custom, it is not popular with Arabs born in Arabia. However, those of us who came to this world on the east coast of Africa, who grew up with Africans and mulattoes, readily took to this custom despite being derided by our Asian siblings and relatives, so long as the father did not catch us in the act. As soon as we left him, the sinners among us succumbed to the betel nut, although in my case not until many years later.

With no shortage of pastimes, this interlude also passed quickly, until the gunshots and drum rolls of the Indian guard reminded us of sundown and our fourth prayer. Of all the daily prayers, none was conducted as quickly as this one. Anyone who did not plan to go out (we and our mothers always had to get special permission from our father or his deputy, although this was denied in only the rarest of cases), or anyone who was not expecting company from outside, invariably had someone to visit in the house or was visited by siblings, stepmothers, stepchildren, and secondary wives. We had coffee and lemonade, fruit and cake, joked and laughed heartily, read out loud, played cards (but never for money or any other winnings), sang, listened to native African music on the *sese*, sewed, stitched, and made lace, all depending on what anyone felt like doing.

It is therefore very mistaken to assume that women of rank in the Orient do absolutely nothing. That they do not draw, play musical instruments, or dance is, of course, well-known. But is this the only way to pass the time? People there are, without exception, easily contented and do not feverishly chase the perennially variable amusements and pleasures we pursue here. When judged on the basis of attitudes prevailing here, Oriental people may indeed appear to be Philistines. —

Male servants are let go in the evening, so they can return to their homes and families outside of the house. The eunuchs also have external lodgings.

The oil lamps in the rooms and corridors are mostly left to burn throughout the night, and only the candles are extinguished at bedtime. Young children above the age of two are no longer put to bed at a set time. They fall asleep whenever they feel like it. It was not unusual for children overcome with sleep to simply lie down wherever they might be and fall into a deep slumber. A few slaves would have to carefully pick up the sleepy heads and carry them to their cots, often across long distances, without them even noticing.

Bedtime for those who did not go out or who had received their guests usually came around ten o'clock. Many, however, love to stay up until midnight to stroll across the flat and well-maintained rooftops under the bright moonshine, a pleasure like no other.

The fifth and last prayer session is supposed to take place at about seven thirty. However, many in the house are busy with visits or other things right then. It was therefore determined that one could postpone this prayer time all the way to midnight. In that case, then, the last prayer is, as a rule, conducted just before bedtime.

When it is finally time to go to sleep, a well-to-do lady is waited upon by two female slaves, who are both tasked with easing the mistress into sleep and watching over her. One massages all the limbs, as in the morning, and the other swings the fans back and forth, until they can slip softly away. Members of the high-ranking and wealthy world also get their feet washed in eau de cologne and water beforehand, which is extraordinarily refreshing. That such women go to bed in their full attire, with all their jewelry on, has already been mentioned.

CHAPTER SEVEN

Our Mealtimes

As described, we had two mealtimes a day. Our brothers and nephews that lived outside the house, married or not, joined us for breakfast whenever the father was in the city with us. By contrast, I cannot recall a time when he would have eaten at his sons' places or anywhere else on the outside.

Our dishes were set up on the long *sefra*. It was much like a billiard table with short feet, except that ours was a lot longer, with a rim the breadth of a hand. The whole thing was no more than ten to fifteen centimeters off the ground. We do not have separate dining rooms, and so the *sefra* was simply placed on the gallery. Although we owned random pieces of European furniture, such as sofas, different types of tables and chairs, and the stray wardrobe (there was a lot of European furniture in the father's room, but more for show than actual use), we were consummate Orientals at mealtime and simply sat flat on the floor, which is to say, on rugs or mats.

The table order was strictly observed according to rank. The father always took his place at the head of the *sefra*. Next to him, on both his right and left, sat my oldest siblings. We little ones (only after turning seven) were last in line. We had no concept of mixed seating and no visitors at the table.

The food itself consisted of various dishes, often as many as fifteen. Every meal featured rice prepared in one of many different ways. Our favorite meat was lamb, our favorite fowl, chicken. Plus we had fish, Oriental breads, and plenty of cakes and sweets. The many eunuchs were usually lined up some distance from us, ready to respond to any special requests.

That included when the father really liked a certain dish. The eunuchs would often hand him plates that he would fill for the younger children who were not yet allowed to eat with him, or for individuals who were sick. He would always summon me to a specific corner in Bet il Mtoni where I would get such a filled plate. Even though we, of course, were served the same food as the adults, it was naturally much nicer to get it as a special selection from the father, and he, too, took much pleasure in it.

Upon taking their seats, everyone said grace softly but audibly: "In the name of Allah, the All-Merciful," and upon rising as well: "Thanks be to the Lord of the Universe," and so on. The father was always the first to be seated and the first to rise.

Unlike here, individuals do not get their own separate plates. Instead, all the various dishes (except the rice) were served on numerous small plates that were arranged in meticulous symmetry along the length of the *sefra*. We would then eat in pairs of two per plate. Rice enough for five to six people was served pyramid-shaped on a type of large platter, and everyone helped themselves with their fingers from where they sat. We rarely ate vegetables.

We never drank while eating. Sharbet and sugared water were available only after the meal was over. We also rarely spoke at meals, at most when the father explicitly addressed one of us. Otherwise, we kept quiet while we ate, which, not to be underappreciated, has its benefits. Fruit or flowers were also never placed on the *sefra*.

A few minutes before and after the two main meals, well-appointed male and female slaves stood near the table with water pitchers, soap, and hand towels at the ready, so we could wash our hands before and especially after we ate. Of course, we ate solely with our fingers. Knives and forks were superfluous and emerged from their hiding places only when we served Europeans. Meat and fish were already pre-cut by the kitchen into bite-sized pieces. Spoons were used only for whatever was not quite compact enough for cutting.

After the hands were washed, it was customary for people of refinement to perfume them as well, so as to remove any residual odor.

Fruit was never enjoyed right after mealtimes, but rather beforehand or somewhat later. Everyone would have a large quantity of fruit, corresponding to seasonal availability, brought to their rooms.

By contrast, eunuchs would regularly distribute genuine mocha in dainty Oriental cups that sat in gold or silver saucers, a quarter or half hour after mealtimes. The coffee is thick, boiled down to its essence, but then filtered completely clean. It is always consumed pure, without milk or sugar, and served without other food, except perhaps to enjoy a bit of finely-cut areca nut.

The coffee is always poured right when it is ready to be enjoyed. The act of pouring calls for very special dexterity, by which the slaves fill the little cups, much like beer poured with foam, in a long and rapid stream. This takes a quick motion of the spout downward as much as possible, followed by an equally quick return of the spout upwards, without spilling even so much as a drop. The coffeepot is made of tin with a brass coating. An assistant follows from behind the coffee pourer with a tray full of additional, empty cups and a large back-up coffeepot. If the group is still gathered, their duty is swiftly carried out. But if the group has already dispersed, they must pursue everyone individually, seeking them all out wherever they may be, to serve them all their precious drink.

Coffee, of course, as everyone knows, is cherished in the Orient and consequently handled with meticulous care. As proof, suffice to say that coffee is roasted, ground, and boiled only for immediate consumption, which means it is enjoyed completely fresh several times a day. Neither boiled coffee, nor roasted beans are ever stored. Any that are no longer fresh are thrown out or at most given to the lower house servants.

The second and last principal mealtime occurred punctually at four o'clock in the afternoon. It was in all respects like breakfast, so I am spared any further description. After that meal, it was rare to partake of anything other than coffee and fruit until the next morning at nine o'clock.

VUE DE LA VILLE DE ZANZIBAR
(État de Zanzibar)

CHAPTER EIGHT

Birth and Early Years of a Prince or Princess

The birth of a prince or a princess may not have been greeted with thundering cannon shot, but was nonetheless an important event for us that caused much happiness and, unfortunately, much envy as well. The father and relevant mother were always elated about the birth of a newborn, and we young children always shared their joy wholeheartedly. That is because a newborn brother or sister had to go through many ceremonies, all of which became family festivities that catered especially to us youngsters. In our family circle, these birth celebrations happened about four to six times a year.

Muslims are not familiar with male obstetricians. Instead, they turn only to female midwives for advice, even though these midwives are paragons of ignorance. Most of them come from Hindustan and are much preferred to the native ones, although I could not say why, since a Hindustani midwife knows as little as an Arab or Swahili one. This much is clear, that when a brand new mother and her child stay healthy and alive, it is but thanks to God and her own solid health, rather than her extremely simple-minded midwives. I later heard much from my married friends about their extremely barbaric methods, which I must naturally refrain from recounting here.

After the newborn is thoroughly washed in warm water, a bandage is wrapped around its torso and a vegetable-based, heavily perfumed powder is spread on its neck and underarms. It is then dressed in a tiny shirt of pure cotton or muslin. With the little baby laid on its back, and hands and legs straightened

47

out as much as possible, a broad cloth is used to wrap the baby from bottom to top, up to the shoulders, tightly bringing in both arms and legs. The child stays imprisoned like this day and night for forty days, with but a brief respite from bondage twice a day to be bathed and dried off. The goal of this bandaging is to ensure a flawlessly straight posture for life.

Despite the many servants, the mother always keeps watch directly and lovingly over the child. The spacious crib, skillfully carved out of the finest wood and imported from East India, is rocked non-stop by alternating slaves, often with gusto. Depending on the season, it may also be covered by a lace or gauze curtain as a mosquito net.

Only rarely does a mother nurse her child, and when she does now and again, then usually just to pass the time. Every child has one or two wet nurses at its full disposal until the age of two.

If the newborn is a girl, then right at the end of the first week, her ears are pierced with a sewing needle and red silk thread, usually six holes per ear. Within a few months, they are already bearing the heavy gold rings that stay on forever. Anyone not wearing earrings is mourning a loved one.

On the fortieth day of a child's life, a very special ceremony takes place: the shaving of the first hair. The chief eunuch does the shaving according to prescribed formalities, which are not complete without heavy doses of incense from a type of gum arabic (much like the incense in Catholic churches). These first hairs have a special status. They may not be burned or thrown in the trash, but are instead buried underground, thrown out to sea, or hidden in some crack in the wall. About twenty to thirty people attend this festive ceremony. It is the only time the chief eunuch serves as barber, which he does while in constant danger of negligently crushing the vulnerable soft spots on the little baby's head. After this precarious work, he, along with the rest of his numerous assistants, always receives an appropriate gift of honor from the father.

This is also the day the child is released from its body wrapping forever. Now the child is adorned with rings on the arms, feet, and ears, and dressed in a silken shirt and *kofije,* a little cap made of gold brocade, complete with ear cuffs. Not until then is the child ready for public viewing. Up to this point, only the parents, the most essential slaves, and the new mother's very closest and most devoted friends have been allowed to see it. This reflects the widespread belief in the evil eye and sorcery of all kinds. —

Indisputably, little Oriental children at this age look much prettier than European ones, if only because the latter are kept too much in white. I have now been in Germany for many years and still cannot conclude otherwise. Even my own children looked perfectly drab in their baby garb. The contrast was just too great whenever I thought of my younger siblings, nephews, and nieces in their winsome attire, while seeing my own children in their European outfits.

The heavy perfuming already starts with the smallest children. Everything that is theirs, clothing, bed sheets, bath towels, and diapers, is bestrewn for the night with wondrously fragrant jasmine (different from the one we have here), then freshly smoked before use with ambergris and musk, with a final sprinkle of rosewater. But it is worth remembering that doors and windows stay open practically year-round, all day and night, which has the fortuitous effect of circumventing any harm from this fondness for fragrance.

To protect children from the purported evil eye, they are draped with amulets from the fortieth day onwards. Called *hamaje* or *hafid*, they are especially common with the lower classes, who use all sorts of objects. An onion, for example, or a piece of garlic, small seashells, a piece of bone, and the like are worn by young children in leather pouches tied around their left upper arm. Instead of such amulets, the higher classes use selected verses from the Koran, which are engraved on gold or silver plates hung from matching chains around the neck. Boys keep these sayings only up to a certain age, whereas girls frequently keep them longer. The girls especially love the *hurs* (the guardian), a mini-book with very tiny print, about seven centimeters long and four to five centimeters wide, that is placed in an elegantly crafted gold or silver case and fastened to a necklace. Anyone wearing such an amulet, on which God's holy name is engraved, must never set foot in an unclean place, surely a testament to the boundless veneration devout Muslims have for their God and Maker! —

In addition to breast milk, it is not long before children are served milk soup several times a day, made of milk that is cooked with rice flour and some sugar for a very long time and then served from a cup with a long spout. Bottles were not yet in use in my time. But that is all children are given to eat until they get their teeth and can eat anything.

Children are seldom carried. They are preferably just placed on a rug-covered floor, where they can roll around to their hearts' delight.

When a child makes its first attempts to sit upright, it is time for another celebration, one that is geared exclusively to all the youngest siblings. To further encourage participation in the sitting party of our little brother or sister, something special was always baked or cooked that day.

Mother, nurses, and child come dressed in their absolute finest, wearing their most precious jewelry. The child is placed in a medium-sized, square wagon that sits on very low wheels and is filled with cloth and cushions. The celebrated child's legs are placed on either side of a small rod that rises perpendicularly from the axle. All the other little children gather around.

In the meantime, corn kernels have been roasted in a special manner until they open up to the size of a thimble and become as soft as wadding. This is mixed with lots of very small silver coins, and the mixture is then poured on the child's head. Immediately, all the siblings pile on to raid their little brother or sister. And yes, this can easily become life threatening. —Many other children in our circle between four and ten years of age were often invited to join these parties as well.

As long as children lack the strength to wear sandals (the wooden ones for girls and women are called *kubkab*, the leather ones for boys and men are *watje*), they simply run around barefoot. Since the *watje* are significantly easier to wear than the *kubkab*, very young girls are initially allowed to walk with *watje* until they have the skills to take on *kubkab* for the rest of their lives. —Neither young nor old, male or female, wears socks. Only higher-ranked ladies need them now and again for horseback riding, since custom requires that they cover their ankles.

Already at the age of two to four months, the father presents a child with two or three attending slaves, in addition to its wet nurses, who from then on become the child's property. The older the child becomes, the more slaves it receives for personal service. If one of the slaves dies, the father finds a replacement or gifts a corresponding amount of money. —Up to a certain age, young girls wear boys' caps in the house as well.

Every prince stays in the house with the women until he turns seven, when he undergoes the Mosaic rite.[10] Naturally, ceremonies are also a big part of this process, culminating after the child's recovery in a special celebration open to all dignitaries and top officials. Whenever possible, this event takes place out in the countryside, with the father present. It also features food and entertainment for the public, usually lasting three days.

This is also the time every young boy gets his very own docile mare. His escorts can get their mounts from the stables, where a couple hundred Arab horses

---

10 Presumably a reference to circumcision, one of the ceremonies included in the Law of Moses that traces back to God's covenant with Abraham.

are always available. This way boys early on become very proficient riders, acquiring an amazing degree of agility and flexibility otherwise seen only among trained circus riders. Since we do not use regular saddles or stirrups, it takes much more skill to sit tight than here. And the father took an unconventional approach whenever his sons got in trouble on outings. Not only the sons, but also the escorts had to reckon with getting punished. The father assumed they must have been way too lenient with their princes, especially in light of the tight responsibility and strict instructions he had given them.

The fact is, none of us was ever spoiled in our upbringing. The father's great love of justice and his incomparably noble character came with equally firm consequences that knew no weakness. We had to obey all our teachers and caretakers. We knew any complaint that made it to him would no doubt leave us in shame, if not slinking away in tears. This strictness taught us due deference toward such individuals. As we grew older, we also became increasingly aware of our deep moral indebtedness to them.

The wet nurses, even if they served only briefly in that role, were especially revered and benefited from this special recognition their whole lives. They always start as slaves, but, as a rule, gain their freedom in recognition of their dedication and sacrifice. African nurses, in particular, usually excel in their extraordinary devotion and attachment. Even the most anxious mother can fully entrust her child to the nurse, who considers herself a second mother and steps up to that role. What a contrast with the lack of interest and heartlessness shown by nurses here! How often have I felt compelled to lecture some total stranger on a public walkway after watching her brutal treatment of the poor little creature in her care.

This contrast between the wet nurses here and there may be mostly explained by the poverty that forces the former to entrust their own beloved children, with considerable sacrifice, to utter strangers. These nurses serve their masters only for the money. They are not interested in whether the children in their care are called Saul or Paul. Their thoughts and feelings are naturally with their own children. And what mother could hold that against them!

How very differently an African wet nurse takes to the child entrusted by her mistress. She has already served her mistress for years and was perhaps even born in the same house. Not surprisingly, she has few personal interests, having always made her master's concerns her own. Add to this the most significant factor, that such a wet nurse only rarely, if ever, has to give up her own child, but can instead readily keep it with her. The nurse's child receives the same food as the little master or mistress, the same milk soup, some of the same chicken, and so on, and the same with the bath, and even the used clothes it inherits. And after the mother finishes as wet nurse, her child continues to be a playmate of her second care. Even when the child remains a slave, it is given preference over all other slaves, and only bad people would ever break the bond with their milk brother.

Yet there is also one very bad trait that African wet nurses have. They are known to tell young children three to five years old fantastical and often very harrowing stories and fairy tales, both to entertain them and to keep them quiet. Of course, the lion (*simba*), the leopard (*tshui*), the elephant (*tembo*), and the many witches (*watschawi*) feature prominently in these fables that are terrifying even for adults.

In general, there is no question that childcare is much easier in the South than here in the North. Notably, children there are spared the never-ending coughs and colds, and all that entails. Children there are also very self-reliant and resilient, despite all their comforts, partly because they are freer and less constrained (both in their settings and clothing) to naturally play and romp as they please. They may not know anything about regular gymnastic exercises, but it is not uncommon for a lad of ten to twelve years to launch into an ardent sprint and leap over one or even two horses. High jumps are generally very popular, and everyone does their best to outdo the others.

Swimming in the sea is practiced no less eagerly, with everyone basically self-taught. Shooting also starts very early and is exercised with much passion. Mock battles are especially popular. Hours are spent on them from youth onward. Even though young boys usually walk around armed to the teeth, carrying as much powder and lead as any adult, it is very rare to hear of any careless accidents. —

The young princes, as already mentioned above, lived in the paternal household only up to a certain age. After that, each young prince was assigned his own house to take care of himself and, as a rule, his mother, if she was still alive. The father granted him a fixed monthly allowance, designed to match the son's circumstances, with which he had to cover his needs. Additional amounts could be expected for a marriage or an addition to the family, as well as for exemplary conduct, but nothing more. Only when the father's ships arrived annually, with a new load of goods, did all the siblings that lived outside the father's house and their families show up to receive their allocated shares, whether needed or not. As to anyone who had the serious misfortune of letting their expenses exceed their allowance, it was never made easy for those debts to be repaid. The father hated nothing more, and whosoever disgraced himself this way once took great care never to do it again.

If war broke out, as was unfortunately so often the case in Oman, then all the princes, even those that were still underage, had to head out and join the fighting, just like every common man.

The upbringing was strict overall, but that only increased the respect and reverence of the sons for the father. As a child, I sometimes watched with amazement as the older brothers rushed ahead of the slaves to straighten the sandals the father had slipped off before entering the room. The older brothers also appeared in the paternal household several times a day, as soon as the father himself was there, and then took part in the meals.

About the upbringing of a princess, there is little to say. The first years are basically the same as for her brothers, except that the sons have much greater latitude to leave the house after their seventh year. The only aspect worthy of note at the birth of a princess is the wide comb, usually of silver, that is placed, to suit the local fashion, under the back of the newborn's head to flatten it for later. —If a princess marries one of her cousins, of which there are, to be sure, many more in Oman than Zanzibar, then she naturally leaves her paternal home in exchange for her husband's. And yet her paternal home, the one true bulwark against all of life's hardships, always remains open to her as a place to live. Or if she prefers, she can move in with a brother. Every sister has a favorite brother and vice versa; the two stick together in both joy and woe and support each other with both advice and assistance. As laudable as this custom may have been, and as fortunate for those involved, it also frequently and understandably, given the size of our family circle, provoked jealousies among siblings. It can take a strong disposition to rise above it all.

Often it was up to a loving sister to intercede with the father about a favorite brother's mishap. The father tended to favor his daughters and rarely left their pleas unanswered. He was especially obliging with his older daughters. As a rule, he would walk towards them from far across the room and then let them sit beside him on the sofa, whereas the adult sons and the rest of us children had to stand respectfully before him.

View of Stone Town by Rosa Troemer

CHAPTER NINE

School in the Orient

School (*mdarse*) is of very scant importance to Orientals in general, and so it is for us. In Europe, school is at the center of the State and the Church, for royal and regular citizens alike. Educational resources have a major bearing on every individual, as to both character development and future prospects. In the Orient, by contrast, the *mdarse* is completely tangential. For many, it does not even exist. But before I allow myself further commentary, I want to report on some of what we called school in our house.

At the age of six to seven, all the siblings, both boys and girls, had to enter the *mdarse*. The girls only had to learn how to read, while the boys had to learn both reading and writing. Bet il Mtoni and Bet il Sahel each had only one female teacher to lead classes, whom the father had brought over from Oman. Whenever the teacher got sick and had to stay in bed, we were very happy. There was no available replacement, so we simply got time off.

There was no designated classroom. Class took place in an open gallery, with unhindered access by pigeons, parrots, peacocks, and bobolinks. From there, we could also comfortably look into the courtyard and greatly amuse ourselves with scenes of the lively activity down there. The schoolroom layout consisted of but a single, gigantic mat. School supplies were equally basic. We needed only a Koran on a stand (*marfa*), a little pot with homemade ink, a bamboo pen, and a well-bleached shoulder blade from a camel. The last item was in lieu of a blackboard. It is easy to write on it with ink, and nerves are spared the aggravating scratching sounds on slate. Our slaves usually took care of wiping off the blades.

First, just as here, we had to learn the very complicated Arabic ABCs. Then, in the absence of any other schoolbooks, we began to read the Koran, followed, as mentioned, by writing lessons for the boys. When students are still at a rudimentary level, they all read in unison and usually very loudly. But that is the extent of it, since what is read and learned is never explained. That is also why at most one student out of thousands understood enough to interpret, word for word, all the thoughts and directives in the Islamic holy text, even though eighty out of a hundred had learned half of it by heart. Reflections upon the holy text are actually considered irreverent and unauthorized. People are simply supposed to believe what they are taught, and this rule was strictly followed.

Bright and early at seven o'clock, after having enjoyed some fruit, we had to assemble on the mat that had been rolled together overnight and was now swept clean, to await our stern teacher. Before she showed up, we exalted in wrestling, boxing, jumping, risky acrobatics on the balustrade, and other childish antics. At the bend in the gallery, we put up a watchman, who would flag a sighting of our teacher from afar with a forced cough. In an instant, we seated ourselves on the mat, a picture of utmost innocence. When her steps got closer, we popped up like rubber balls to respectfully extend our hands and wish this dreaded person a good morning. She always held her despised bamboo cane in one hand and carried a large brass inkpot in the other. We stood in proper order before her until she took her seat, after which we could take ours. Encircling the teacher, we all sat together cross-legged on the mat.

Now she began to pray the opening surah of the Koran, considered the Muslim Lord's Prayer, whereupon we responded in a chorus, closing with the familiar *amin* (not *amen*). Then the lesson from the previous day was reviewed, followed by some new reading or writing. In this way, lessons would regularly go until nine o'clock and then, after finishing breakfast, again until noon, when it was time for the second prayer.

All of us were allowed to bring some of our slaves to school to let them participate in class. They sat at a distance behind us, while we grouped ourselves however we pleased. We had neither fixed seats, nor differentiated classes. We also did not have the feverish excitement that erupts here when grades are given a couple of times a year. If anyone made especially good or bad progress, or distinguished themselves through especially good or bad behavior, the relevant mothers and the father would be told about it directly. The teachers were under explicit instructions from the father himself to punish us quite thoroughly if there was ever cause to do so. Wild as we were, she did have ample need to resort to that nasty cane.

Beyond reading and writing, we learned only a bit of arithmetic, namely, up to one hundred in written form and one thousand orally; anything more was apparently harmful. Little effort was made to teach grammar and spelling. Only over time, with much reading, was it possible to figure out the rather difficult *ilnahu*[11] on one's own. Back home, I had never heard of any of the bodies of knowledge, like history, geography, science, math, and all the rest, much less learned them. Not until coming here did I have the pleasure of discovering all those academic subjects. But whether the modicum of added knowledge that I have painstakingly acquired here leaves me better off, compared to the others over there, remains an open question for me. One thing in any case is clear: I have never been so swindled and cheated as during the time when I was most informed. Oh, you happy folks back home! You cannot fathom, even in your dreams, all that is part and parcel of this holy civilization! —

As for the so-called home-work for school, which takes up so many hours here, that was naturally quite out of the question with our approach to schooling.

The teacher, no matter how dreaded she may be, is held in especially high esteem by all her students. They would never fail to grant her due respect, and they always approach her, even later in life, with utmost regard. It is not unusual for someone to call upon the teacher as a last resort to help mediate a dispute. This somewhat resembles the way devout Catholics relate to their priests.

Oriental school children have at least one thing in common with their European counterparts: the natural instinct to try to win over their teachers with gifts, basically to bribe them. When my children here frequently asked me for a few coins to buy a bouquet or a flowerpot for Miss So-and-So, I could not help but think back to my own school days. This behavior lies deep in mankind itself, not in a particular nation. Before I had even an inkling of Germany and all its school children, I together with my siblings carted all sorts of things, preferably all sorts of snacks, to our teacher to gain her precious favor. We laid the best French bonbons, which our father took care to give us every day, at her feet. But the recipient, who to our joy, I am sorry to say, often endured major tooth pain and had to let us run free, was not always thrilled with our gifts. She claimed we were simply out to make her sick and exacerbate her tooth torments. And to be honest, I am quite sure we never really wanted this poor lady to get any meaningful relief from her hollow teeth.

---

11 *Al-nahu* or *al-nahw*, literally "the way," defines the Arabic rules of syntax. Credit for the Arabic word goes to Professor Emeri van Donzel, *An Arabian Princess Between Two Worlds*, page 211 (1993).

The duration of our schooling was never fixed. What there was to learn had, in any case, to be learned, whether it took a child one, two, or three years to get there. That depended totally on the child's natural abilities.

Lessons in handiwork did not belong to the school curriculum, if I may put it this way. This task belonged to our mothers, who almost universally had a ready, in some cases exemplary, competence in sewing, embroidery, and lace making. As a result, in this area, too, we had a wide range of training experiences, with learning heavily dependent on interest and inclination. I have sisters, for example, who are so talented they would have no issue whatsoever if they ever had to earn their daily bread through their own handiwork, while others would find it impossible to sew even a single button. —

Public schools are also available, but only for the sons of poor parents. Anyone with even moderate means keeps a private teacher. If necessary, the master of the house could also enlist his clerk to teach the lessons, although for girls naturally only while they are still very young.

That is what little I know to report about our schools. It is, of course, a natural topic for me, this comparison between these schools and the German ones, between hypereducated European school children and ignorant Arab ones. I was born and raised there, so I can speak firsthand from experience. I have lived here for many years and sent my own children to school, with every opportunity to develop my own views. I may even have an edge over natives, who, being so accustomed to some things, may not see what a neutral observer coming from a different culture might notice right away. I have absolutely no desire to set myself up as a judge—and precisely for this reason, it may interest some to become acquainted with my thoughts.

In general, I find that Europeans set overly high demands on schools to the same extent that Arabs set overly low ones. No people has yet found the right middle road, and none will find it. These contrasts will endure, not to be overcome, as long as the world continues to exist.

There is hardly anything more that children can be taught beyond what they are already taught here, which they are taught in such abundance that their juvenile brains cannot possibly retain it all. Once children enter school, parents no longer have anything of them. In addition to school hours, children are so overloaded with their many homework assignments that there is often little prospect of a comfortable family life together, nor the ensuing regular influence on their character development. The whole blessed day is but a never-ending rush and push from assignment to assignment. And how many of these assignments have no enduring value for the children! How much of it requires laborious learning and yet appears designed to recede into obscurity again as soon as possible. To let such things steal time away from children when they could instead be spending it with their families is surely wrong.

Meanwhile, these poor beings are crammed together five and more hours a day in a cage-like room, a so-called classroom, filled with indescribable heat and pent-up air. Why is anyone here still surprised when a school child gets sick? Young ones are nurtured and cared for at home, as much as possible, and then the school air makes these efforts all moot. How do some of these school children look; it pains the heart to see these pitiable beings! Was our open-air gallery not better? And what good is the highest-level education when the body is destroyed by its acquisition?

Generally, respect for elders was practiced not only towards parents, but also teachers and caretakers, in a way that went well beyond what we consider common practice here.

In my opinion, academic learning is emphasized much too much here. Everyone wants to advance more and more through their education, until no one is left to be a worker. Priority is placed on learning and knowledge. When the majority of people attain such lofty educational goals, then their desires and their justified and unjustified demands in life are naturally also on the rise, which leads to a more challenged and aggravated ability to exist, with all its consequences. Yes, the mind may be extraordinarily educated, but meanwhile the heart is ignored and pushed aside.

I was truly shocked to come across a statistic about the mentally ill, which indicated that the vast majority of these unfortunate cases were former students at high schools or institutes of higher learning; presumably many fell victim to academic pressures. I could not help but reflect on my homeland, where we do not need insane asylums and where I only ever came across two cases of insanity, one an African woman and the other from Hindustan.

As already indicated: My intention is not to cast judgment on all European education, something I am in any case unable to do. I simply wanted to share a few of my observations that have convinced me that schools and education here also have their share of negative aspects. It will accordingly be no surprise that it has always been and remains an open question for me if it is in fact appropriate for Europeans to lament as yet "unenlightened" folk, and if they should even be allowed to use external force to instill their enlightenment in them. Some will scoff and shrug their shoulders, but regardless! I can state with great certainty that those who believe it is in the interests of such peoples to have education and enlightenment brought to them are sorely mistaken. As an Arab woman that was born and raised in what Europeans consider a totally backward sphere, I know best how little resonance the European educational approach would find in the Islamic Orient.

With peoples that have other beliefs, who actually desire European enlightenment, as with the Japanese, the matter is different. May they find their way in, as best they can. Muslims, however, face innumerable elements in the European upbringing that are absolutely antithetical to their strictly religious point of view. How often people here demean the half-cultured Turks? And yet, they have endeavored, more than is good for them, to become civilized, if only to an extent. In so doing, they have merely weakened themselves, without reaching their goal, because European civilization conflicts with and runs counter to all their basic beliefs. Civilization simply cannot be compelled through force. One should in fairness allow other peoples the free and unencumbered right to continue to cultivate their national views and institutions, which have been developed over the course of centuries, undoubtedly through mature experience and practical wisdom. Above all, a pious Arab would be deeply violated by enlightenment attempts that start with the kind of scientific teachings that are at the core of European education. It would shock his whole being. Speaking to him of the laws of nature would cause him the most acute internal conflict when he sees in the whole of the universe, down to the minutest detail, with unshakeable faith, but one thing: the all-steering, all-overseeing hand of God!

Probing the deepest meaning of nature and all creation will surely always be an elusive quest for our limited human capacities. In my reading, I once came across quite an appealing reflection. Given our short duration on earth, humans were compared to dayflies that have seen the light of day in the Strasbourg Cathedral. In the same way that these little flies could not even begin to absorb this entire marvelous construct in all its details in the course of a single day, so, too, our short lifespans cannot come to know, much less understand, all the wonders of this world. May wise people continue to study and explore, but may we not fill the heads of our children with so much knowledge that they are then unable to comprehend. In seeking to keep the right balance here as well, may we above all, and I say it again and again, not forget the heart for the head.

CHAPTER TEN

Annual Provisions, Personal Care, and Fashion in Our House

Here in Europe, the paternal head of a household who provides a monthly or quarterly allowance to his wife and unmarried daughters is absolved from any further need to care for their upkeep. Things were quite different in my father's house. Zanzibar has no industry to speak of, and therefore also no factories. All clothing and all fabric for the entire population are acquired exclusively from abroad.

My father would thus undertake some amazing bartering to cover the massive needs of his houses. Every year several of his own big sailing vessels, as many as necessary, were loaded up with our local products (especially cloves) and sent to England, Marseille, Persia, East India, and China, where our local agents set about procuring whatever we needed in exchange. The captain in charge was always handed an endless shopping list, most of which invariably constituted items for our daily care.

The annual day of distribution for these items depended, of course, on the successful return of the ships. Our household naturally awaited these ships with increasing impatience. Their arrival signified the start of a new season for us, and our whole regime depended on their cargo for the entire subsequent year.

Even the younger children found these ships steeped in a special magic. They brought us all those wonderful toys from Europe. When on one such occasion, the first time the father gave me a finely dressed doll, which could cry and had front teeth, I was beside myself with joy.

Once the ships had successfully returned, a date was quickly set to distribute the contents to everyone in our house, old and young, high and low. Even before that date, the younger brothers beseeched and beset the captain of the ship to find out what special toys were on board. Twenty to thirty crates were always filled to the brim with toy horses, little wagons, dolls, whips, fish and ducks that followed magnets, music boxes in all sizes, harmonicas, flutes, trumpets, small guns, and more. If these items did not live up to our expectations, that was bad news for the captain. He was personally responsible for everything, had the broadest powers to act, and but one overarching order to follow: Always buy the best you can find and spare no costs.

When the distribution finally began in both Bet il Mtoni and Bet il Sahel, it always lasted three to four days, until every one of the hundreds of people had received their proper share. The eunuchs took care of the unpacking and sorting. My older siblings undertook the actual distribution. Envy, resentment, and jealousy were, unfortunately, never more evident in our house than during these days of delight.

The fabric for our clothes, whether luxurious or simple, was handed out in whole bolts, and it was up to everyone individually to exchange their excess with others. This took place on a large scale, often lasting a fortnight. Since we had no tables, cloth was cut while sitting on the floor, making it not uncommon for a lady to accidentally, in her zeal, cut into her own attire.

Also to be distributed were musk, ambergris, countless oriental fragrances, rose oil and rose water, saffron (which, in combination with other ingredients, is essential for women's hairstyles), silks in all colors, gold and silver threads (tinsel) for handiwork, and woven gold and silver buttons, in short, everything that belongs to an Arab lady's upkeep, plus a certain amount of Maria Teresa coins, naturally apportioned by rank and age, to cover the cost of other miscellany.

Now and again, a few fashion-addicted Oriental ladies will have spent more than their allotment over the course of the year and would thus have to ask the father or their husbands for special supplements. Such entreaties were presented only in the greatest secrecy, as Arab heads of households were not enamored of excessive waste, any more than here, and the petitioner was sure to get an unwelcome bonus lecture on top of any extra funds.

As is the case everywhere, our house featured not only wasteful characters, but also frugal ones. These held the laudable view that slaves were not just for luxury, as was normal for the noble and wealthy classes, but should instead become revenue generating. Their slaves were accordingly trained in a variety of crafts, like sewing, stitching, and lace making for young girls, or as a saddler, carpenter, or the like for older boys. Whoever took this course was naturally less likely to run out of pin money, whereas the others had to relinquish their cash to outsiders, making it hard to balance receipts and expenses. Slaves that had acquired special skills were also accorded greater status and would, in the event of a possible release, be better positioned to establish themselves. In Oman, where relatively few slaves are kept, it is the norm to teach them all a specific craft, so they can benefit both their masters and themselves. Slaves were thus often first sent from Zanzibar to Oman to, in effect, be raised and trained. They naturally became more valuable as a result.

If anyone happened to be visiting on distribution day, and the father heard of it, then this guest would also, according to rank, get a share of whatever was being distributed, even if it was just hard cash. Any leftover cargo was put in storage and intermittently distributed throughout the year to our kinfolk from Oman.

Since summer never ends below the equator, and the four seasons are known in name only, our yearly arrangements were considerably simplified. It would have gotten quite complex if we had had to take care of fall, winter, and spring at the same time. The monsoon, which lasts six to eight weeks and during which the temperature drops to about +18°R,[12] is the only winter we know there. In this time of year that was more wet than cold, we wore mostly velvet and other thick fabrics. We also tended not to wait until nine o'clock to enjoy some food, but took our tea and cakes earlier.

Every bit of our attire was prepared by hand. We knew nothing of sewing machines back then. Our apparel benefits from a simple cut that is the same for both men and women. The intolerably unhealthy practice of corseting has not yet affected Orientals, to the preservation of their precious organs. So it is not the cut, but the fabric and adornment that distinguishes the Oriental outfit. By contrast, people here are soon bored by sticking to one thing, although we need not settle whether lack of variety properly characterizes Oriental attire. One thing is certain, however, that "fashion" and its constant variability does

---

12 Noted using the Réaumur temperature scale with freezing of water at 0 degrees and boiling at 80 degrees, the equivalent of 22.5°C and 72.5°F.

not enrich the economy. To the contrary! Everyone can see for themselves how much family stress, and how many domestic scenes, could be avoided if we were more measured in our need for fashion. This addiction to always dressing in the latest style has unfortunately become so widespread that everyone is forced to participate *nolens volens*, regardless of whether they can or care to.

I have absolutely no intention of reversing the unreasonable fashion practices here or recruiting enlightened Europeans to become Philistines. I simply want to state that in point of profligacy, European women far surpass their Arab counterparts. How much it takes to stay even somewhat fashionable here: a paletot or shawl for the spring and so-called summer, a raincoat for the winter, lots of dresses, lots of hats (plenty of ladies have a special hat for every dress), various umbrellas also matched to hats and dresses, and so on. How modest by comparison is the wardrobe of an Arab woman!

The clothes of an Arab woman, regardless of rank, consist of only one ankle-length garment, a pair of pants (no bloomers), and a head scarf, as can be seen on the frontispiece.[13] The fabric varies greatly. Rich people prefer gold brocade in the most diverse patterns, velvet and silk with ample adornment, and only plain, light calicos and muslins for hot days. The garment and pants never have the same pattern. And care is taken not to allow the length of the garment to cover the rich embroidery of the pants and the two golden ankle bracelets, one of which is adorned with numerous bell-like gold pieces that pleasantly chime with every step. The headband, which is wound around the forehead, features two long ribbons with large tassels that hang down the back or either side of the head. The actual silk head scarf reaches down to the ankles.

When an Arab lady wishes to go out, she throws on her *shele*, which serves as shawl, paletot, jacket, raincoat, and duster all combined. This is a large, black, silk scarf, fitted with gold or silk trim according to the wealth and taste of its bearer. An Oriental woman wears this one and only covering until it is completely worn out without ever going out of fashion. Even the fanciest and wealthiest women make it a point to never own more than one *shele*.

During the monsoon, the finer Arab ladies in the house also wear a *djocha*, a kind of paletot that reaches down to the ankles and is made of cloth richly adorned with gold or silver embroidery. The *djocha* is worn exactly like the paletots here, which is to say never on its own, but always over the other regular clothes. It is open in the front from top to bottom and held together only at

---

13 Page xviii.

the chest level with gold braiding. Older ladies prefer a thick and sumptuous Persian shawl to the *djocha*.

This is thus the only piece of clothing that has any association with winter. Beyond that, of course, we have scant need to protect ourselves from the cold, since it never goes below +18° in the wet season.

Apropos, worth mentioning here, we also kept a kind of heating apparatus, and a very comfortable one at that. A brass bowl, roughly twenty centimeters deep and thirty centimeters wide, seated on three legs, each fifteen centimeters high, would be filled with glowing coals and placed in the middle of the room. This coal fire disperses an extraordinarily mild and pleasant warmth that draws everyone to the *mankal*. The very popular corn harvest happens during the same season, when corn is prepared in many different ways. A favorite is to shuck the fresh cobs, which grow significantly larger than here, and lay them for roasting on the glowing coals of the *mankal*; just five minutes, and they are ready to eat. As the corn on the cob starts to get done, it emits a steady popping noise, which was always great fun for us children. —Windows and doors almost always stay open, even with this small-scale heater.

Bet il Ras by Rosa Troemer

CHAPTER ELEVEN

On a Plantation

I mentioned previously that my father owned forty-five plantations that were scattered across the whole island. Each one had about fifty to one hundred, on the big ones up to five hundred, slaves as workers, under an Arab manager. Only two of these plantations came with real palaces, while six to eight had larger cottages, and the rest contained only staff and farm buildings. Consequently, we had access only to the first ones for longer stays.

During times when my father was in the city, we were unable to take a plantation outing all together because a portion of his governing entourage always had to stay with him, and he personally was too caught up in his business affairs to accompany us. But for us children and adults, it was always great fun to visit a plantation. My older siblings gave the good-natured father no peace until he permitted some of us to ride over without him.

Preparations for these outings were always quite involved. It was no small matter to ensure the plentiful upkeep of such a throng of people on a plantation that was often one or two German miles hence, for which everything was carried on the heads of slaves. Already three days prior, several hundred slaves were engaged to transport what was needed. Much to the dismay of the cooks and chief eunuchs, who had to take care of the entire company, these transfers resulted in considerable loss of food and heavy spoilage along the way, so they always had to provision double of what was actually needed. The plantation managers at the other end got the greatest benefit, since they were allowed to keep any leftovers for their own use.

Most participants remained sleepless with joyful anticipation the night before. Already that evening, they had inspected the snow-white passenger donkeys, whose tails were now colored red with a plant-based dye called *hinna*. Any of the ladies (namely, the *sarari*) who did not have their own donkeys would borrow from friends and acquaintances, or have them supplied by my brothers and the eunuchs. And yet, it was not unusual for someone to get left behind if she neglected to organize her transport on time. This was just something the father never concerned himself with; in this respect, everyone was on their own.

If the plantation we wanted to visit was on the coast, the matter was naturally much easier. In those cases, no one ever had to stay home for lack of transport. Our ships always put enough row boats at our disposal. Our provisions also benefited. Peacefully stowed in the boat, they naturally had a better chance of reaching their destination than when inconsiderately thrown back and forth by slaves at a large number of rest stops on country roads.

These outings seemed especially designed to bring out the ardor for all the extensive finery that Oriental women possess. Everything was mustered, everything was applied, lest there be any chance of lagging behind the others. And for any beauty facing the great misfortune of not having her new outfit ready on time, she would rather forgo the event entirely, lonely and alone.

As a rule, the departure time was set early at five thirty, directly after the first prayer. Leading up to this time, our courtyard was filled with such a confused and frenzied cacophony of voices and noises that anyone with weak nerves could have been brought to despair. Fortunately, people there are equipped with unusually robust nerves. The regular lifestyle, freedom from worry, and magnificent ocean air keep such nervous maladies from our shores.

The traffic on our two stairways backs up continuously. There are shouts down the stairs, shouts up the stairs, screams, and hefty pushes. Slaves exchange crude profanities and then resonant slaps in the face. The saddled animals, who have already been waiting an hour, are restless and start to add their pleasant donkey voices to the overall racket. All the while, they are earnestly endeavoring to indulge in their favorite activity, to roll around on the ground, never mind their rich adornment and charming tack. Their supervising slaves have their hands full just keeping them in check. And in the meantime, impatient travelers have already saddled up.

After everyone has inspected their animals in the courtyard, the animals are routed up over the elevated pitch to the street, where their owners mount. The weak and delicate eunuchs also ride along, while the stout African slaves must run the distance on foot. And thus begins the most amusing ride one could ever imagine. Great, but usually harmless, pranks are mixed in with cheerful joking, causing so much laughter that it can be hard to stay in the saddle.

The snow-white donkeys present a most picturesque sight, so richly decorated with little gold and silver plates that chime pleasantly with every step, and their lightly elevated saddles resting on fancy saddle pads. No less stunning are our foot runners with their exquisitely polished weapons and their clean, white attire. As the sun climbs higher, the more elegant ladies keep these African speed runners by their sides to be protected from the blazing heat with wide-reaching parasols that these runners carry as they stay apace. Other slaves trot along with small children straddling their shoulders. Somewhat older children, but not yet old enough to ride their own horses, are each assigned to ride with a eunuch.

We had to pass through the city while it was still twilight, and during this time, the whole company kept close together. But as soon as we were out in the open, all discipline came to an end, and everyone rode ahead at their own pace. Any efforts by the eunuchs to keep a closed caravan were in vain. Whoever felt themselves astride a fiery mount had little interest in holding back for the sake of the whole, and the eunuchs could call and shout in their delicate pitch however much they wanted. After having set out all together, as if by command in one big crowd, we reached our destination strung out in various larger and smaller groups.

There we were greeted by the first and oldest of our slaves at the plantation and, if the Arab manager was married, by his family. Being a man that adhered to custom, he himself was not allowed to be seen by any of us during our entire stay.

We always left for such outings on an empty stomach, and thus arrived with that much more appetite to enjoy the countless delicious fruits that had been set out for us. The first opulent main meal was served immediately afterwards, which the ensemble ate in our various groupings, as we did back home, according to rank. When the meal was done, everyone took off to do whatever they pleased. No one had to worry about spectators here, where only the dear cattle lowed under the magnificent trees. Here, everyone could be completely unrestrained and indulge to their hearts' delight. The group came back together as a whole only for mealtimes and prayers. All prayer requires cleansing, and since there was no water on parts of the island, that was reason enough to have to head home.

Over the course of the day, neighboring estates would send their invitations, and other neighboring ladies would announce their visits. Both invitations and visitors always applied to the whole family. In practice, though, outside guests were hosted exclusively by my older siblings, while invitations could be accepted by anyone who wanted to attend.

Our ability to live simply in the lovely South, since we hate to make a fuss, is evident in our mass outings. It would have been impossible to provide beds for all the many participants. Instead, everyone, whether of high or low rank, just lay down on their pile of saddle blankets and, in place of a pillow (ours always being round, much like the French), put their arms under their heads.

What we consumed on these occasions can hardly be described. I have already mentioned the extreme amounts of provisions brought over by hundreds of slaves over the course of many days. But that was not enough. Our kindly neighbors insisted on showing their good graces by sending daily shipments of massive amounts of cooked and uncooked food. As a rule, this was followed by various discomforts, much like the Christmas sicknesses here. —

Good old Ledda, the customs manager, was permitted to greet us, as a man of a different faith, even though Arab men were strictly forbidden to do so. He was unusually loyal and had a touching personal attachment to our whole house. Especially for us children, this grey-headed star worshipper took every opportunity to make us happy. On every one of his holidays, and ours as well, he made sure to share all sorts of delightful gifts from his Indian homeland, in particular many sweets and baskets of fireworks (*fetak*). As soon as he heard that we were planning a trip to the countryside, he made a special point of bringing such gifts. Every evening we then had fun burning the widest assortment of products made by talented Indian pyrotechnicians.

The evenings were otherwise filled with watching Africans play games and dance, which they did in the garden under the open sky. Native dancing is nowhere near as ugly and unpleasant as some travelers have claimed in their books. On the other hand, I, too, initially took a total dislike to European dancing. The eternally twirling pairs just made me dizzy, even when I was sitting still in my chair.

Hindustani dancers were also frequently brought out to the plantations to regale us in the evenings with their artistry. These dancers are extraordinarily talented and, even though they are not compensated as richly as in Europe, they quickly become very prosperous, regardless of their expenditures, and are able to return to their homeland with satisfaction. Even so, they get but minimal respect from us.

69

Such evenings in the Orient are truly romantic. Picture a large group, featuring an array of complexions, elegant, but very colorful and creatively dressed, gathered in a large circle, whether standing, sitting, or squatting, and filled with hearty laughter and harmless jokes in the relaxed manner of the South, and all that in lush greenery under the most magnificent trees, while bathed in the intense light that shines down from the tropical moon. You have to have experienced it to be able to imagine it. Not until late, very late in fact, would the gathering disperse, and the visiting ladies would mount their donkeys and ride home.

A whimsical little French girl by the name of Claire, along with her two wild brothers of fourteen or fifteen years of age, the children of a French consular doctor and very good at Swahili, were often included on these outings and knew how to liven things up with their songs. Claire precipitated general laughter one evening, on her first overnight with us, when she appeared—in her traditional European white nightgown.

For extended stays, our father might occasionally come out to visit us, but always returned to the city by evening. Horsemen then continuously circled back and forth to maintain a seamless connection between us and the city, as a kind of postal service.

Come harvest time, we preferred to avoid such outings because that would have disturbed the slaves too much in their work. The clove harvest comes upon us so suddenly and transpires so quickly that it is challenging to gather the whole bounty in good condition within the short time available. The rice harvest also has to be completed right away, whereas sugar cane, coconuts, sweet potatoes, and the other farm products could tolerate more of a delay. Cattle are never used for farming. Farm tools are practically nonexistent; we do not have even the most basic plow. Everything has to be done by hand. To turn the soil, we use spades. Rice ears are tediously cut by the bushel with standard small and straight knives. The master or mistress may even join the clove harvest, so as to motivate and energize their slaves. Africans are known to resist work, and they need very sharp and steady oversight to be productive.[14] That kind of ongoing control is, however, totally untenable for the clove harvest. A better method is to require a daily quota of cloves from each slave based on age and ability. Those who bring in more get extra wages; those who neglect their duties can expect commensurate consequences.

---

14 The author has been criticized for racist statements in her *Memoirs*. The translator provides some reflections in "On Controversy" on pages 243–51.

Only the actual harvest requires effort. Little is needed leading up to the harvest. The soil is so incredibly rich that it needs no fertilizing. And the general practice of burning straw on the fields fortuitously keeps the soil from depleting. —

The father always set the exact length of our plantation stays. He would determine the day we were to be back in the city between six thirty and seven thirty in the evening, after nightfall. At our departure, the plantation manager's family would receive suitable gifts hand-selected by the father, and our nearest neighborhood women usually accompanied us a bit down the road. The father always sent out about one hundred to one hundred and fifty soldiers that ran alongside the long procession. Despite their heavy load of weapons (at all times bearing rifle, shield, lance, saber, and dagger), they still managed to keep up with our mounts.

Even on these trips, the mandatory six o'clock evening prayer was not to be missed. And so the whole company would stop somewhere, typically in Ngambo or Mnazi Mmoja (both towns lie just outside the city), and settle into prayer mode. Everyone carried a small mat that they kept especially clean, on which to pray under the open sky. If, as often happened through negligence of the servants, a mat went missing or was even left behind at home, a huge leaf from the *moz* (banana) tree would be sent for as a substitute. We are allowed to pray on plant material only.

Darkness would quickly descend. As we returned to our mounts, a great number of colossal lanterns were lit. We then rode in almost fairy-tale splendor back into the city.

Macshale from the Harbour

CHAPTER TWELVE

The Father's Voyage

I was about nine years old when the time came for the father to go back to his old Omani empire, as he did every three to four years, to personally manage the situation there. Up to that point, my oldest brother Tueni (often called Sueni, but that is less correct) had represented him in Muscat, both as regent and head of the family.

This time my father had an especially urgent reason to travel to Oman. The Persians had made several incursions near Bandar Abbas on the Persian Gulf, which were not so significant on their own, but could have easily led to military entanglements. This small piece of land within Persia, with its controlling location at the entrance to the Persian Gulf, had given us nothing but trouble since its conquest and proved very costly for the father. It was taken from us again later, which was surely no bad fortune. Until then, the Persians gave us no peace, for which we could hardly blame them.

We had no steamboats back then, only sailing ships. We were thus very reliant on the wind and entirely dependent on its moods, which frequently delayed travel. Travel preparations took at least eight to ten weeks until everything was procured and in place. It took especially long to bake the so-called long-duration cakes that were needed to feed about a thousand heads over a ten-week period. Salt-cured meat was unknown to us, and food preserves, even if we had had them, were *haram* (unclean, contrary to the food laws) and not something we could enjoy. Instead, a colossal number of livestock had to be ferried along, including about a dozen milk cows. Incalculable quantities of fruit were added to the cargo. All forty-five of our plantations had to deliver fruit to the ships for days on end.

All the sons were allowed to participate in the trip, but only a few daughters, given the inconveniences that women generally cause. A couple of the *sarari* were taken along as well, but only the most favored ones.

In fact, not many of us wanted to go to Oman. The proud Omani women treat the Zanzibari women as an uneducated lot. This condescension even carried over to our siblings. Family members born in Oman deem themselves extraordinarily distinguished compared to us Africans. They believe that our upbringing among the natives has of necessity rubbed off on us. They consider our coarsest feature to be that we, how horrid! speak another language besides Arabic. —

As already mentioned several times, many of my siblings and many more of my relatives lived in Oman, most of whom were quite poor and depended on the support of our father. All of them expected presents when the father arrived, and so the travel load grew even larger.

At this time then, everyone's thoughts gravitated to their loved ones in far-off Asia, which caused the otherwise languishing correspondence to liven up. But this is where the inability to write would become a major obstacle. One had to witness the great predicaments that arose to truly appreciate the scale of the distress. Letters had to be written by someone else, and, at the other end, strangers would then have to read them to the recipients. My brothers and any literate male slaves were more than overloaded in this task, and when they were no longer able or willing (yes, that also happened), then this letter writing had to be outsourced, for better or worse, to complete outsiders. That these letters very seldom meet the mark goes without saying.

Here is an example: One of the beauties calls to her slave: "Feruz! Go to this-and-that *kadi* and tell him, he should write a sweet letter to my friend in Oman. Pay him whatever he charges for the letter." And then Feruz is loaded up with a host of details that the *kadi* should include in the letter. The *kadi*, however, is under time pressure with a dozen such letters to be written, and so it is no wonder when the various assignments get wildly mixed up. Triumphantly, Feruz returns to his lady: "Bibi, here are the letters!" To play it safe, this lady then goes to another literate person to have the letters from the *kadi* read back to her. She is soon astounded, and her dismay increases with every additional word. The letter is totally inaccurate. Where she wanted to offer condolences are congratulations, and vice versa, and so on. Every letter must therefore be written multiple times by multiple people until it is more or less in shape for mailing.

Everything was finally ready. The three-masted ship *Kitorie*, meaning "Victoria" (named for Her Majesty, the Queen of England), was assigned to the father and his family, and the other two or three were for the retinue, servants, and baggage. The number of travelers in relation to the total number of ships was thus very large. Notably, however, Orientals take up less space and do not require their own separate cabins. When night arrives, everyone looks for their own spot on the upper deck and lies down on the personal mats they brought along.

The retinue and servants embarked first. Then around five in the morning came the women and, toward midday, the father with his sons. My brothers Chalid and Madjid and the younger ones accompanied the travelers to the ship and stayed there until the anchor was raised. With a twenty-one gun salute, the father gave his last farewell to the country and family members that stayed behind. —

Right away our house fell into an unfamiliar quiet, even though the place was still overcrowded. We could tell the head of the family was missing, and a sort of solitude reigned despite the masses of people. My brother Chalid acted for the father, as the oldest son in Zanzibar. He stopped by our house multiple times a week to check on our well-being and went just as often to Bet il Mtoni to check on the inhabitants there, especially to take requests from our venerable stepmother.

As the leader of the family, Chalid was very strict, and we often had reason to complain about his harsh treatment. Here are two examples: A fire once broke out in Bet il Sahel, which, fortunately, was quickly extinguished. We understandably flew into a panic when it started and rushed toward the house doors, only to find them locked and tightly guarded by soldiers. Chalid had immediately ordered the doors closed, so there could be no chance that we might recklessly, in broad daylight, emerge to the eyes of the public.

Another time, he brusquely expelled a distant relative, who was very influential in Zanzibar, from a mosque because this man had had the temerity to ask him in that space for the hand of one of our sisters. For months thereafter, this poor suitor could not present himself at the daily official gatherings, nor in this mosque where Chalid tended to pray. Destiny, however, saw to it that this rejected fellow took another sister of ours home with him a few years later, after the father and Chalid had died.

To the chagrin of many, the father had appointed Chole to be the female head of household at Bet il Sahel and Bet il Tani during his absence. It was easy to understand why this bright light of our house found no joy in her leadership role. How could it be otherwise when this post engendered nothing but jealousy and lack of gratitude? Despite her good nature, there was no way to satisfy everyone; she was as human as the rest of us mortals. Impossible demands were made of her, and no one cared about the limits of her power. She could hardly help the fact that the father favored her, but the jealousy was simply too great and robbed any sense of perspective from those who thought ill of her. —

In the meantime, our three-masted ships often sailed back and forth between Oman and Zanzibar, bringing frequent news and gifts from the father. Whenever these ships docked, there was understandably much joy. The place would always be full of people rushing around, with lots of noise and lively gesticulating, the way only those in the South can.

Sadly, not long after the father's departure, our brother Chalid was called back to the Lord. The regency transitioned to Madjid, now the oldest son, who knew how to win over all the hearts with his kind nature.

Finally one day, a ship arrived from Muscat with the joyful news that the father was ready to leave Oman and return to Zanzibar. The news spread quickly and raised the spirits of the whole country. Our father had been gone for three years and was indeed missed at times. Even those who were not lovingly attached to him at least looked forward to the endless supply of gifts for young and old that he always made sure to bring back from Oman. The whole place was full of anticipation, and preparations worthy of our greatest celebrations were happening everywhere.

But the time passed in which the travelers could have readily reached Zanzibar, and still there was no ship in sight. The house and the country eventually became restless. Arabs love to probe the hidden future with so-called clairvoyants, and in Swahili lands, in Zanzibar, this custom is especially pronounced. Even Hungarian gypsies would have a lot to learn from their Swahili counterparts. What the latter practice in terms of lies and deceit is beyond description. On the other hand, gullibility knows no bounds.

Understandably, no stone was left unturned in seeking any possible explanation for the three missing ships, and so these fortune tellers were trafficked in droves through our house. They were brought in from miles away, often from the furthest corners of the island, especially from the tribe of the *Wachadimu*. If the fortune tellers were elderly, they were seated on donkeys and triumphantly trotted in.

An unusually bizarre appearance came in the form of a woman, who, it was said, or more precisely her unborn child, could foretell the future. We had never seen such a monstrosity, so of course, she had to be called in for questioning. It was on an afternoon (the scene is forever indelibly marked in my memory) when this soothsayer, or seemingly sacred person, who was possessed of an unnaturally large circumference, strode past me. The child, which she had allegedly carried under her heart already for years, was virtually omniscient. It could report on everything, from what was happening high up in the mountains to what could be seen deep down in the oceans. Now it was going to tell us about the fate of the father and explain why his arrival was so delayed. With a distinct, but very squeaky voice, this enormous being recounted her vision, while the whole, sizeable assembly sat spellbound. From afar, it saw several three-masted ships on the high seas headed toward Zanzibar. It wanted to ascend the mast of the father's ship to see what was going on there. After a short while, it described in minute detail what each person was doing at that very moment. To conclude, it told us to bring copious offerings to ensure the continued good favor of the sea spirits, so as to guard and protect the travelers from harm. The instructions of this exceptional child were of course strictly followed in every detail. All the professional beggars, of which we have legions on our lovely island, were able to indulge for days on end in the abundant meat, chicken, and rice, not to mention clothing and cash, that we had distributed to them.

I was later ashamed to realize we had all simply fallen victim to a ventriloquist. At the time, we were all convinced that this amazing child had the ability to unveil the invisible world, all the secrets that were totally hidden from human perception. Whether this woman was indeed a fraud that fully intended to deceive us, I am not sure. No one had ever heard of a ventriloquist, and therefore no one could have come up with that explanation. Maybe this woman herself had no clear sense of the matter. Maybe she actually believed, when she heard those strange tones for the first time, that this was an unusually precocious and privileged child and then only gradually became a sophisticated swindler.

We do love all things mysterious in our parts; the more esoteric and opaque the matter appears, the more we buy into it. Everyone believes in invisible spirits, both good ones and bad. When someone dies, their room is thoroughly fumigated with incense for days in anticipation of the expected, frequent return of the pining soul of the deceased, which usually prefers the room where it died, where no one likes to enter, certainly under no circumstances at night.

And superstitions abound. For sickness, betrothal, pregnancy, and all manner of events, people seek the help of fortune tellers. They want to know if the sickness can be cured and how long it will take; if fortune will smile on the betrothed; if the expected child will be a boy or girl; and so on. If the opposite in fact occurs, which naturally happens time and time again, the soothsayer always has a plausible excuse at the ready. She says it must have been her unlucky star on that particular day—better luck next time. And people accept that. Whoever takes up this kind of business does not fare poorly and is soon a made man or more precisely, a made woman.

Muscat Harbour
from the Fisherman's Rock

A View of Muscat from the East

CHAPTER THIRTEEN

News of a Death

Time slipped away, day after day, week after week, with no sign of the father. The long wait was shortened only by the never-ending dealings with the soothsayers, so there was at least some good in that, even if their prophecies never came true. Finally one afternoon, while we were still at prayer, the happy news spread that a fisherman had seen several ships with our flags far out on the high seas, although stormy weather kept him from getting any closer. That could only be the father! Everyone rushed to put on their festive outfits that had been ready for weeks, to welcome the long-awaited father with the greatest joy. We always preened and adorned ourselves like this for loved ones returning from travel or even after victorious battle, while we wore decidedly simple and unadorned clothes to express our sorrow on a day of departure.

Even as we made the fisherman swear to us over and over again that he was telling the truth, we sent a mounted messenger to share the news with our venerable stepmother in Bet il Mtoni. The courtyard became active with slaughter, cooking, and baking, the chambers were richly perfumed, and everything was put in the best order. According to the fisherman, we could expect the ships to arrive within two to three hours.

Madjid rushed out with his retinue to reach the father. They set off in two cutters, fighting against a massive storm that threatened to obliterate them and their boats at any moment. They hoped to be back in our midst at the latest by seven that evening, together with the father. But man proposes and God disposes.

Time passed. Seven o'clock had long come and gone, and still there was no sign of the ships. An unusual disquiet gripped the whole city, but mostly our house. We sensed that something was amiss, although not quite that, which we were soon to learn. We feared that Madjid and his escorts could have lost their lives in the raging gale, and this horrible discovery naturally would have delayed the father's arrival. Eventually the view prevailed that all the ships, large and small, had gone under in the storm. Conjecture was heaped on conjecture. No one, not even the youngest children, wanted to go to bed before those we awaited had happily arrived.

And then a message suddenly spread that no one wanted to believe. The whole palace was said to be surrounded by several hundred soldiers keeping strict guard. Everyone rushed to the windows to see for themselves. The night was pitch black, and all we saw in all directions were the glowing fuses of soldiers' weapons, a sight that could only add to our already petrified spirits. And to make matters worse, we were informed that the soldiers were not letting anyone pass, neither in, nor out.

What has happened? Why are we locked in? Everyone wanted to know. Principally, though, we debated back and forth about who had issued the order. Madjid had, as much as anyone knew, not yet returned, and even his own house—where we could clearly see figures pacing restlessly back and forth in the bright lights—was also guarded by sinister figures, just like ours.

With the eunuchs and all the other male slaves sleeping outside the house, we were in especially dire straits. The whole building contained only women and helpless children. A few fearless women showed great courage and pushed forward to the front hall on the ground floor where only one more door separated them from the designated security room, where they could readily speak with the guards through the hall windows. But these men proved hard and heartless, as they kept to their orders and withheld all information. When the shrieks and queries of the slave women got to be too much, the guards swore high and holy that if they did not settle down, they would simply shoot them down.

We cried and hurled accusations at the invisible power, which clearly was an evil one. The children cried and screamed everywhere and could not be calmed. The pious prayed to the Almighty. It was a spectacle that defies description. Had anyone happened upon the dreadful disarray of this night of horror, they surely would have thought themselves in an insane asylum.

Morning was already dawning, and still we had no idea why we were being treated as hostages or where Madjid might be. Even with all our fear and agitation, we dispersed into groups at the appointed time for morning prayer duty. But alas, who can describe our utter dismay when we finally saw our fleet, clearly anchored before us with flags at half-mast. How unspeakable the lamentation when our gates opened in the early morning, and our brothers came to us without the father!

Only then did it become clear to us for whom the ships mourned, what irreparable loss we and our country were meant to endure. Our dear father is no longer! On this trip from Oman to Zanzibar, amidst but a few of his children and faithful followers, he had been called to meet the Lord, whom he had always served with the greatest humility! The gunshot wound to his leg, that had plagued him for so long, had finally put an end to his precious life.

This departed soul was not only the most caring head of his family, he was also the most conscientious ruler and true father of his people. How beloved he was could be seen in the widespread grief at his passing. Black flags waved from every house, and even the very poorest hut had set out a small black cloth.

We learned details of the father's illness and his last hours from Barghash, who was on the same ship and with him at his death. We also had Barghash to thank that the precious corpse had not been lowered into the bottomless sea, as required by Islam. Barghash had spoken forcefully in favor of taking the father back to Zanzibar, and even had him preserved in a coffin to enable the transit. His natural devotion to the dear father led him to do this, but in so doing, he violated our traditions and customs, our religion, even more. For us, coffins are completely unacceptable. Every one of us, from prince to pauper, all of us in the same way are to be returned directly to the lap of Mother Earth, back to that from which we came.

Now we also discovered why we had been so strictly guarded the night before. Madjid, with his retinue, had suffered greatly in the storm and feared they would go under. Their small vessels, which were designed only for coastal runs, had had to sail far out to sea to reach the ships. By the time they arrived, Barghash was gone. As the eldest son on the flotilla, he had taken command and, with land in view, had ridden off quietly to take the body to shore and bury it secretly and unseen in our burial ground.

This maneuver arose from an old tradition that any disputes over the throne were to be handled in the presence of the body of the deceased father or brother, with the expectation that filial devotion would, as a rule, benefit the rightful heir. But Barghash wanted to win the lordship for himself. Knowing that such a formal rite would favor Madjid, he decided to thwart it altogether.

He opted instead for blatant force, above all hoping to blindside everyone while they were still reeling from news of the death.

He had therefore, immediately upon landing, ordered our house and Madjid's to be surrounded, with the goal of capturing Madjid there. And yet, his plan failed, since Madjid had already set out to sea. Barghash later sought to explain his measures as an attempt to forestall a potential revolution. —

And so Madjid, who, as already mentioned, had ruled Zanzibar as the acting head following Chalid's death, retained his position and proclaimed his status as ruler that same morning. But we still hung in the fearful uncertainty about whether he was truly our leader, or if our oldest brother Tueni, who continued to stay back in Oman, might not seek to wrest his entitlement by force.

CHAPTER FOURTEEN

Our Mourning

Our mourning was full of rituals. For starters, all of us, young and old, had to remove our fine clothes and were allowed to dress in only the most common black cotton. Our richly embroidered face coverings were replaced by plain, black fabric. Creams and perfumes of any kind were strictly off-limits, and anyone who sprayed rose oil or even rose water just once onto their clothes was considered heartless, or at least decried by all as a coquette. All the adults refrained, at least initially, from sleeping on their beds. Like the father, who slumbered directly on the ground, so, too, his beloved, if they wished to express their devotion, had to deny themselves such comforts.

For a full fortnight, our house was like one of the largest hotels in the world. During this time, anyone and everyone could come and eat their fill, whether prince or pauper. In keeping with long-standing custom, especially the favorite dish of the deceased is always cooked and served to the poor in massive quantities.

All wives of the deceased man, without exception, from those of noble birth to purchased slaves, must observe a special religious mourning period that spans a full four months. These poor souls are obliged to grieve for their husband or master in a dark room. They cannot intentionally step into daylight, much less sunshine. If a *terike* (widow) ever has to leave her artificially darkened room and go through the open gallery, she must throw a dark, heavy scarf over her mask, covering herself to the point where she can barely find her way. During this time, the eyes become extremely sensitive to light and can only slowly resume direct exposure after the mourning period comes to an end.

Right at the start, widows are formally tied to their status through specific ceremonial words uttered by the *kadi*, a kind of priest, to whom they of course appear fully covered. He then also has to expressly free them from this widow status with a special ceremony when the four months are over. There are other dark and superstitious rites that widows are subjected to on the day of their release. Above all, they must simultaneously undergo a complete cleansing, from head to foot, while each one is flanked from behind by a female slave that clangs two sword blades over the head of her mistress in a regular rhythm (poor people may have to use nails—the material must be iron). Given the number of widows the father left behind, there was no way to conduct the ceremony in the baths, which were too small for this purpose despite their great expanse. And thus, the cleansing of all these women was undertaken on the beach, making for a peculiarly animated and outlandish spectacle.

From then on, the widows wore different clothes. Only now could they contemplate remarriage. Although previous access to them had already been restricted to male family members and our personal slaves, this was even further restricted after the four months, so that no one but our brothers could see our mothers. —

In our first year of mourning, some of us went regularly on Thursday evenings, the eve of the Islamic Sunday, to visit the father's gravesite. It was a rectangular structure with a large dome, in which other siblings of mine also rested in peace. After reciting the first sura of the Koran (effectively the Islamic Lord's Prayer) and other verses, and pleading to the Almighty to show mercy to the departed and grant forgiveness for their sins, we would pour precious rose oil and rose water over the graves and waft smoked ambergris and musk, while wailing loudly about the painful loss.

Muslims maintain an unwavering belief in immortality, and accordingly also believe that the soul of the deceased is permitted, now and again on special occasions, to visit the former site of its own earlier being and its relatives, naturally unobserved. That is why we like to go to a beloved gravesite and share all our joy and pain with the immortal soul of the deceased, who still pays intimate attention to us in the afterlife. In short, we honor the dead in all ways. One can be confident that a decent Muslim, who swears by the head or the name of his deceased, would sooner perish than violate the sworn oath. —

As long as our mothers were in mourning, our houses kept to their usual routines. We, of course, could not conduct any business during this time. But we also had to first settle our affairs with our siblings in Oman. A ship was immediately dispatched to share the news of the misfortune that had hit us so hard. How would Tueni, who was the father's oldest son and by rights entitled to be his successor, react to all this? Would he come to an understanding with Madjid, or did we have a violent family quarrel looming on the horizon? Such questions were in daily discussion.

After quite a few months, our brother Muhammed arrived in Zanzibar as the representative of our siblings in Oman, primarily to participate in the distribution of the estate. And then he returned to Muscat as quickly as possible, the moment his task was done. Muhammed was considered the most religious of all our family members. From youth onwards, he had cared little for the world and worldly interests. As an enemy of all that glittered externally and all material goods, he had never embraced his status as prince. He put little stock in riches and never wore elaborate attire, in lieu of clothes that were very modest and plain. Since Omanis were not accustomed to much pomp, he found the Zanzibari opulence all the more off-putting. So much grandeur made him feel outright unhappy. Hence his great haste to be able to return without delay to the simpler conditions of our original Asiatic homeland.

The question of succession remained unaddressed. Madjid, who held the power in Zanzibar, made no issue about whether Tueni, who now took full control of Oman, was on board with his illegitimate position, and Tueni in turn never formally recognized him as the Sultan of Zanzibar. Later they came up with a sort of compromise, through British mediation, under which Madjid was to pay his older brother an annual sum. Madjid, however, kept to the agreement but a short while and soon stopped making payments, since they could easily be seen as a kind of tribute to, and he as a vassal of, Oman. Tueni could do nothing about it. He had battles of his own to fight in Oman, and his means were no match for the wealthy ruler of Zanzibar, should he have wanted to exert his rights by force. Lacking a formal, contractual basis, Oman and Zanzibar have ever since continued as two separate kingdoms, independent of each other.

By contrast, the siblings were able to agree on a distribution of the father's private estate with Muhammed's engagement. We have no nation-state in the European sense and therefore have nothing that stems from this label or concept. In particular, we have no concept of government income or expenditure. Whatever customs duties came in were simply private assets of the ruler, our father. With these and especially the profits from his plantations, considering that he was also the largest landowner on the island, he covered all costs and filled his treasury. In turn, at least in my time, we also had no income, property, business, or other taxes, unlike the many we have here.

All these private assets were distributed among the siblings. Even the military ships were handled this way and accrued to Tueni and Madjid as offsets from their shares under an agreed formula. Islamic law gives significant advantage to sons over daughters in matters of inheritance, under a justification that a man has a duty to maintain his entire family, which a woman does not. And so, we sisters received only half as much as our brothers.

Even I was declared of age, together with my brother Ralub, my former playmate in Bet il Mtoni, although we were both barely twelve years old. This was early even for our customs, but it was simply an unusual time for us all, and one upheaval followed another. We thus received our inheritance just like the others and were standing on our own two feet at twelve years of age. Our still younger siblings remained under Madjid's guardianship, who kept custody over their assets.

In his last will and testament, my father had instructed that any of his women without children should be cared for as long as they lived. By contrast, the mothers of his children received only a relatively small, one-time payout. He may well have assumed that we would care for our own mothers, but in this way, the mothers ended up entirely dependent on their children, the mother owning practically nothing, and the child everything. But the father had gauged his children correctly. I can, to the credit of all my siblings (we totaled thirty-six still living at the time of his death), gladly certify that not one disappointed his admirable trust in them. They all loved and respected their mothers as before; no one ever took advantage of their privileged position. Indeed, that would have been extremely damnable. A mother is always a mother, whether she is a born princess or a purchased slave. She needs neither rank nor riches to forever have a rightful claim to the greatest devotion from her child.

Not long after distribution of the inheritance was completed, our once-crowded house became empty and lonely, at least in comparison to earlier times. A number of my siblings, together with their mothers and personal slaves, moved out of the father's houses to establish their own homes. Chole, Shewane, Aashe, my mother, and I chose not to follow this example right away, and so I continued to live with them and my mother for some time at Bet il Tani.

Changes also took place at Bet il Mtoni, with Zemsem moving out to her new plantation where she stayed until her subsequent marriage, and Mettle also transferring a short time later to hers. It was, in fact, necessary that some of us leave the big houses, now that we were able to live independently and unrestrained, according to our own tastes. We needed to make room for our younger, underage siblings.

Having been collectively cared for out of an admittedly massive common pot during the father's lifetime, this now, of course, changed things. Everyone who had received their inheritance henceforth had to take care of themselves. Conditions were unchanged only for the underage siblings, alongside their mothers and slaves, and the women without children. Their care was now Madjid's responsibility, so that all their wealth and earnings were naturally at his disposal.

Sultan Madjid bin Said

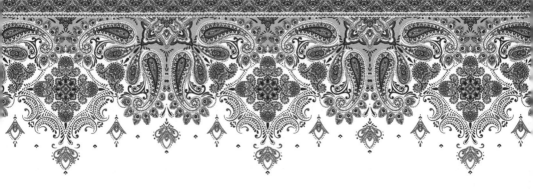

CHAPTER FIFTEEN

Personalities and Stories of My Siblings

Over the course of my narrative, I have already spoken about my siblings, some more, some less. How many siblings I had overall, I do not know. Certainly, a large number had already passed away before the father died, and I do not believe I exaggerate when I put the total around one hundred. When the father died, we were thirty-six, eighteen sons and eighteen daughters. If I were to list each one and recount the personalities and fates of them all, European readers would hardly take interest. And yet, I cannot help but say a bit more about at least some of them, so as to highlight a series of characteristics and traits that illustrate the life, traditions, and customs of my homeland more clearly.

1. Sharife

Our father, who managed the government himself and personally oversaw everything, had little time for his younger children. He directed all the more loving attention to the adults. This raised considerable jealousy among the host of little ones, who, like the older brothers, had to stand before him as stiff as sentinels, while the older daughters were allowed to join him on the sofa. My childish jealousy found its target mostly in my sister Sharife, while for my brothers, it was Hilal.

Sharife, the daughter of a Circassian, was a blinding beauty with the complexion of a German blond. She also had a sharp mind, which made her a loyal advisor to the father. Whether in war or peace, he discussed everything with her, and, as I was later told, only rarely or almost never had cause to complain about her counsel. Certainly, proof again that Oriental women rate more than mere simpletons.

She had only one period of disagreement with the father. Following her heart, she married a cousin whose character the father deemed substandard for the husband of his favorite child. After that, she avoided the father's house until his disapproval finally subsided. She had chosen well and remained the exclusive wife of her husband. Her only child, Schnun, a most beautiful young boy that she loved passionately but raised very strictly, was my playmate. Every Friday, when he came with his mother, he would bring me a little something, especially when the monsoon (Arabic *mossem*) sent the ships from Muscat to us. Sharife had many connections there. She loved Muscat above all and lived out the end of her life there while accompanying the father on his last trip.

2. Chole

When I got to know Bet il Sahel, as I mentioned, Chole became my ideal. She was particularly close to the father, and her charming manner, effervescence, and grace totally won him over. Never again have I come across a woman that was as perfectly proportioned as Chole. She had excellent taste in how to dress, and everything looked good on her. Even when everyone showed up in their finest velvet from Lyon, she could wear a simple calico dress and stand out from all the rest, like a born ruler to her underlings. Her judgment in all aspects of fashion was considered as unerring as that of Empress Eugenie in her time for all of Europe.

Chole's mother, who was from Mesopotamia, had such excellent discretion and intelligence that the father gave her top oversight of the household in Bet il Sahel. Chole's own much older, proper sister Aashe always caused Chole much suffering, which she bore with touching fortitude. Whenever other sharp tongues sought to disparage Aashe to her, Chole always coolly brushed them off. Only I knew how deeply her sister's behavior pained her, for she divulged all her suffering to me, withholding no secrets from me, despite my young years. "Oh my God, Salme," she often exclaimed in tears, "what have I possibly done, how can I help it, that the father chooses to favor me? Do I not share everything I get from him with her? Am I to blame that the father constantly calls for my help?"

Sadly, many in the house showed her the same resentment. If people needed her to put in a good word with the father, they would flatter her. Then in no time, her loving support was forgotten. She assisted her mother in overseeing the household, and the father later transferred full responsibility to her. That was fodder for many new complaints. It was impossible to satisfy everyone in the overcrowded palace. If the extreme heat caused even one chicken, one piece of meat, one fish to spoil, if plantation fruits arrived late or were squashed, if goods procured for the residents did not meet their expectations, if Turkey had a bad rose harvest with insufficient rose water and rose oil for our huge consumption: Chole was to blame for it all. She was made responsible for everything.

What people resented even more was that the father took her into the treasury with him or even sent her there alone. Her enemies would have liked to search her at the exit every time, treating her just like the pearl divers in the Persian Gulf, to make absolutely sure she absconded with nothing for herself. So great was this spiteful jealousy and resentment. And then one day, these numerous adversaries were confronted with the appalling news that the father had given her a very pricey, opulent crown, ordered especially for her from Persia. This truly marvelous tiara consisted of many golden, diamond-laden palms, with one large palm in the center flanked on both sides by more palms that decreased in size all the way to the capstones at the ends. It was not suitable as actual headgear, but instead constituted a valuable asset for times of need. Considering how much every Oriental woman loves jewels, it is not hard to understand that such a magnificent gift only increased the number of Chole's enemies. Even the father was bitterly resented for this kind of preferential treatment, although he was clearly in no position to satisfy all the wishes of his large family.

And how did Chole handle this envy? That was her best quality: She always stayed equally gracious, equally accommodating toward everyone. She never had a single thought of revenge or retaliation. Her attitude was always: "If the father is satisfied with what I do, then that must suffice for me."

Chole cared faithfully for me as a child, and later became my dearest friend. When she moved from Bet il Sahel to Bet il Tani after the father died, our relationship grew especially close. We were always together. I ate at her place, or she at mine. We talked long into the night and sought our rest side by side. How much influence she won over me will become clear later. She kept her love for me all her life. In 1871, after the death of my husband, she commissioned a letter to me, as she was unable to write herself, saying I should send her one of my children for her to adopt. I was unable to take her up on it, as the child would have had to become Muslim.

Her generosity and gentleness became truly proverbial. Her subordinates were very well kept in her services. She forgave all their mistakes and always put in a good word for the slaves of others. I, for example, had a Nubian slave who had mastered the art of cooking while in a Persian household in Oman. As good as she was for my physical well-being, she soon became insufferable, since anything that came near her went missing. None of the many warnings and unmaskings made a difference, so I finally decided to sell this thief. When Zafrane, so the name of this fiend, found out, she ran in the dead of night to my Chole's plantation to plead for her benevolent help. As skilled as she was in garnering Chole's sympathy, I had no choice but to keep this dangerous person for the love of my sister.

After the father died, Chole (who received no more than the rest of us) used her inheritance to acquire one of our most beautiful plantations, which the father had frequented most often. Complete with a gorgeous palace and splendid furnishings, this cost her a hefty sum and brought little income. And yet, she paid no mind to such calculations in her devotion to the father, who had loved her like the apple of his eye. She gladly made the greatest sacrifices simply to own his favorite refuge. Every year, around the clove harvest, she would spend two to three months in Sebe, as the plantation was called. I have such unforgettable memories of those days, as I ambled with Chole, hand in hand, under the wonderfully fragrant trees in the garden, and as we conversed innocently and easily with the many slave children or sat in the deep window bank and watched people go about their day.

The sumptuously furnished room of the father was never used and only opened for distinguished guests upon special request.

Her hospitality was grandiose, and Sebe's beauty always drew many guests. The rarest of plants, otherwise unknown in Zanzibar, decorated the garden, and everything was carefully nurtured by the cherished caretaker, just like in the father's times.

A most charming stone building stood in front of the formidable wall that encircled the garden, in the shade of a marvelous tree, larger than the largest oaks we have here. It had only one room, with a marble floor, ceiling-high wall mirrors, masses of colorful lanterns, and scores of cane chairs. Whenever he spent time in Sebe, the father would drink the evening coffee here with his male associates. Now we could visit this beautiful and refreshing place undisturbed, to enjoy ourselves like children and remember our dear father.

The much beloved, much envied, and much despised Chole is no longer of this world. I had to lose her in the year 1875. She was said to be the victim of a treacherous poisoning, although the matter was never fully clarified. She remains close to me always!

3. Aashe

Seldom has nature been so capricious when endowing two proper sisters as in the case of Chole and Aashe. While Aashe had a small figure and dark skin, Chole was tall with light skin. Where Aashe was completely disfigured by smallpox, Chole was the perfect Oriental beauty. And while Aashe presented a formal, closed, yes, even cold manner, Chole was charming in her natural generosity and goodness, even if, on the other hand, Aashe did surpass her in intellect. The contrasts could not have been starker. Asian relatives coming for a visit could never believe that Aashe and Chole stood before them as two true sisters.

Poor Aashe was acutely aware how much her face bore the pockmarked scars of smallpox and therefore rarely appeared unmasked. She always stayed covered, even among her siblings and servants. Understandably, she cared little about her appearance. Relative to rank, she dressed very plainly and looked almost shabby next to other family members. A single Abyssinian slave, who was very adept at finery and hair care, served her simultaneously as hairdresser, milliner, and chamber maid.

By contrast, she was acknowledged far and wide as the top food connoisseur, and indeed, no one making the rounds would have encountered a cuisine as fine as what she offered. Others accordingly sought to place young people under her experienced kitchen staff to learn the many secrets of the proper art of cooking. Even my brother Madjid took up her services. Every day he had her staff prepare five to eight dishes, for which he paid a fixed monthly sum.

With her intelligence, she was often engaged to referee and always showed sound discretion with the right answer. This sharp mind especially did wonders for her finances. She conducted her business masterfully, a compliment that only few of us deserved. Her accounts were never in the red, not even prior to the harvest that was essential for replenishing our purses. Big spenders, on the other hand, were wont to call her stingy now and again. —

Her favorite brother was poor Hilal. She was unusually devoted to him and cared for his oldest son Suud in every possible, motherly way after his death.

4. Chadudj

Chadudj, Madjid's sister, is already familiar to the reader. Although preferred in our house to Aashe, she lived with Madjid, whom she loved above all else, and therefore had less contact with us.

In later years, she assumed the role of mother for our twice-orphaned, youngest brother Nasor. Weary of life after Madjid died, she headed with him to the final refuge of Muslims, to Mecca. There they were both, one after the other, soon called from this world.

5. Shewane

When I moved into Bet il Sahel, Shewane became my playmate. She was older than me, but closest in age of all my siblings. Gifted with a clever mind, strong build, and a look that would have subdued a lion, she was bound to play an important role in the house. She basically appointed me her errand boy. Every day I was made to feel her admonishing hand, and, as thanks for my service, I received at most a flattering: "You white monkey!" She was the daughter of an Abyssinian, a people known by us for both their heated temperament and intelligence. And I came from a "white" mother, which subjected me to various attacks by my darker siblings. But nothing like what my brother Djemshid had to endure, having inherited not only the hair, but also the blue eyes, from his blond mother.

Early on, not long after the father's death, Shewane also lost her mother and her only proper brother Ali, whose markedly different character had made him more popular than her. Half grown, she stood alone in a world that was so different from what she would have wished. She felt no warmth for any of the many brothers except perhaps Madjid, and then only out of her devotion to Ali, who had been his close friend.

Her truly majestic figure and the almost classical beauty of her face lent her a dignity that impressed everyone. Her main character trait was a well-developed sense of independence. She could never get herself to seek advice from anyone, and no one quite knew what she was about. Unable to write, she was taken advantage of by a cunning African slave, who thoroughly fleeced her. Despite her gruff approach, she was extraordinarily benevolent, and towards her subordinates, she was strict, but always fair.

She sought out the handsomest and choicest slaves and overloaded them with the most precious weapons and jewels. Everything around her radiated with the splendor and riches of fairy tales.

I was the only sister who managed to get along with her, more or less, despite all the rough treatment I had had to endure in my younger years. When I occasionally found an opportune moment to open up with her about how much others criticized her huge expenditures, specifically her extensive display of slaves, she would respond quite calmly that she was well aware that she did not have long to live and wanted to bestow some of her wealth on poor people during her lifetime, or use it up as quickly as possible herself, so there would be nothing left for us to inherit. She was rich, having taken on Ali's considerable fortune, in addition to her own share of the father's estate. But she still stayed on in the father's house, even into her later years, which was generally disfavored.

Shewane had no interest in the opinions of others. Even though she lived under the same roof with hundreds of people, she looked to no one and lived only for and among her many slaves. For this reason, we also did not learn of her grave illness until it was too late. Angered by Chole's and my alleged unkindness, she refused to receive any more visitors from that time on. No matter how much our hearts bled, we could not go against her will. She always got her way. And when she realized that her flourishing life was being undone by an unstoppable case of galloping consumption, she made all those around her promise high and holy that no one, other than the woman who washed her corpse, would ever see her dead body. Her command was strictly observed. As soon as Shewane passed away, her room was firmly locked. Only after the corpse had been washed, bestrewn with camphor, and wrapped in white linen seven times around, including her face, all as prescribed, only then were we allowed to go to her. Speechless, I knelt before her corpse and embraced her, not heeding the fearful individuals that warned me of contagion and sought to pull me away. In such moments, even if only briefly, our normally very controlling egoism relents.

Despite our considerable differences, I was devoted to Shewane with all my heart. I always defended her, and anyone who could see past her abrupt style and peculiarities was bound to love her. Her pride and ambition made her some enemies, especially among older people who chose not to tolerate them. And indeed, precisely this pride was one of her many riddles, considering that her soul was filled with a strong and deep faith.

Even on her deathbed, she still looked after her city slaves and the higher-ranked land slaves. She not only gave them freedom, but also gifted them all her costly weapons and jewels, in addition to an entire plantation for their livelihoods. All those who had taken such care of her should no longer need to earn their upkeep after her death.

6. Mettle

Mettle was, like Shewane, the daughter of an Abyssinian, but no one could tell because of her light complexion. During the time I lived in Bet il Mtoni,

95

she and her brother Ralub were my playmates. Their mother was completely paralyzed from an illness and could do little to take care of her children. That, however, did them no damage, and they both became exemplary, upstanding people.

This poor suffering mother had to live on the ground floor that was otherwise used only for the major storerooms, a space that was hardly suited for an infirmary. Musty basement air filled the room in which my siblings grew up.

In front of this room, directly by the banks of the murmuring river Mtoni, a special resting place was set up, not quite a meter high and three to four meters square. Here the sick mother could sit or lie the whole day, while being attended to by her good children and slaves. Her stepchildren and their mothers enjoyed stopping by and checking in. My mother, in particular, sought to read to her from the Koran and other holy texts, since she was unable to read, like most other women that came to us as adults.

Mettle and Ralub were a rare pair of siblings, filled with the dearest childhood love for their mother and always seeking to make the poor woman happy. Mettle, who was a couple of years older than me, was especially good-natured. She always gave in to our wishes, the best playmate in the world. —

After the father's death, Mettle became my nearest neighbor in the countryside. We visited each other daily when we were on our plantations. Only merry Ralub loved to disrupt this peace by frequently surprising us together with his friends. That always created hapless confusion, since we were not supposed to be seen by strangers, but that was Ralub's whole point. —

Mettle lived the rest of the year in Bet il Mtoni, even after her mother's death, until she married a distant cousin in the city. Two sweet twin boys were her sole joy. I could stop by whenever I wanted, and she would always have a boy on the arm or both on her lap. No one was more unassuming or content in our house, and in this, she was the complete opposite of Shewane. But even that found the displeasure of some, who considered such modesty unbecoming of a princess. Then Mettle would declare firmly, she would always stay the same, whether interacting with a prince or a pauper; her nobility would remain undiminished in their eyes. "That I do not always run around in silks and velvet, that is my business. Does it make me any less worthy than my siblings? Am I not always still the daughter of my father?" I am ashamed to admit that I had absolutely no sense for this philosophy at the time. It was only later, after I had occasion to reflect on her wisdom, that I came to give it my full endorsement.

7. Zeyane

Zeyane and Zemzem are true sisters, the children of an Abyssinian mother. When we were still living in Bet il Mtoni, there was, as mentioned, a deep friendship between my mother and Zeyane. Zeyane in turn had a soft spot for me and spoiled me more than my mother considered beneficial. Our rooms were spaced far apart, so that I had to traverse two stairs and the whole courtyard to get to Zeyane and ZemZem. I accordingly always ended up staying there that much longer, often five to seven hours a day, which left my mother quite frustrated. Messenger after messenger would come to pick me up, all to no avail. At last my mother would come herself and then end up spending the afternoon or evening with the sisters as well.

I can thank Zeyane for introducing me to making lace. She had become very skilled in this. Either alone or together with my mother, she created the most beautiful designs, which no one was allowed to see until they were deemed a completed success.

Zeyane made friends everywhere through her benevolence. She never tired of caring for and consoling sick and helpless beings.

In Bet il Mtoni, the women could go out wherever they wanted during the daytime, as long as the father and his male retinue were not present. We often saw Zeyane head out in the company of one or two slaves bearing packages, on the way to this or that official's family, where she always left thankful hearts behind.

As the day of our move to Bet il Watoro neared, my mother and Zeyane shed many passionate tears. They were well aware that they would rarely see each other after this. Zeyane hated the city and could not often get herself to go there. My mother, on the other hand, would be too busy with her many duties to frequently visit Bet il Mtoni.

On the last day, I ran over to Zeyane very early while my mother was busy, so I could be with her as long as possible. She was overcome with tears, overloaded me with parting gifts, gave me boiled eggs the way I liked them, in short, tried to show me all her love. And she urged me to be well-behaved and devout and give my mother much joy.

It is impossible for me to describe this departure from her. It made that much more of an impression on my young sensibilities to go straight from Zeyane to our very rigid stepmother Azze bint Sef for last farewells with my mother.

8. ZemZem

Far more beautiful than Zeyane, ZemZem possessed all the good and noble qualities of her sister, who passed from us much too early. Only later when ZemZem and I became plantation neighbors did I get to know her better. She was by nature extraordinarily practical. Averse to any exaggerated displays of luxury, she preferred all that was pure and simple. Everything under her prospered to an extent rarely seen in an Arab household. On the whole, if I may put it this way, she came the closest to the German ideal of a *Hausfrau*.

She was very motherly to me, as I had been the favorite of her dearly beloved Zeyane. Whenever I did something wrong, which was unfortunately quite often, she would gaze at me for a long time, silently, with her big, soulful eyes. "Oh, what a pity," she would then say, "that your good mother had to leave you alone in this harsh world so soon. Yes, if Zeyane were still alive, she could have been your second mother, and you would have stayed a child much longer. Since that is of course what you still are, a child without a proper understanding." And she would soothingly finish with these words: "But do not be upset with me that I speak to you like this. I do it only for my love of Zeyane, who held you so dear. See, others do the same stupid things, but I would never think to reproach them for any of it."

She was especially helpful to me in agricultural matters. For hours, she would ride with me through the plantations and draw my attention to this or that good practice. Once she even turned to my *nakora* (a type of inspector): "Your mistress is simply still a child (*mtoto* in Swahili) and does not understand the first thing about these matters. That is why you need to make an even greater effort for her, and whatever you do not understand, you can always check with my *nakora*." That was hardly flattering for my conceited self-esteem, but since she meant so well, I could not be angry with her.

Not until relatively late did ZemZem end up marrying our distant cousin Humud. (We try to maintain the custom of marrying amongst ourselves to preserve the blue blood.) He was the one who, in the mosque, had dared ask Chalid for the hand of a different sister and had then been harshly rejected because of the affront. After Chalid's death, he tried his luck again with his chosen one directly, but without success. His aggrieved ambition had no desire to play the scorned suitor for long. He turned to ZemZem, and she accepted his overture. The wedding was celebrated without delay, plainly and absent any fanfare, since Humud was extraordinarily stingy despite being one of the richest people in Zanzibar. He did not even observe the basic standards of traditional Arab hospitality. And on top of that, he was fanatically orthodox and flaunted his strict piety for show, which most people saw as pure hypocrisy, since he was capable of the worst cruelty in response to the slightest cause. Naturally, no one loved him, and many despised him, even if everyone shied away from openly crossing this rich and influential man.

I seldom saw ZemZem after her marriage, but she seemed happy enough in her union with this much disliked man. Presumably, in her practical way, she also knew how to handle him well.

9. Nunu

I also want to share some details about a sister that nature treated very badly, who deserved our pity. Nunu was the daughter of a Circassian we called Tadj (meaning crown) because of her striking beauty. Tadj had been given special attention by the father, which caused much jealousy and resentment. When her child was born, with the same stunning beauty, but completely blind, many considered it just retribution for the mother's guilt in securing the father's favor. The poor mother suffered bitterly because of her child. Her grief was abated only by the firm belief that everything was as God willed it. But she also did not have to bear the sight of her blind child for long, as a case of dropsy soon snatched her away.

Poor, blind Nunu was then on her own. But here, too, it held true that God's help is closest when the need is greatest. An extremely dutiful Abyssinian slave made a sacred promise to the dying Tadj that she would diligently care for Nunu until the very end, never to desert her. She kept her promise in exemplary fashion and protected her little mistress from all the trials of life. She took instructions only from the father, who in his love naturally cared for the poor blind girl far more than all his other children. To be sure, this, too, generated all sorts of disparaging talk.

Nunu was the wildest, most misbehaved child I have ever seen. She was a horror for all mothers with small children. From the age of six to ten, she made a mission, as crazy as it sounds—of scratching out the eyes of all her younger siblings. As soon as she heard that a new brother or sister had been born, she would ask if it could see with healthy eyes. Eventually it was easier to lie, and then one could clearly see her joy in learning that others, too, would never see the sun and the moon. The most bitter envy filled her little heart.

Nunu had a better sense of her surroundings than one would ever expect of a blind person, and she moved around with great ease and speed. She ranged all over the place, and everywhere she went, she caused great mischief, like a dreadful little hurricane. Whatever she could get her hands on, porcelain, glass, especially our fine Asian water carafes, she shattered with great pleasure.

I must mention another one of Nunu's peculiarities. She wanted to be treated like someone with full eyesight. As soon as the cannon shot announced the sunset, she demanded that her room be lit. She wanted to choose the fabrics for her outfits and always stood in front of the mirror when her slaves dressed her. If she heard that one of us had nice hair, nice eyes, or nice eyebrows, then nothing was more urgent than to subject the relevant part of the head to an often very precarious examination, after which she would opine nonchalantly whether her expectations had been met or perhaps exceeded.

As time went by, to our general relief, Nunu became more reasonable and composed. She no longer needed to be constantly feared, but could instead be appreciated for her good sides and even come to be loved. The poor, unhappy being then also lost her loyal caretaker, after having lost both father and mother. Since she was in no position to live on her own and still needed some degree of guardianship, our sister Aashe took her in and kept a joint household.

10. Shembua and Farshu

Two of my nieces, Shembua and Farshu, who went to school with me, played with me, and later belonged to a political party with me, must also be mentioned. Back then, they lived across the street, and, since streets in Zanzibar tend to be narrow, we were able to have direct conversations from window to window, without having to resort to our well-developed sign language. We talked about personal care and household matters, and we even indulged to our hearts' content in—politics. Only with respect to the last topic did we take security measures by posting innocent-looking servants at the house corners, who could alert us to an approaching enemy by dropping a cane, coughing, or whistling softly. But of this exciting time, I will share more later.

Shembua and Farshu were my brother Chalid's only children. They had had such deep love for each other since childhood that they never wanted to be apart. This resulted in considerable conflict with their respective mothers, who bore deep-seated jealousies toward each other. Shembua, who was a good bit older than her sister, was by nature sweet and modest, while Farshu was the total opposite. Shembua was so very accommodating that she was practically a mother to the latter.

Chalid, as one of the father's favorites, had received a sizeable fortune that his two only children inherited. In keeping with their deep attachment to each other, they resolved not to divide their inheritance, but hold it jointly throughout. This simply increased the jealousy of Farshu's mother, an Abyssinian, who ultimately demanded that her daughter give up this title in common. Farshu was by nature very stubborn and refused to comply, instead declaring firmly that as long as she and her sister remained unmarried, they would not divide their fortunes. With relations already on a razor's edge, this left her mother feeling deeply aggrieved, and without a word, she left the house and child forever, taking only a small pack and a few funds. At first no one knew where she had gone, but were consoled by the hope that she would return to Farshu once she calmed down. But this was never the offended's intention. Rather than see her daughter again, much less live off her mercy, she chose instead to earn her keep through needlework. I have already mentioned how a widow is almost entirely dependent on her children after the husband dies.

The unhappy mother kept totally out of sight, while her means lasted. Only when her last *pesa* was spent did she seek out my older sister Zuene, who had been close to Chalid, in Bet il Mtoni. There she remained under the condition that Zuene make no effort whatsoever to reunite her, as long as the daughter did not of her own free will acknowledge her injustice. Quite unbelievably, Farshu remained indifferent to this news and made no effort to reconcile with her mother, not even when her mother became sickly. It made no difference that she was widely rebuked, or that I repeatedly reminded her of her filial duty; Farshu stayed obstinate and unyielding. One would hardly have imagined such harshness in this delicate little being, and yet her gorgeous eyes betrayed the adamant resolve behind her decisions. Soon after my departure from Zanzibar, Farshu's life was snatched away by a bad case of consumption, and I never could find out whether she had reconciled with her mother before her death.

The most beautiful property owned by my nieces was the superbly magnificent plantation Marseille, a name that reflected Chalid's predilection for France and everything French. All the walls, except in the prayer rooms, were covered with mirrors that made for a glorious effect in the shimmering light. The floors in the chambers had inlaid black and white marble tiles, whose coolness in the South cannot be overstated. With an ornate clock, whose strokes upon the hour revealed figurines that danced and played musical instruments; round powder room mirrors that variously distorted their reflected images; large, round quicksilver spheres, like the ones we see on occasion in gardens here; and other works of art, Marseille Palace felt like a veritable museum, especially for simple folk that were little acquainted with civilization, meaning primarily our relatives from Oman. How often did I hear these words of wonder: "By God, these Christians are real devils!" Marseille and life there were ideally suited for conveying a true sense of the Orient to unfamiliar outsiders.

What wonderful days I spent there. With my nieces' love of emancipation and their well-known tolerant attitudes, this was a place where we could freely circulate, and the house was always full of guests. There was no end to the comings and goings. Non-stop we could hear forerunners and foreriders yelling *sumila! sumila!* (make room! make room! in Swahili) and slaves announcing new arrivals. Only cheerful guests, seemingly without a care, were to be found here. Those who thought to stay for three days were often rallied by the kind hostesses into staying a fortnight, which the fathers and husbands simply had to accept.

Each day was spent relishing the utmost informality. Everyone could do whatever they pleased without being considered impolite. That is true hospitality, when it poses no constraints, but offers full freedom. Only towards evening, as the sun went down, did the guests come together to spend time in the large rooms illuminated by countless shining candles and lanterns or in the park under the dazzling moonlight until one or two in the morning. When there was no moonlight, tall piles of wood, soaked in palm oil, were fired up at various locations, where we could avidly converse late into the night.

This place of radiance and joy was later destroyed. My brothers Barghash and Abd il Aziz entrenched themselves in the palace, despite our outrage, during our plot against Madjid. This is where the decisive battle took place. The entire property was ruined, and my nieces took a great loss. Even so, they had enough other wealth to absorb this downturn and resisted any further discussion; it was not worth the talk! —

11. Hilal

Of my brothers, I want to highlight two of them, Hilal and Tueni, both unhappy, one through his own fault, the other a victim of his own son.

Our religion is known to forbid Muslims the pleasure of all alcoholic drink, and our sect, which also forbids smoking, is much stricter on these points than, say, the Turks or Persians. Now, at one point, an ugly rumor spread in our family that our brother Hilal (meaning new moon) had been seduced by Christians, especially the French Consul at the time, to give in to drinking. He suddenly began to experience inexplicable fainting spells and soon the smell of wine became evident. The poor man could no longer rid himself of this evil spirit that had taken hold. Hilal was one of our father's favorite sons, and this caused the father bitter grief. To correct this wayward soul, he initially put Hilal under house arrest, but soon had to banish him entirely from the family.

Our sister Chadudj was especially close to Hilal and had the most to suffer for him. He continued to visit her often in the father's house, even after being banished. With much difficulty and at great risk, he would enter secretly and spend the night with her and his other loyal friends in a dark room, so that no light would betray his presence. No one ever had the heart to let the father know about these touching visits. Because the father kept him on very limited terms to make sure he had nothing left to spend on alcohol, Chadudj always gave him generous support, though hardly in his best interest.

Hilal succumbed increasingly to the effects of this harmful passion. He had fewer and fewer sober moments and soon death put an end to his sad state. Despite all that had happened, our father felt an unspeakable grief for his beloved son. He often locked himself away in his prayer room, and traces of his tears could later be found where he had knelt in prayer to his Lord. Indeed, he even expressed his pain in words, something he otherwise never did, and repeated over and over: "Oh my misfortune, oh my despair for you, Hilal!" —

Hilal left behind three sons, Suud, Fesal, and Muhammed. The youngest, Muhammed, was adopted by my otherwise childless stepmother, Azze bint Sef. I do not know what gave her the idea; perhaps she did it out of love for our father. Muhammed really knew how to win Bibi Azze over completely, a feat the rest of us never managed. Up to that point, she was known to be very exacting and frugal. No one could believe their eyes when Muhammed began to allow himself the greatest profligacy, naturally with her money. Although none of us had ever thought of owning dogs, Muhammed went ahead and ordered a whole pack from Europe, including some superb specimens we had never seen before. His entire life was consumed by the upkeep of these dogs, which of course were never tolerated in the house, along with several especially beautiful horses. These dear creatures naturally could not be expected to live off leftovers. A whole special cuisine, with no shortage of variety, was arranged for them. The plumpest chickens, the best cuts of meat, the biggest fish all wandered into the huge pots. Rumor had it that these dogs, as well as the horses, did not just drink cheap water, but rather—champagne. I do not know if that is true, but either way, Muhammed stirred up much negative talk borne of envy and resentment, after drawing many enemies through his extravagance and having but few friends.

Suud also projected in every way that he appreciated the lifestyle, customs, and practices of Europeans. He was the most like his father.

Hilal's third son, by contrast, was completely different. While Muhammed and Suud tended to luxury and the high life, sweet Fesal presented himself so modestly that one would have assumed him to be a normal citizen instead of a prince. He had a contemplative nature that was not drawn to material pleasures, and thus remained a mystery to his brothers. Later he bought a small plantation in my neighborhood and came to visit me often. He seldom went into the city without bringing me a little something, even if it was just a few packs of fireworks, of which I was especially fond.

Misunderstood by his brothers, the poor thing was deeply unhappy. He had a gentle, noble character, the sort that is so easily overlooked in this world. But those who got to know him were soon charmed by his friendly manner and kindness. Having lost his mother quite early, he had hardly ever known love. "That is why I am doubly depressed," he would confide in me, his much younger aunt, "even my brothers consider me totally superfluous and want nothing to do with me. I really do not care if I live or die; I am dispensable to everyone." How my heart bled to hear this good man, who deserved so much love, talk this way. Would such a tired soul, who has nothing left for this world, not find his best chance for peace in a cloister?

After I gave in to my brother Madjid's request to return to the city, no one was more deeply hurt than my poor Fesal. Over time he had gotten so used to sharing all his thoughts and concerns with me, as if I were truly such a sensible aunt, instead of what I actually still was at the time: a very wild and naïve young girl.

12. Tueni

Our oldest brother Tueni was born in Muscat and spent his whole life in Oman. He never visited Zanzibar, and his prejudice against the birthplace of most of his siblings was unshakable. Muslims are not allowed to have their portraits painted, and a deeply ingrained superstition reinforces this rule even more than others. There was also no photography back then. So Tueni remained, for those of us who had never been to Muscat, a completely unfamiliar personality. We only heard of his kindness to others, as well as his courage and determination in battle. His soldiers practically idolized him, and his mere presence instilled great confidence in them. Even as a youngster, he loved war, like our father, and he was the most competent soldier of all my brothers. He apparently spent most of his time out in the camps, thus causing much heartbreak for his wife

Ralie, who was our proper cousin of equal rank and gave him several children.

For all the time our father stayed in Zanzibar, Tueni was his representative in charge. But Tueni usually left the responsibility for domestic matters, meaning the actual governance, to our second oldest brother, the devout Muhammed, who, as mentioned, was filled with a similar dislike of Zanzibar. Tueni had enough to do with the external defense of the kingdom. There were Persians at Bandar Abbas to be fought, and incursions of nomadic tribes from inner Arabia to be defended against. These numerous tribes are all very poor, and many survive only on their pillage. Few desert Arabs own anything more than a camel, some indispensable weapons (gun, sword, dagger, lance, and shield), one or two iron cooking pots, a sack of dates, and, if fortunate, a milk-bearing goat. All the men, big and small, carry their guns into battle, while the wives and daughters follow on foot from afar, ready to restore their men after combat with cooling water, milk, and food. Every year these bands, sometimes stronger, sometimes weaker, would invade Oman and keep the country in eternal unrest. Only a determined and energized ruler could maintain his ground there.

That was the state of affairs when our father died on his return to Zanzibar. If death had reached him while still in Muscat, Tueni would have been in a position to secure his reign over Zanzibar, instead of having Madjid, as the fourth-oldest of our brothers, leverage the circumstances to proclaim himself Sultan of Zanzibar. I have already mentioned how Madjid agreed to make fixed annual payments to Tueni, but soon thereafter pulled back on this commitment. Madjid was widely rebuked for this, especially as Tueni's situation deteriorated from day to day.

The ongoing military runs devoured huge sums, and the missing payments from Zanzibar hit at exactly the worst time. Tueni had to get funding at any cost and found himself forced to levy taxes on various items. Fortunately, no one in Oman thought of taking on debt, which has been the current ruin of other Oriental states. But even these limited charges awakened the specter of discontent. Sadly, those who were displeased succeeded in gaining influence over Tueni's oldest son, Salum, pulling him tightly into their web, until he brought upon himself the darkest sin a man can commit.

One day Tueni returned from a meeting and threw himself exhausted onto the divan to get some rest. Suddenly, his son came forward and demanded the reversal of this tax decree so categorically that his father had to emphatically rebuke him. Salum flew into an extreme rage, pulled out a hidden revolver, and shot down his own unsuspecting father!

This bedazzled youngster did not enjoy the fruits of his bloody act for long. He, too, soon faced retaliation. He had barely installed himself as the ruler of Oman when his brother-in-law Azzan decided to dethrone him. Completely unexpected, Azzan struck the capital Muscat in the dead of night, filling it with plunder and carnage. The tremendous bitterness people felt towards the evil Salum greatly facilitated Azzan's endeavor. No right-thinking person would reach for his weapons to defend a father murderer. There was little resistance to the invading wild hordes, who dragged off anything that was portable and destroyed all the rest. Especially Salum's palace was heavily damaged. Under the most perilous conditions, he managed to flee with his family on one of his war ships, saving but his bare life.

Even his unhappy mother Ralie, along with her other children, barely managed to escape on a ship. She lost everything. And yet, a young Indian merchant, named Abd il Rab (meaning servant of the Lord), later succeeded in purchasing most of her valuable jewels from a Bedouin at a bargain price (said to be three hundred Maria Theresa thalers), and the good soul returned this lost property to the trial-tested princess simply as a gift! —

The invader Azzan was soon chased away by my third-oldest brother Turki, who then suffered the same fate by my younger brother Abd il Aziz (likewise servant of the Lord). This one, a foster child of Chole, had distinguished himself as intelligent, courageous, and energetic. Already at the age of twelve, he had joined us in the plot and battle against Madjid, thereafter spending time in Baluchistan, where we recruit our soldiers. Abd il Aziz succeeded in finally giving Oman a brief period of calm. But even he was unable to maintain his reign for long. Turki returned and empowered himself anew as the ruler, at which point Abd il Aziz sought refuge for a second time in Mekran in Baluchistan, where he remains to this day. —

Surely a sad spectacle, these family feuds, that can be understood only by those familiar with the inbred lust for power of Oriental princes and the passionate nature of Orientals generally. Even I was not to stay unaffected by such sad circumstances. Yes, I, too, had to find my way through it!

CHAPTER SIXTEEN

Status of Women in the Orient

Before I continue with the story of my personal experiences, I would like to bring in a few more chapters that address various aspects of Oriental life. It is not my intent to provide a comprehensive account of all the customs and practices. I do not wish to write an academic tome, but only try to give European readers a more accurate understanding of the more important attitudes and customs of the Orient. Some details will be less interesting, but I prefer not to leave them out, as they may be of interest to at least a few.

I will step right into the most important of all these questions: the status of women in the Orient. This is a rather difficult topic for me. As a native Oriental woman, I am certain I will be considered biased and therefore fail in thoroughly dispelling the distorted and incorrect views that prevail in Europe about the position of an Arab woman in relation to her husband. Despite easier connections, the Orient is still far too much of the old fantasy land, about which one can say just about anything with impunity. A tourist heads off for a few weeks to Constantinople, or Syria, Egypt, Tunisia, or Morocco, and then writes a ponderous book about the life, customs, and practices in the Orient. And yet he has never had a closer look inside real family life. So he contents himself with stories that are passed from mouth to mouth and become increasingly distorted, perhaps from a French or German waiter in his hotel, or that he hears from sailors or donkey drivers, which he records and then uses to pass judgment! There is not much to be learned this way. He simply lets his imagination run wild and then supplements at will. If his book then happens to be amusing and artfully written, it will certainly garner many more readers than the less spicy, more reality-based accounts, and accordingly shape the views of the broader public.

I, too, judged things in Europe for a long time only by their superficial sheen. When I first saw the beaming faces in society here, I naturally came to believe that the interaction between men and women in Europe was much more properly structured, and that marriages would therefore be much happier than in the Islamic Orient. Later, however, as my children got older and no longer required my constant oversight and care, my increasing engagement with the world led me to understand more and more that I had incorrectly assessed people and social relations and allowed myself to be dazzled by outer appearances. I have observed relationships that were called marriages, but whose sole purpose seemed to be for mutually shackled pairs to already enact the torments of hell in this world. I have seen too many unhappy marriages to believe that Christian marriages are really all that superior to Islamic ones, that its participants are so much happier. In my opinion, neither religion, nor current customs and attitudes determine *ab initio* whether marriages will be happier or unhappier. What matters everywhere is whether the married couple has a genuine understanding toward each other. It is on this basis that happiness and peace can arise, from which an inner harmony can ensue, to ultimately make the marriage into a true marriage.

Having learned from this experience, I will make an extra effort to avoid passing judgment, and instead seek to use the following pages simply to report on the position of women in the Orient, specifically in marriage. I only know the precise conditions in Zanzibar, and those in Oman about as well. Nonetheless, Muslim views are still the most authentic in Arabia and among Arabs, and these perspectives form the basis of other Oriental cultures. My descriptions may thus be considered relevant for the rest of the Islamic Orient, except of course for some deviations and off-shoots that have arisen most notably because of their close association with the Christian Occident.

It is definitely wrong to think that Oriental women have less social status than men. A woman of commensurate birth is equal to her male counterparts in all respects. She maintains her rank and the full scope of all emanating rights and entitlements. Only the position of *sarari* is a subordinated one.

What causes an Arab woman to appear more helpless and somewhat less entitled is simply the fact she lives a withdrawn life. This is the custom for all Muslim (and also many non-Muslim) peoples of the Orient, and the higher a woman's social rank, the more stringently she must abide by these restrictions. She may be seen by only her father, son, uncle, nephew, and all her slaves. If she needs to appear before an unfamiliar man, or even speak with him, then the religion requires that she cover her head and body, especially part of her face, her chin and neck, and her ankles. As long as she obeys this rule, she is entirely free to move around during the day and can walk unrestricted on the streets. However, since such coverings are so unpleasant and disfiguring, high-ranking women avoid going out by day and frequently enough envy the Bedouin women who forsake such requirements. If such a Bedouin woman is asked whether she is embarrassed to go out without the required coverings, she will respond: "Such rules are only for the rich, they were not created for poor women!"

Today I am quite willing to admit that these Oriental practices are excessive, but I am not yet ready to pronounce European customs superior. When a stately woman is seen here in her ball gown, one would be justified in deeming her paucity of clothing to be an even greater exaggeration.

Under certain circumstances, the seclusion of women can become quite burdensome, and this custom really does go too far. However, Oriental women need not be pitied as much as we love to do here.

The law allows a Muslim man to possess four lawful, official wives at a time, and if one dies or divorces, he can bring home a fifth. *Sarari*, or secondary wives, can be bought and sold again as often as the man wants and as much as he can afford. I have, however, never seen anyone that really had four primary wives side-by-side. A poor man can of course take only one. A rich man tends to set limits as well, possessing at most two and putting them in separate living quarters, where each can keep her own household.

Needless to say, there are also Oriental women who know to look after their independence. These women first check if a suitor already has another wife and then secure a formal promise in the marriage contract stipulating that he neither take on another wife, nor purchase a *surie*.

In practice then, monogamy mostly rules. However, in those cases where men take full advantage of what the law allows, unedifying dissension will readily arise among the wives. The practice naturally leads to all sorts of resentment and envy, which the hot temperament of Southerners can turn into raving jealousies.

Jealousy can turn polygamy into the greatest torment, and that is a good thing. Many a rich and high-ranking man is put off by the thought of dealing with these daily dramas and therefore sticks with monogamy. And that then significantly limits this vile custom. The fact that there is really no justification or excuse whatsoever for polygamy must be evident to anyone who is right-thinking, and especially to every woman. But now a counterquestion: What is the situation with Christians, with civilized Europeans, on the subject of marriage? I will not even dwell on the fact that the Mormon sect, as self-described Christians, openly practices polygamy in a Christian state. But does civilized European society really consistently treat marriage as being so sacred? Is it not often pure illusion to speak of "one" wife? To be sure, a Christian is allowed to marry only one woman, and that is a major advantage of Christianity. On this subject, Christian precepts seek what is good and right, while Islam permits what is bad. But current practices and practical realities in the Orient significantly dampen the negative effects of the law—while here, despite the law, sin rather frequently gets the upper hand. I am tempted to say that the only difference between an Oriental wife and a European wife appears to be that the first has knowledge of the number, as well as the nature and character, of her rivals, while the other is kept in loving ignorance. —

Naturally, only a rich man can afford *sarari*. Born as slaves, *sarari* are considered free after they bear children. Only in the rarest of cases would a master resell his *surie* if a child dies, and then only if he is very mean-spirited, as a matter of necessity or ennui. If the man dies, then his remaining *sarari* are usually perfectly free; no master lords over them anymore. If one then marries a brother or other relative of the deceased master and liberator, she becomes a legitimate wife as a free person. —

It is a myth that Arab husbands treat their wives worse than here. Religion is a major factor in that it encourages male protection, as though for a helpless child. A faithful, god-fearing Muslim man is as humane as any refined and well-mannered European man. The former is perhaps even stricter with himself, always mindful of the ubiquity of the Lord, as the author of those commandments, and believing firmly until his dying breath in the just accounting for his good and bad deeds.

Of course, alongside its noble characters, Zanzibar also has its share of tyrants, just as we do here, who demonstrate neither the appropriate kindness nor respect that is due their better halves. And yet, I can in good conscience state that I have heard more here about gentle husbands beating their wives than in my homeland. It is different, though, with the Africans. On my plantations, I have often enough had to throw myself between a contentious couple to make peace.

A wife is, moreover, in no way subject to her husband's every whim. If she ever encounters behavior by her husband that she is unwilling to accept, she can always get protection from her relatives, or she has the right to take her complaint personally to the *kadi* if she has no one else to turn to. Often she helps herself.

One of my very dear lady friends was sixteen when she married her significantly older cousin, who was far from worthy of her. Ever the playboy, and believing she would put up with anything, he was rather surprised when he returned home one evening and found a harshly worded message instead of his wife. I had always visited this friend on her plantation unannounced because I knew this dear husband preferred to spend his time gallivanting around the city. One day, however, she came to inform me that I could no longer come without notice because her husband was now staying at home. Full of remorse, he had pursued her and fervently begged her forgiveness. Once he realized how resolute his little wife was, he made sure to never hurt her again. I could share many more such examples of independent Oriental wives.

Spouses greet by kissing each other's hands. They share meals with their children. The wife shows the husband a range of loving gestures, like handing him his weapons when he leaves the house and taking them from him when he returns, or offering him water to drink. In short, she attends to all the little details that make a life together warmer and dearer. These are purely voluntary acts, and she is in no way bound to perform them.

The whole household is the exclusive domain of the wife. She is the undisputed head of this terrain. There is no such thing as a household allowance by which the husband takes care of his wife, but rather both operate out of a single account, except when a man splits his income in two for two wives of equal rank, with separate homes and households.

Naturally, how far the wife's domain extends depends on the couple. Here is an example: I had invited a large group of ladies to one of my plantations. However, since my invitation had gone out rather late, potentially too late for some of them to get their transport animals from the countryside in time, I feared a number of invitees would decline. One of my female friends immediately offered up a whole host of Omani donkeys, complete with all their gear and even the necessary guides. When I suggested that she first speak with her husband to get his approval for such a generous offer, she promptly replied, not to worry, she was not in the habit of getting her husband's permission for such a trifle.

Another female acquaintance of mine in Zanzibar carried much broader responsibility for all the business and investment dealings. She alone managed her husband's large estates, along with his city houses. He was not even aware of how much income he had and seemed perfectly content to get whatever money he needed from her hands. Due to her care and competence, he in fact did quite well.

The job of raising children belongs entirely to the mother, whether as a wife of equal rank or a purchased slave. In this, she recognizes her greatest good fortune. Whereas in England, it is customary, and considered quite sufficient, for the mother to throw a quick glance into the nursery once every twenty-four hours, and in France, the mother sends her children to the countryside under the care of complete strangers, an Arab mother, by contrast, is highly attentive to her children, protecting and nurturing them with the greatest diligence, and hardly ever leaving them alone, for as long as they need motherly care. In return for her devotion, she earns the sincerest piety and deepest love. This relationship with her children more than compensates for the disadvantages of polygamy and makes her family life happy and contented.

It takes having seen the joy and outright exuberance of wives in the Orient to fully appreciate how little truth there is in all the tales of their oppressed, downtrodden status and thoughtless, degrading aimlessness. But visits that are arranged for only a few short moments cannot provide deeper insight into the essence of these conditions. And even when translations about this or that are more or less correct, they hardly amount to a real conversation, not one that goes beyond rudimentary exchanges.

As polite as they are, Arabs dislike having strangers delve into their personal affairs, especially when those strangers belong to different nations or religions. Whenever a European woman came to visit us, she would initially be subjected to intense staring at the colossal circumference of her fashionable crinoline, which would typically fill the breadth of the staircase. The very spare conversation on both sides would rarely go beyond the mysteries of our respective outfits. After being hosted in the usual fashion, perfumed with rose oil by the eunuchs, and then sent off with parting gifts, she would have left none the wiser than when she came. She would have entered the harem, seen the to-be-pitied Oriental women (to be sure, only behind masks), marveled at our outfits, our jewelry, and our flexibility at sitting on the floor, but that is all. She could never boast of seeing anything more than any other European women before her. Eunuchs would escort her up, serve her, and lead her back out, under constant surveillance. Rarely would she be shown anything other than the room in which she was received. Indeed, often she would not even be able to decipher the identity of the masked lady to whom she had spoken. In short, she would have had no opportunity whatsoever to get a good look at Oriental family life and the role of the women. —

One more point is important for a proper understanding of Oriental marriage. When a young woman weds, there is no change to her name or rank. The wife of a royal prince that comes from a common family would never consider herself equal to her husband. Despite the marriage, she remains the "daughter (*bint*) of N.N."[15] and is addressed this way. This also goes for the reverse in the frequent case when a prince or ruler allows his daughter or sister to marry one of his own slaves. He says to himself: My servant also remains her servant, and she therefore continues to be his superior. Although the husband loses his formal slave status upon marriage, he will naturally always refer to his wife as "Highness" or "Lady."

When a man refers to his wife in conversation with another man, something he generally prefers to avoid, he never says "my wife," but rather refers to her as the "daughter of N.N." Or at most he uses the expression *um ijali*, meaning "mother of my family," whether she has children or not. —

It is understandable that couples, who would not have known each other beforehand, often have trouble getting along. Difficult, distressing relations can arise, as happened between my father and Shesade and between Madjid and Aashe. For such cases, Islamic law has the undeniable advantage that divorce is made incredibly easy. It is clearly better that two married individuals with starkly opposing world views and character traits are able to separate in peace, rather than be forever bound in mutual torment, which so often leads to the most horrible crimes. At the separation, the wife gets back her complete assets, over which she also had free disposition during the marriage. If the husband requests the divorce, the wife also retains the gifts he gave her at the wedding, but if she seeks to divorce, she must return them.

I believe all these examples suffice to show that Oriental women are not quite as subjugated and repressed, or stripped of their rights, as is assumed here. How much power and influence some of them are able to wield is amply apparent from the characteristics of my stepmother, Azze bint Sef. She totally ruled over our father. Indeed, matters of court and state often turned on her highly variable moods. Although divided in most things, all of us stepchildren were united in seeking to weaken her influence, but no matter what we tried, it almost always failed. Should one of us want something from the father, it would regularly be deferred up the chain for Bibi Azze's prior endorsement, as there was no matter over which she could not lay some claim before the father could proceed. She knew how to maintain her power across the board until the day he died.

Another example: The daughter of a commanding officer of one of the fortresses in Oman came to Zanzibar with her husband. They were of average means and, as the wife herself told me, "fortunately" without children. By nature, she was

---

15 From the Latin *nomen nescio*, an unnamed person, used here as a generic reference.

113

sharp and witty (a trait that succeeds nowhere better than there), but truly unattractive. Nevertheless, her husband was completely devoted to her and bore her many moods with the patience of an angel. Whenever she wanted to go out, he had to escort her back and forth, like a slave, whether he wanted fresh air or not. He never had control of his own time, and from the moment he finished his morning prayers, his day was hers, whether his lady chose to stay with him or leave him alone the whole day. He was her complete slave.

I want to recognize one more member of our family, someone who especially belies the inferiority myths of Oriental women. My great aunt, the sister of my grandfather, is still today considered the model of a clever, courageous, and energetic woman. When the story of her life and deeds is told and retold, young and old listen with rapt attention.

When my grandfather Sultan Imam of Muscat in Oman died, he left behind three children, my father Said, my uncle Salum, and my aunt Aashe. As my father was only nine years old, this required the establishment of a regency. Against all custom, my great aunt declared categorically that she would run the government herself until her nephew came of age, and she forbade any opposition. The ministers, who had not anticipated such a decision, but had instead secretly looked forward to years of their own rule, had no choice but to obey. Every day, the new regent called on them to report and receive her orders and instructions. She watched over and kept up with everything. Nothing escaped her sharp gaze, to the anger of any who were disloyal and lazy.

For herself, she simply stripped the shackles of proper etiquette. When appearing in front of her ministers, she covered herself only in her *shele*, the outfit a lady wore to go out. Whether the world wished to carp about her approach made no difference, as she followed her own undeterred path with skill and verve.

Soon enough, she was put to the most serious test. She had barely taken up the reins of government when, as unfortunately happens often in Oman, a very treacherous war erupted. Our nearest tribal neighbors believed they could easily overthrow the female regency, and with it our house, to claim the reign for themselves. Burning and killing their way through the land with their hordes, they finally arrived at the gates of the capital city Muscat. Many thousands of people from the countryside had fled here from their ruined provinces, abandoning their land and belongings, to seek refuge and aid. Muscat is well-protected and can withstand a siege. But what good are the most fortified walls when supplies and munitions run out?

In this challenging time, my great aunt proved herself beyond measure and even won over the admiring respect of her enemies. At night, she always rode solo in male attire along the front lines. She managed her soldiers in the most dangerous locations, sometimes eluding an unexpected attack with only the speed of her steed. One evening she set out especially worried. She had learned that the enemy was going to try to bribe its way into the fortress under the cover of night for a total massacre. She therefore decided to test the loyalty of her troops. With utmost care, she rode up in disguise to one of the sentries, demanded to speak to the *akid* (a senior officer) and presented, in the name of the attackers, the most enticing offers. The outburst of anger that erupted from this dutiful sentry alleviated any concern about her soldiers' sentiments, even as it put her life at great risk. They immediately wanted to knock down this apparent spy, and she had to draw on her utmost skill to avoid being killed by her own people.

Muscat's situation became increasingly dire. Starvation was widespread, and hearts were filled with hopelessness. There was no chance for help from the outside. It was decided to try one last, desperate push, even if it meant going down with honor. They had just enough powder reserves for one more fight, but the deadly lead needed for guns and cannons was completely spent. The regent called on everyone to collect every last nail for the guns, and even to search for the right-sized pebbles to use instead of bullets. Whatever iron or brass they could find was smashed and loaded into the cannons. Her Highness even opened the doors of her treasury and had bullets poured from her Maria Theresa thalers. Everything was offered up, and lo and behold, this desperate effort paid off. The enemy was fortunately caught by surprise and scattered in every direction. More than half of their troops were left behind, dead or wounded. Muscat was saved. Freed from her heavy load, this courageous woman dropped to her knees and thanked the Almighty in ardent prayer for his merciful help.

After that, she reigned in peace and was then able to transfer the kingdom to her nephew, my father, in such good shape that he could focus on other, more distant goals, above all to conquer Zanzibar. That the acquisition of this second empire was even possible is in part thanks to her, my great aunt.

That, too, was an Oriental woman!

117

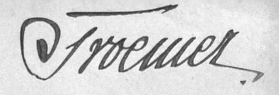

Memoiren

einer

arabischen Prinzessin.

━━◈ Zweiter Band. ◈━━

Dritte Auflage.

Berlin.

Verlag von Friedrich Luckhardt.

1886.

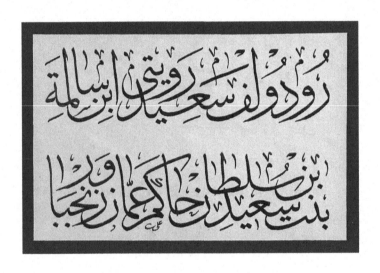

120

Memoirs of an Arabian Princess

Volume 2

On the preceding pages, the end paper and title page are from an original edition of Volume 2 that belonged to either Rosa Troemer, the author's youngest daughter, or a member of her family. The bookplate on the previous page is from Rudolph Said-Ruete, the author's son and brother of the translator's great-grandmother.

All footnotes in the following pages were added by the translator.

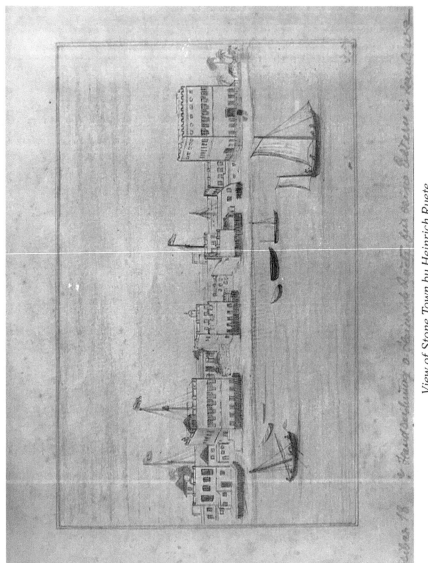

View of Stone Town by Heinrich Ruete

CHAPTER SEVENTEEN

Arab Matrimony

In general, in Arabia, the father or head of the family arranges the children's marriages. There is nothing unusual about that, and it also happens in Europe, where young men and young girls have the greatest freedom to interact. We have all heard about the irresponsible fathers here, who have plunged themselves so deep into debt that they have no way out but to hand over their pretty or genteel daughters to their creditors as sacrificial lambs; or how fun-loving mothers push their children into unhappy marriages simply because they would rather be rid of them at any price.

No less tyrannical parents can be found among Arabs as well, those who disregard the happiness of their marrying children and tune out any pangs of conscience. But it is not generally an abuse of power when parents there make choices for their children. The isolation of women makes this support necessary. No one disputes that, despite all the customs and laws, there may still be encounters with men from time to time that can lead to more interaction. But as a general rule, a young girl will neither see her prospective husband, except perhaps through a window, nor speak to him until the wedding night. And yet, he does not stay a complete stranger. His mother, sisters, and aunts practically compete to describe him as aptly as possible and fill her in on anything that could possibly be of interest.

Often the two already know each other from their childhood. Until their ninth year, girls can interact with boys of the same age and get to know them this way. And so it may happen that the former playmate later remembers his female friend and asks the father for her hand, having of course first sought her opinion through her mother or sister.

With virtually all candidates, the cautious father leads with the following question: "But where did you actually see my daughter?" "Oh," comes the response, "I have never yet had the privilege of seeing your honored (*mahshume*) daughter. But I have heard my family speak all the more of her virtues and charms."

Only when the candidate for marriage completely fails to meet the father's requirements does the suitor get an immediate rejection. As a rule, however, the father gives himself ample time to consider the matter and observe his daughter and her mother. Eventually, he mentions with studied indifference that he is thinking of inviting some men over in the next days, and when his wife or daughter ask whom he plans to invite, he proceeds to casually list out his friends. If he perceives a certain joy upon mentioning the name of the applicant, he can rest assured that there is full consensus between his family and theirs. Only then does he reveal to his daughter that N.N. has asked for her hand and solicits her opinion. Her yes or no is almost always dispositive. Only a despotic and callous father decides unilaterally, without first ascertaining his daughter's approval or disapproval.

In these questions, too, however, our father maintained his sense of justice and laid the fate of his children in their own hands. My older sister Zuene had just turned twelve when a distant cousin, Suud, came to him for her. The father was upset at receiving this request while she was still so young, but also could not bring himself to dismiss the bid out of hand without first having informed his daughter of it. Zuene had lost her mother, for whom there was really no adequate substitute at this crucial age. Still half a child, and lacking good advice, she found the thought of becoming a married woman so amusing that she insisted that Suud not be turned away, and the father let her prevail.

It is quite common for us that children in their earliest youth are already promised, and yes, even married. Two brothers, for instance, had made a solemn promise to have their children marry each other. As it turned out, each had only one child, one a boy and one a girl. As soon as the boy turned sixteen or seventeen, while the girl was still seven or eight, talk turned to the forthcoming wedding. The mother of the boy was my plantation neighbor. A very smart and prudent woman, she often complained to me about the harsh insistence by her husband and brother-in-law that she take in a young child that she would first have to care for and raise, instead of receiving a daughter-in-law. The mother of the young girl was no less dismayed that anyone would even think to tear her child away so soon. The combined efforts of the two mothers succeeded only in having the wedding postponed by all of two years. I left Zanzibar not long after and therefore cannot report what became of this relationship. —

The formal engagement is ceremoniously announced to all friends and acquaintances. Beautifully dressed female slaves, often as many as twenty, go from house to house bearing the announcement and invitation to the wedding celebration, for which they reap ample gifts.

At this point, the house of the bride's parents becomes unusually lively, with the wedding often taking place just a month later. Regardless, the engagement period never lasts long, and there is also little to prepare in the blessed South. People in the Orient would never dream of the many indispensable necessities that Northerners must have, and an Arab bride would be rendered speechless at the sight of a European trousseau. Why do people here love to burden themselves with so much ballast?

An Arab bride, by comparison, is sent off with relatively little. Depending on rank and wealth, her trousseau consists of precious clothes, jewels, slaves, houses, plantations, and cash. She receives gifts not only from her own parents, but also from the parents of the groom and the groom himself. All of this becomes her own personal property. When her parents' estate is divided after they have died, this trousseau is never netted from her share.

Considerable effort goes into preparing the bride's clothing. An elegant lady must change her outfit two or three times a day in the week after the wedding. A specific bridal costume, like the white dress and white veil here, is not customary in the Orient. The only requirement is that the bride wear brand new things, from head to toe, while color choices are entirely up to her. Some may even dazzle with all the colors of the rainbow, and yet their attire is anything but tasteless and ugly.

In addition, special perfumes are prepared, as they play a major role in wedding celebrations. That includes *riha*, a very costly mixture of pulverized sandalwood, ground musk, saffron, and large amounts of rose oil that is rubbed into the hair, as well as a pleasantly aromatic incense mixed of the wood *oud* (a type of aloe resin), the finest amber, and much musk. An Oriental woman can never have enough perfume of any kind.

Add to that the baking, the production of all sorts of confections, the procuring of animals for slaughter. In short, all hands are fully occupied.

Meanwhile, the bride has to subject herself to various uncomfortable and burdensome customs. She must spend the entire last week in a dark room, where she refrains from all embellishments and finery. This is supposed to make her appear all the more beautiful and graceful on her wedding day.

She is a tormented being during this period, with one visitor after another. All the old women she has ever known, especially all her former nurses and nannies, whom she may not have seen in years, now seek her out, all with open hands. The chief eunuch who once shaved off her first hairs pays a call with special pride for this past honorable service, seeking her continued goodwill— and a token. He receives a precious shawl, a ring for the little finger of his left hand, a pocket watch, or some guineas.

The groom is spared from being cooped up in a dark room, but otherwise suffers no less. Anyone who once served either him or the bride comes to him as well, thereby carting off a double load of gifts.

During the last three days, the groom stays home and is seen only by his closest friends. Now the interaction between the two families becomes even more intense. There is no end to the exchange of greetings and gifts between the bride and bridegroom.

Finally, the big day arrives. The wedding ceremony normally takes place in the evening at the home of the bride, not in the mosque. A *kadi*, or if none is available, a man generally known to be devout, officiates the marriage. Strange as it may seem to Europeans, the bride herself, the principal person, is not present at the formal ceremony. She is represented by her father, brother, or some other male relation.

Only if she has absolutely no male relatives does she appear personally before the *kadi* to be bound to the bridegroom with the usual ceremonial words. In this case, she enters the empty room alone, mummified beyond recognition, after which the *kadi* enters, followed by the bridegroom and witnesses. After completion of the act, during which the voice of the bride is barely discernible, the men again exit first before the newly wedded wife rises and returns to her chambers.

The wedding ceremony is followed by a rich meal for all the men who are present, including the bridegroom, complete with heavy smoking of *oud* and perfuming with rose oil.

The handover of the bride takes place three days after the wedding. Countless hands are then busy preparing and bedecking her to the utmost. Towards nine or ten in the evening, she is then escorted by her female relatives to her new home, at which point the bridegroom immediately enters, accompanied by his male relatives. At the threshold to the private chambers, the men take their leave of the bridegroom, and the women take their leave of the bride, with profuse congratulations and blessings. The guests then head to the gender-segregated social rooms on the ground floor to begin the joyful celebration that carries on for days.

After the bridegroom enters the bridal chambers, the proceedings always follow certain rules of etiquette. If the woman ranks higher than the man, she stays seated when he enters and waits for him to address her. She continues to leave on her elegant mask, which jealously covers her face. To ask her to de-mask, and to show his love and respect, the young husband must place a gift worthy of his means at her feet. For poor people, a few pennies may suffice, while the rich give significant sums.

As mentioned, starting with this evening, the house of the young husband becomes a center of hospitality for the next three, seven, or fifteen days. Friends, acquaintances, and even non-acquaintances are welcome and may eat and drink to their hearts' delight. Of course, no wine or beer is served, and even tobacco smoking is forbidden by our Ibadi sect. Nonetheless, people are extraordinarily full of happiness and cheer. They eat, drink almond milk and lemonade, sing, perform war dances, and listen to passionate speeches. Eunuchs spread *oud* incense and besprinkle guests with delightful, cooling rose water from silver bowls, which regrettably wafts away so quickly.

The ladies linger together until about midnight, while the men may spend the entire night in this house of joy, until the breaking dawn calls them to their duty, to prayer. —

Honeymoons are, of course, unknown in the Orient. The young couple is much more likely to spend the first week or two at home with each other, hidden from the outside world. The young wife receives guests only after this period is over, and then her chamber overflows every evening between seven and midnight with friends and acquaintances bringing her all their best wishes.

CHAPTER EIGHTEEN

Arab Visits Among the Ladies

I have repeatedly referred to the many visits we made to our friends and acquaintances, and the many we hosted. It may well be of interest to learn more about such socializing among Arab ladies, how we interact, what we talk about.

If we wished to visit someone, we usually sent elegantly dressed female slaves to convey our intentions the same day. Only rarely did we dare show up unannounced on good luck. All city visits are made on foot; we only ride out to the countryside. We also dress in our finery for such occasions, not just to show respect to the friends we are visiting, but also to flaunt our clothes and jewels in the hopes of outshining the others. The same as here!

That said, an Arab woman may not show her face. It stays covered with a mask, often at home and always on outings. This is not like the Egyptian mask, which is ugly and hard for breathing. Our masks were very elegant, stylized in black satin and decorated with gorgeous lace made of colorful silk and gold and silver threads. They consisted of two main parts, connected by a thin support, one part covering the forehead and the other covering the nose and part of the cheeks. The eyes and lower part of the face were left completely open. The mask was fastened with either silk strings entwined with gold or meter-long gold or silver chains wrapped multiple times around the head, which also kept our headscarves in place.

Rainy days, uncommon as they are, dampen the mood because there is no chance to socialize outside the house, and we are stuck within our own four walls. Not everyone in the Orient has an umbrella, this indispensable companion in the North, and it is not always easy to borrow one when going out. The middle class, and Africans now and again, carry enormously large umbrellas imported from India, which are covered in yellow, green, or very occasionally black oilcloth.

I hardly need to mention again that Muslim ladies may not, as a rule, go out on public streets in broad daylight, but rather only in the early morning hours or evenings after the sun sets. There were no streetlights when I grew up in Zanzibar. We had to carry our own light in order to wind our way through the narrow, mostly crooked and dirty streets. Lanterns thus became objects of great luxury. The larger ones were one to two meters round. The prettiest ones had the form of a Russian church, with a large dome in the middle ringed by four turrets. In each tower, a bright candle threw its light through white, red, green, yellow, or dark blue panes onto the street. Every upper-class lady was preceded by two to six such lanterns, depending on her rank and means, all carried by escorts chosen from among the few slaves with enough strength to handle them. Regular citizens, by contrast, contented themselves with one lantern.

The train of every traveling lady additionally consisted of a whole host of armed slaves, who tended to look more battle-ready than they really were. These escorts always carried a high price tag. Their weapons, aside from the gun and revolver, were fully adorned with precious gold and silver and quite expensive. This did not, however, deter the rascals from selling them for a song, or pawning them off for a pittance to a usurer (these fine men are usually Hindus or Banyans),[16] only because the reckless knaves wanted to quench their thirst with *pombe* (palm wine). A mistress had no choice but to reclaim the weapons for ten times the price, or arrange a new outfit for the scoundrel, along with a well-earned, exemplary punishment.

Ten to twenty armed slaves would thus proceed with their lanterns, two-by-two or in whatever combination of orderly rows, at the head of a high-ranking lady's train. Behind this distinguished lady, who was sometimes accompanied by an Arab woman, a group of well-dressed female slaves would form the end of the train.

If a bystander, whether of high or low rank, was encountered en route, the slaves would motion him out of the way or detour him into a side street, open door, or shop until the train went by. But this worked consistently only with the family

---

16 Among its mix of cultures, Zanzibar had a significant Indian population, known primarily as Banyans, both from the convenience of the alternating monsoon trade winds and the Sultan's preference for their business and administrative capabilities. Interesting details can be found in G. Dale, *The Peoples of Zanzibar: Their Customs and Religious Beliefs* (1920); located in the Leiden University Libraries at NINO SR 739a.

of the Sultanate. Other fine ladies did not always fare as well in securing clear passage, and the rougher street folk were especially disinclined to move aside.

The long procession of richly clothed pedestrians and the colorful sheen of lanterns in the dark and narrow streets made for an enchanting sight. Even though good behavior in the Orient also calls for keeping as calm and quiet as possible when moving around in public, our lively nature would invariably break through, as the group proceeded loudly and jokingly enough for curious onlookers and eavesdroppers to be drawn to their windows and doors or lured onto their low, flat roofs.

Frequently, I would happen upon a sister or encounter a friend that was on the way to visit me. At that point, we would continue together, causing the train to swell to double and sometimes triple its length.

Having arrived at our destination, we allowed our arrival to be announced according to local custom. To be sure, we did not wait around in a dark corridor or anteroom until the lady of the house had finished her toiletries, but rather followed directly on the heels of the person announcing our arrival. Visitors were then received inside or, on moonlit nights, up on the clean and flat, balustraded roof.

The hostess sits on her *medde*, a kind of horizontal cushion about ten centimeters high and made of the finest brocade, and leans against the *tekje*, a large, square cushion placed against the wall that is also made of brocade. It is not our custom for the hostess to step forward, whether warmly or politely, every time a guest comes in. She does so only to show her personal affection for the guest or out of respect for her guest's higher rank and status.

An Arab woman is generally very reserved with respect to complete strangers, whether the strangers are of high or low rank. That is in contrast to closer acquaintances. As soon as a close friendship is established, any difference of rank or birth disappears.

After the arriving guests have kissed the hostess's hand, head, or hem of the shawl (while those of equal rank simply shake hands), they take their rank-appropriate place. Only a lady of equal rank may seat herself unbidden on the *medde* and claim the comforts of the *tekje*, while those of lower rank take their place at a certain distance on the mat- or rug-covered floor.

The mask stays on, as does most everything else, including the thin, light *shele*. Only the shoes are removed. Instead of the wooden sandals (*kubkab*) that are normally worn at home, we go out with elaborately stitched *kash*, a kind of slipper with a broad heel. These shoes are readily slipped off before entering the room, a custom that everyone, from ruler to slave, follows. It is then the unenviable task of the many slaves standing at the door to arrange the shoes in pairs, despite looking mostly the same, so the guests can immediately slip them back on for departure. Here, too, a strict protocol applies. The shoes of the highest-ranked guest are placed in the middle, with those of lower rank placed around them in a semi-circle.

Soon after a guest arrives, slaves pass around little cups of coffee, and this ritual is repeated every time a new guest arrives. Fresh fruit and confections are also enjoyed. Everyone can just take as much as they want.

The hostess is similarly spared the need to keep up the often rather forced conversation that counts as good etiquette here and takes the greatest effort. No, everyone is completely at ease and chats freely about whatever comes to mind. Without theatres, concerts, balls, or circuses, conversation topics are already rather limited, and no one there loves witty quips about the weather either. Instead, conversations are mostly about personal matters and agriculture, with all that pertains. Everyone with a higher rank is active in farming, perhaps not as experts, but with great interest.

Guests can freely indulge a good mood, and laugh and joke, without having to worry if their reputations might suffer as a result. In addition to all other advantages of the South, its residents are mostly cheerful, upbeat, and content. Why not, with nature, always sunny and bright, setting such a good example? Under a clear sky beaming with full sunlight, the melancholic spleen never gets the upper hand in the South. And nature is so bountiful, generous to excess, that people are guaranteed whatever they need to live, with nary a care.

The master of the house is not allowed to enter the rooms of his wife, daughter, or mother during visiting hours. Only the ruler and his immediate male relatives are exempt from this rule, except that the presence of an equally ranked female cousin would also bar any unannounced visits by my brothers and nephews.

This custom becomes very uncomfortable when a lady visits her friend for the whole day, say early from half past five in the morning until seven in the evening. The men in the house sometimes have considerable trouble staying out of the way. That is surely burdensome. But, in this case as with other special customs, Orientals do not feel put upon in the slightest. This is how they grew up, they know no other way and cannot compare, it all feels absolutely normal and right. Everywhere the force of habit and its penetrating influence! I do not deny that many things in the Orient may appear excessive or even exaggerated when considered more objectively. But is Europe the only place that is free from such lopsided perspectives and behaviors? Over there, the strictest restraints between men and women; over here, the most unbridled freedom. Over there, constant coverings and masking, despite the heat; over here in the cold north, full cleavage; and so on. These are certainly extreme contrasts, but we exaggerate here just as there. In my opinion, the happy middle has not yet been found anywhere.

Evening visits by the ladies can easily last three to four hours when filled with the liveliest conversation and gesticulation. And then finally, it is time. The slaves are roused from their deep sleep to form an orderly procession. Meanwhile the lanterns have been allowed to burn during the whole visit, completely unnecessarily, but such is the fashion.

After the hostess hands each visitor a parting gift, be it but a trifle, and everyone says good-bye, the train is set in motion to return home. If I end up leaving the house at the same time as a sister or friend, it always takes a while to disentangle the confusion of retinues on the street. Our path is still traceable long after we pass through, given the intensity and sustained fragrance of our heavy perfumes. We must all be home by midnight at the latest, since that is the deadline for the nighttime prayer. —

Arab women have another special advantage over European women. They are under no obligation to express thanks for the social occasion to which they were invited. They need not feign or pretend. Is it not bad enough to sit through a boring gathering without having to then also show gratitude for it? How often have I heard ladies give their most flattering compliments to the hostess for a lovely time and then stand outside the door and unload their biting critiques. What an abhorrent charade! Would we not stand closer to our merciful Creator if everyone tried especially hard to stay open and honest toward their fellow humans? Why the eternal masquerade?

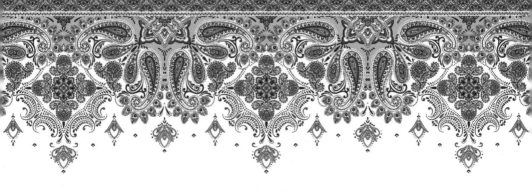

CHAPTER NINETEEN

The Audience;
Interactions Among Men

It is a long-standing custom that the ruler grants his male relatives, ministers, and other officials, as well as anyone else who wants to see or speak with him, open access two times a day, namely after breakfast and after the fourth prayer. The designated hall for this gathering (Arabic *barze*) was on the ground floor of our house, right by the sea, whose waves at high tide always splashed the base walls of this wing, and from whose expansive and lively setting the windows looked out onto a magnificent view. The hall was large, but often not large enough for all the visitors that came. The interior had the same simple character as every Arab room. Beyond rugs, floor-to-ceiling mirrors, clocks, and a large number of chairs along the walls, there were no other furnishings.

Because no high-ranking Arab ever travels unaccompanied, there was always a throng of several hundred attendants at the door. Anyone who could find room took a seat on the stone benches that ran the length of the house wall. The latecomers had to stand in the open palace courtyard to wait for their exiting masters or friends. Those were always interesting sights for us. For this audience, men always appeared in their full state regalia, with turban, tunic down to the ankles (*djocha*), and sash tied at the waist.

At home, Arab men wear white caps that are often nicely embroidered on heads that are clean shaven once a week. When they go out, they put on a turban (*amame*). Building a turban requires a certain dexterity. It takes some men half an hour to construct them properly. That is why removal is handled so very delicately, since even the smallest misstep can cause the whole thing to fall apart. But anyone who cares about his looks reconstructs a new turban every time he goes out. The cloth that is used for turbans is relatively plain and costs less than five to eight dollars. The fabrics used for sashes (*mahsem*) are much more expensive, with prices ranging from twenty to two hundred dollars. These are silk fabrics, richly interwoven with gold and silver threads. Someone of higher rank normally owns a whole series of sashes that are swapped out, much as men do with their neckties here. Older and devout people, who are less bound to fashion, just wear plain white or black silk *mahsems*.

An Arab man's outfit is naturally not complete without, as already often mentioned, his weapons. His wife, daughter, or son normally hand them to him when he is about to go out.

Before the men enter the gathering hall, they remove their shoes, which is when the different ranks become apparent. The lower-class men take off their *watje* at a distance, the higher class right at the door. But this is not the result of some despotic decree; the practice is completely traditional and voluntary. Arabs show their due respect at every opportunity, according to custom. Above all, they harbor pious, instinctively royalist sentiments toward their ruler and his whole house.

Once the gathering hall is full, the Sultan makes his way to greet the distinguished attendees. The official procession in my father's time always took the following order: First came an African guard unit, then a company of younger eunuchs, after them the chief eunuchs, and finally our father in advance of his sons, with the youngest at the very end. Downstairs at the door of the *barze*, the guard unit and eunuchs formed a lane through which the father and his sons entered the room. All rose to greet him, and the same ritual was then repeated when he left the gathering in the same orderly procession. Our father also showed due respect to all in return. When someone of high rank took his leave, the father would accompany him a few steps, while all others stood to rise.

Coffee was only rarely served to the morning audience, but always in the evenings. This audience was simultaneously also a legal proceeding in which my father handled the main matter quickly and efficiently, and knew how to resolve difficult questions with Solomonic wisdom. People were free to come and go, and this freedom of movement was in some ways contrary to the otherwise very ceremonial style of Arabs. Anyone could present a matter, request, or complaint and seek a response. Virtually everything was handled only orally, since business affairs were not settled in writing. Petitioners would usually have to come and present their matters directly. Smaller matters were typically delegated for decision to the relevant ministers, *kadis* (the appointed judges), or chief eunuchs. The audience lasted about one and a half to three hours. Those who did not get their turn or came too late to push their way into the overflowing *barze* were summoned anew by the chief eunuchs, and their items then topped the agenda for the next day.

Between the ages of fourteen and sixteen, princes are permitted to attend the audience, after which attendance becomes mandatory. Similarly, every man of rank must show respect for his ruler by being present every day, unless deterred by something especially urgent. If someone goes missing several days in a row, slaves are sent to find out the reason for the absence. If this person is lying infirm, he can be certain that the ruler himself will soon pay a visit. Not even the most contagious diseases, like cholera or smallpox, are deterrents; God decides and ordains all! The female caretakers of the sick person, as well as the wife, mother, daughter, and sister, must of course vacate the room as long as male visitors are present. When, however, someone remains absent from the gatherings without justification, then resentment, even hostility, is presumed.

Every distinguished Arab has a *barze* on the ground floor of his house, set apart from the women's quarters, where he spends his time and receives his friends and acquaintances. The floor is usually laid out in black and white marble tiles from France. Rugs or mats are not used, so as not to diminish the pleasant coolness of the stones.

The men pay their visits during the same hours as the women, with evenings after seven being the favorite time. When Arabs go out, they must have a specific destination. They have no inkling that one could, or even should, take a walk for health reasons. Any European seen pacing back and forth on his roof is presumed to be praying in his peculiar Christian manner. —

I need not add anything about the social practices and interactions among men. They are just like those of women, except that men naturally discuss more of the general questions that affect the well-being of the city and country and take a keen interest in the events of the last audience with the Sultan, the various petitions, the many cases, that were decided. Europeans are readily able to attend male gatherings, especially the audiences with the Sultan, so that our patriarchal activity, with all its good and bad sides, is more familiar to the North than the sequestered lives of Oriental women.

ﺐﺹ

ZANZIBAR FROM THE SEA.

CHAPTER TWENTY

The Time of Fasting

Everyone has probably heard that Muslims have to fast for a full month, every day, the whole day, as long as the sun can be seen in the sky. Islamic fasting is nothing like the Catholic version, which amounts to child's play by comparison. Fasting is obligatory for all Muslims, and children are expected to start when they reach twelve years of age. Because my mother was very devout, she had me practice the sacred month of *Rumdân* already in my ninth year. (We pronounced it *Rumdân,* not Ramadan, the way it is usually written here.)

It is certainly not easy for a nine-year-old child to spend a full fourteen and a half hours every day without being allowed to eat or drink. The hunger is not nearly as tortuous as the horrible, indescribable thirst that impacts someone living in the Tropics. At my age, I naturally had a weak grasp of religion, and so I am ashamed to admit that I initially snuck a little water here and there. Under my mother's penetrating questioning, I remorsefully confessed my sin and received her pardon on the condition that I would never again disobey the sacred religious commands. During the first days, I was so totally dazed that they let me sleep as long as I could to take off some of the pressure. The rules are applied extremely strictly. To be considered fully compliant, even intentionally swallowing one's own spit is not allowed. Thirst can drive people to insanity. My poor mother, who normally followed every commandment with the utmost strictness, was so extremely beset with thirst one day that she forgot herself and in a stupor emptied an entire earthen jug filled with water in a single draft, despite the father's resonating warning voice from on high. As a consequence, she had to fast an entire extra day.

At four in the morning, our ship sends out a cannon blast to signal the start of the fast. Anyone in the midst of eating must stop immediately. Even someone with a cup in hand, ready to take that last quenching sip for the next fourteen and a half hours, has to set it aside, untouched, the moment the cannon shot is heard. No healthy adult may from that time on eat or drink anything. People, love to sleep away the day and then stay up late into a pleasure-filled night.

At six the sun sets. It is time for the evening prayer, after which fasting can be interrupted at six thirty. The loveliest fruits, and above all precious drinking water in cool, porous clay pots, have already been set out to offer languished individuals an initial respite. Soon the family gathers to enjoy a truly epicurean meal that amply rewards the harsh deprivations. Considering how contented Arabs usually are, and how simply they usually live, they become veritable gluttons and luxuriate in food and drink during *Rumdân*.

At this time, life is especially sociable, and everyone comes together in the evenings, or rather nights, for religious songs, rhetorical speeches, and storytelling, while eating and drinking throughout. At midnight, the first cannon shot resounds and wakes anyone who has to prepare the night meal (*suhur*). This is then served between three and four in the morning. Small children that were sent to bed at nine or ten are woken up for it. The *suhur* is rarely shared in a group, but rather eaten individually in each person's own room.

That is how the month goes by. At the start, there are plenty of fainting spells. One can almost watch people become trim and thin. But gradually, people get used to dealing with the privations, they do not sleep as much of the day away, and many who until now were seen only at meals and prayers again appear regularly on the gallery.

Everyone is supposed to adhere strictly to the fast, and masters are expected to order their slaves to comply as well. Those who provide household and personal services, who can be controlled, are held to this standard. On the other hand, the plantation slaves, who mostly have no religion, are free to decide if they want to fast or not.

Children and sick people are excused from fasting. However, once the sick get well, they still need to make up what they missed within the same year, by fasting the full number of missed days back-to-back. The same applies to those who have been on a difficult trip. And pregnant women facing imminent delivery may, if the conditions are challenging, postpone their fasting duty as well. Of course, they would rather avoid facing all the deprivations later alone, when it is so much harder. If a woman delivers during *Rumdân*, she must stop her fasting immediately and may not resume until at least two weeks have gone by. But the strictest rule always applies, that every missed day must be recouped later. Someone who is injured with loss of blood, or is suddenly indisposed without being sick, still has to fast for the rest of that day and also make up the lost time after the fasting period.

Of course, fasting is not merely an outward trial. During this time, devoted Muslims focus primarily on their inward contemplation. They seek to discover and improve their moral failings, to pray for forgiveness of their sins, much like when good Christians prepare themselves for holy communion in the Holy Week before Easter. Even dangerous animals are spared, and extra efforts are made to do as much good as possible. In this way, *Rumdân* is a heartwarming time. People become more conciliatory, kinder, even the ones who are hardened to the core. These long, drawn-out sacrifices undertaken in the service of the Lord bring them closer to Him. And so they are lifted and bettered, some admittedly perhaps only for a short while, but others for their whole lives.

Above all, the traditional hospitality of Arabs achieves a high point during this time, essentially becoming a religious duty. Every man with a family and household feeds strangers, as many as he can find, even people whose names he does not know. The prayer leader of the mosque that he frequents is often simply instructed to send him a set number of strangers every evening for a meal. These are not just poor people, but often men of higher birth and wealth who are foreign and miss their homeland now more than ever in this holy time. To fill in for such guests is always a pleasure for the truly hospitable Arab. No one considers it inappropriate to be served by someone who is poorer, and no one would dream of offering to compensate the host. That would be a severe insult. Truly, egoism cannot take root where such principles prevail, and blessed are those peoples for whom love of their fellow man or woman is an unassailable duty.

The month of *Rumdân* has its similarities to the weeks before Christmas here. We also have to come up with various presents that are distributed on the first day of the following month of *Shewal,* one of the two most sacred holidays of Islam. Handcrafted items are seldom given as presents and then only to the closest family and friends, never to those outside the inner circle. Just as here, such projects take a lot of time to complete. On occasion, I would even spot some lonely soul hiding away, plaguing herself, eager and afraid, trying to finish a delicate piece of work under the bright light of the African moon.

Most gifts are bought as finished products. For this, goldsmiths do the best business. This trade is totally in the hands of Hindus and Banyans, who are known for their cunning, lies, and deceit. Very skilled in their craft, they have managed to drive all Arab goldsmiths out of business. In the lead-up to the holidays, their business is booming. Orders come in one after another, and they take them all in. To ensure that our orders would be ready on time, we usually had to send a few armed slaves to the master smith's workshop to monitor his progress and keep him from working on other orders. That may sound very drastic. However, nothing short of this approach, devised by one of my sisters, proved effective against these Hindus and Banyans, who, as indicated, are the worst swindlers. Their word is not reliable, and they are extraordinarily craven.

Among the favorite gifts are weapons of all sorts. Europeans may consider it strange that an Arab woman would give expensive arms to her husband, brother, adult son, or to-be-betrothed. But such weapons are exactly where Arabs place their greatest extravagance. They are always on the lookout for beautifully crafted pieces and can never get enough of them. Price is never an issue when it comes to procuring a weapon.

Weapons and jewelry are thus at the top of the list for holiday gifts. But there is plenty more that can be given: regal horses, white travel donkeys, and—an atrocity for civilized Europeans—even slaves!

The month of *Rumdân* always passes quickly with all these pressures and purchases. In the last week and often earlier, baking and other household preparations for the imminent celebration begin. The closer the first day of *Shewal* comes, the more the excitement and expectations rise. Everyone is feverishly trying to get their presents and households ready on time.

The night before the 27th of *Rumdân*, the "Night of Value," in which Muhammad is said to have received the Koran from heaven, is considered especially sacred. Prayers that are raised to the Lord on this night can surely count on being granted.

Finally, the last day of *Rumdân* arrives, the 29th or 30th day. It is well-known that we measure by moon months of 29 or 30 days, so that each year amounts to only 355 days. Everyone is now eagerly trying to spot the rising moon. The new sliver of the crescent moon has to actually be seen before the fasting can end. What luck that Muslims almost always look up at the clear and bright sky of the South, which is rarely clouded over like in the bleary North.

Anyone who owns a telescope or opera glass is much envied. The popular instrument is passed from hand to hand; friends and acquaintances from all around ask to borrow it briefly. Our father sends people with sharp eyes onto the roof of our fortress, which still stands from the days of Portuguese occupation, and to the tops of ship masts, to keep watch for the emerging moon from both land and sea.

In the evening of the 29th day of fasting, everyone is tense with anticipation. By the minute, one or the other person thinks they just heard the cannon shot announcing the happy discovery. Every little sound is taken to be the real thing, forgetting in our excitement that shots from ships directly in front of our house always give the palace such a shake that we not only hear, but also feel, the blast. Finally, the actual shot roars. Exultant cheers fill the whole city, and everyone wishes everyone *id mbarak* (blessed festival).

So much for the city. The matter is more complex in the countryside, where direct support of the ruler is missing, and no official signal tells everyone when to stop fasting. Those who live on distant plantations usually send riders into the city to await the cannon shot and then return with the official news that the new moon has in fact been seen. Others let slaves ascend the crowns of the highest coconut palms to watch the horizon from various locations on their properties. Occasionally such a look-out makes a mistake, believing he has spotted the narrow crescent moon when it was in fact just the delicate wisp of a rising cloud. Fasting is then immediately interrupted, only to later discover that fasting is still ongoing in the city, which is what counts. There is hardly a more bitter disappointment for Arabs than having to make up for lost fasting time when they were so ready to celebrate.

CHAPTER TWENTY-ONE

The Small Festival

Baking, as explained, has already been underway for a week. The last few days have also seen major purchases of animals for slaughter, like oxen, sheep, goats, gazelles, chicken, ducks, and doves (we do not eat veal, and Muslims are strictly prohibited from enjoying pork). The stalls are all full, and many of the animals that will be sacrificed for the feast have to be kept in the courtyard. Wealthy people are tasking their eunuchs with exchanging the Louis d'ors and guineas into Maria Theresa thalers to distribute to the needy during the celebration, especially all the poor and humble immigrants from Oman, who have never seen gold currency.

As soon as the cannon shot bursts out, the joyous news spreads far and wide that the next morning is indeed the day of the "small celebration." Life in Arab households becomes even more picturesque, exciting, and over-the-top. Hundreds of beaming folk forget their usual measured steps and run about urgently, here and there. Everyone wants to wish their loved ones all the best and many blessings. With such joyful religious excitement, it is not uncommon to see two enemies extend their hands in reconciliation because they hope to have attained this state with their all-merciful God in the time of introspection and examination. The giddy commotion, the hundred voices calling in many different languages, the agitated complaints of slaves overloaded with work, all this hardly lets anyone get any rest that night.

The service workers in particular get no rest. The slaughterers (slaves) hastily throw themselves onto their bellowing, shrieking, and squealing victims, ending their lives with the prescribed words "in the name of God, the All-

Merciful." Following strict rituals, the throats of the cattle are slit, heads quickly removed, and slaughtered carcasses immediately skinned. Then it is off to the kitchen where they are prepared overnight for the next day's feast. On this evening, our slaughter yard looked like a sea of blood from all the butchered animals, and a humane vegetarian would have fled the scene in dismay. Our local vegetarians in Zanzibar, the Banyans, were horrified by our celebrations and made sure to stay far from our abattoirs. They are manufacturers, but, at the same time, they are loan sharks and the worst throat-slitters in the world. Hated bitterly by their victims, they are gruesomely mocked and derided on these occasions. Under the pretense of this or that lady still wishing to buy something for the celebration, it is a sport to lure these lower-class Banyans—who would never miss a chance to make a deal—into this bloody arena and make a mockery of them. It is a bitter taunt, for these star-worshippers have at least one good side, which is that they stay extraordinarily faithful to their religiously-prescribed vegetarian views.

The ladies, who already cannot sleep a wink with the rowdy noise from all the commotion, also have an array of important wardrobe concerns roiling in their heads. Three completely new outfits are commissioned for the three days of the festival.

An important part in the presentation of a fashion-minded Oriental lady, especially at major celebrations, is played by *hinna*,[17] which is made from the leaves of a mid-sized tree and creates a red coloring on the hands and feet of women and children. The poor *hinna* trees, which almost never get to enjoy their full leafy bounty, look much like dry rods during festival times. Every little leaf has been stripped off, and it takes six to eight weeks for new ones to appear. It is a sad sight to see those trees standing there, so bare against the ample foliage of the other trees.

Oriental women have two main uses for this entirely indispensable *hinna*: as a cure for bumps, heat blisters, itches, and the like, and as a beautifier. The small leaves alone, which are like myrtle leaves, are insufficient to produce either result. They first have to be dried, pulverized, and then supplemented with the juice of several limes, which are smaller than the lemons we have here, but much juicier, plus a bit of water. The mixture is kneaded together into a firm dough, placed in the sun for a few hours, probably to promote acidification, and then reworked with lime juice to soften the mix again.

---

17 *Lawsonia inermis*, also known as henna, of the Lythraceae family that includes crepe myrtles and pomegranates.

Now the beautification of the lady in question can begin. There she lies on her precious bed, ideally flat on her back, and may not move. First, the *hinna* paste is expertly applied flat on the feet about an inch high above the sole and on the toes, which, being undefiled by pinching boots, have retained their natural form. The top surface of the feet is not colored. Big, soft leaves are layered on the *hinna*, and then the whole thing is wrapped tightly in cloth. This is then repeated with the hands. Here, too, only the insides of the hands are covered in a half moon shape, plus the fingertips up to the first joint in a thimble shape, and then that is all wrapped up. And thus the proud beauty has to lie there, bound up the entire night and not allowed to move, or risk blemishes if the mixture shifts. Only the designated areas may be dyed red. If, say, the back of the hand or an additional finger joint picks up the color, that would be considered very unsightly.

Mosquitoes and flies, attracted to the bright lights, may descend in droves upon this helpless body, but no matter how much they plague her, she cannot defend herself. The situation is less severe for the higher-ranking ladies. Female slaves must keep watch and take turns to fan these vexing creatures away from their mistress until the break of dawn, after which the mixture is carefully washed off. The next night this trial begins anew. Three agonizing nights are needed for this part of a lady's regimen to achieve a very nice, dark red color, which then also tolerates all the washing to last up to four weeks.

I recall reading somewhere that it once was fashionable in France to get one's hair done by a particular, especially skilled hairdresser. For the large public holidays, this much sought-after coiffeur already had to start his work the day before to satisfy all his many customers. Those who were first in line then had the pleasure of spending the entire night stiff and stuck on their armchairs to avoid undoing their stylish hairstyles. This reminds me vividly of my own young years in the Orient, although our vanity tortures were even worse than the one described here.

Older ladies and younger children are spared these torments. For them, *hinna* is only used as a cooling wash in a more liquid form.

The day of the festival dawns. By four o'clock, everyone is up and about. They all take extra time during morning prayer to give special thanks to the almighty Creator and Guide of the world for everything he has granted us, all the blessings, and all the misfortunes, which he has imposed on us to test us.

Around five thirty, morning prayer is over. Decked-out ladies can already be seen here and there rushing across the gallery to show off their clothes and jewels to others, for in an hour the pomp and splendor will be so widespread that no one expects to stand out enough to be closely regarded and admired. The comparison to a full ballroom would be apt, except that outfits in the North predominate in so much pale and monotone white attire. In the Orient, only the liveliest color combinations get acclaim. It would surely strain the eyes of a fashionable European lady to see an upper-class Arab woman in her fashion regalia, wearing a shirt-like garment of red silk, featuring various patterns of interwoven gold threads and covered with lots and lots of gold and silver strands, paired with pants of bright green sateen! Quite naturally, she would find this rather too eccentric. The same thing happened to me, when I first saw people in Europe dressed mostly in gray on gray or black on black. This is what I am supposed to wear in the future? These civilized colors really grated on me, and it took a long time before I was able to subject myself to this purported fine fashion.

At six o'clock, a first shot resounds from our ships, punctuated thereafter by one shot after another, to celebrate the Festival of the Faithful. If foreign ships are in the harbor, they join in with their twenty-one gun salutes. All Arabs shoot their weapons in joyous celebration, sparing no powder on this day. A stranger would surely think the city is under bombardment. All ships are decorated, with flags waving on every mast and yardarm, both on our own ships and those from elsewhere.

An hour later, all the mosques are overflowing. On this day, every Arab shows up to say a special festival prayer to his Lord. Hundreds that no longer find room in the houses of worship pray in front of and beside them on the open streets. Muslim prayer involves significant bodily effort, as it requires a very deep and continuous bow, with the forehead down low, touching the flat earth, to honor the Almighty. Nothing, not even thunder and rain, is allowed to interrupt the prayers of a believer, and the duty to pray in or near a mosque is heightened during major festivals. Our father, too, took his place shortly before the hour in the nearby mosque to pray, accompanied by his numerous sons and an unending entourage.

Meanwhile, the already massive undertaking in our house escalates even more in preparation for the scores of well-wishers that will start arriving when the men return from the mosque. Repeated cannon shots announce the end of the prayer hour. From this point on, everyone can fully indulge in their long-denied daily pleasures. The fast thus continues even into the first hours of the first day of the new month, coming definitively to a complete stop only when the shared prayer in the mosque concludes.

We women waited in the father's chambers for his return. This location also gave us the best vantage point to watch the flood of people coming to see the father, all of whom could then confirm the culinary skills of our cooks while at it.

When the father entered the room, everyone rose and went toward him to wish him good fortune, one after another, and reverently kiss his benevolent hand. The distinguished upper-class hand, of both genders, has much to withstand on days like this in the Orient, and it is washed and perfumed until late into the night. Only people of the same rank kiss each other's hands. The middle class kisses people with higher rank on their lowered heads, or more properly on their headcloths. A common woman is allowed to press her lips only to the feet.

The time for distributing gifts was now approaching. The father went into the treasure chamber with my sister Chole and the giant chief of the eunuchs, Djohar, both of whom faced considerable envy for this proof of trust. Many highly-coveted items emerged from the vault: expensive, expertly crafted weapons with inlaid stones; Oriental jewelry of every kind from the most spare to the most ornate designs; the rarest of fabrics specially procured from Persia, Turkey, or China for this day; rose oil and other fragrant oils in large carafes, whose contents were sorted into smaller bottles; and lots of gleaming gold coins.

Distribution by the father naturally took place on a broad scale. There was no way he could remember all the jewelry pieces his women and children already owned and what they especially wanted. So he would usually check their wishes several days beforehand, to see if they might like this or that item. But people tended to turn to Chole as well, so she could remind him of their individual desires during the selection process.

Eunuchs sorted all the gifts in the presence of the father. Every item was noted with the name of the recipient on a strip of paper and then delivered by the eunuchs to each individual. Understandably, these items were subjected to careful examination immediately upon receipt, while the messenger was still present. Frequently, eunuchs had to relay gifts back to the father, along with discerning comments that this or that item was not quite useful, but some other item or two would be more desirable. And sure enough, recipients mostly got what they wanted. Our father was so extraordinarily good-natured and accommodating that no one who appealed to his generosity ever did so in vain.

The father gave and gifted with full hands, but never received in return. It is a nice and endearing custom in Germany that children, according to their ages and circumstances, give their parents gifts for Christmas and birthdays. The head of the family in the Orient fares poorly by comparison. Arab children, big and small, never give their fathers anything.

Up to this point, I have addressed only gifts from the father to our family, but his obligations hardly ended there. On this day, everyone expected something from him. He had to think of all the official Asian and African chiefs who were in Zanzibar at the time, all state officials, all soldiers and their officers, all sailors and their captains, the managers of his forty-five plantations, and finally all his slaves, which may have numbered more than six to eight thousand. Naturally, all these gifts reflected the ranks of the recipients. The slaves, for example, received simple fabric for clothes.

On top of that, there were the hundreds of humble poor, some of whom were still coming by for festival gifts two weeks later. Poor people did well everywhere, since wealthy people all made great efforts to care for them.

Similar activity as in the city also took place at Bet il Mtoni. Here, too, massive amounts of presents were handed out. To us, it was almost miraculous the way the treasure chamber never fell short of the sizeable demands that had to be met over the course of these three days, especially in terms of cash—evidence that our father also must have been an excellent businessman.

CHAPTER TWENTY-TWO

The Big Festival

Muslims celebrate only two major festivals annually, which must be rather unfathomable to Catholics with their many holidays. Two months lie between the small festival and the big festival, which is usually described in Europe and Turkey as the Great Bayram.

This celebration is like the earlier celebration, except more beautiful, more grandiose, and for the people, even more dignified and solemn. It is the time of the great pilgrimage to *Mekke* (the way we pronounce Mecca), which all devout Muslims aspire to undertake at least once in their lifetimes. The horrors of cholera and other plagues that often claim many thousands of pilgrims do not trouble the faithful. Every year countless droves set out anew to plead for full forgiveness of their sins in the holy city of the Prophet of the Almighty. The poor must traverse great distances on foot, and their travel by ship, where they practically lie on top of each other, is horrendous. But trusting in God, they set out with their lives in His hands. Truly, such confident faith, which eschews no effort, no discomfort, no danger in pursuit of a religious duty, may justify expectations that prayers will be answered.

This greatest Islamic festival occurs on the tenth day of the twelfth month of the year and lasts three to seven days. Many already start observing it on the first day of the month with a voluntary nine-day fast, exactly as the devout pilgrims in Mecca do.

Whoever can afford it gets a sheep, to be slaughtered on the first day and distributed to the poor. The law requires that this sacrificial sheep must be the best that can be found, indeed flawless. It should be correct in all aspects, without even a single missing tooth. A totally flawless sheep is of course hard to find, and we would send a few slaves on reconnaissance of the whole island already two weeks or more ahead of time. If they failed to find anything suitable, they would have to travel to the African mainland to try their luck in the interior, where there was more selection. In this way, expenses got quite high, and the actual purchase price would go even higher. Herd owners knew full well how much the Arab royals needed a model specimen, for which any sum would gladly be paid. Neither the person putting on the sacrifice, nor his family or slaves, were allowed to enjoy the meat of the sacrificed animal, not even the smallest piece. None of it stays in the house; all of it belongs to the poor.

The big festival is the most significant event of the year for the poor. It represents one of the best Islamic customs there is: a broad self-taxation to benefit the needy.

In the real Orient (excluding Turkey, Egypt, and Tunisia because of their mixed cultures), people have no concept of government bonds and securities. The phrase "investing money" has no meaning there. Assets are primarily held in tangible form, as in fully-paid plantations, houses, slaves, jewelry, and major coins. If there is anything left at the end of the year from the harvest, rental contracts on housing, or any other income, religious precept requires that a tenth of it must be paid to the poor.

At the same time, Arabs must have their entire fortunes in precious stones, gold, and silver appraised by experts, with a tenth of the total valuation also to be gifted to the poor every year. As such, a wealth tax with a voluntary self-assessment.

All of this happens without any control by the authorities. Everyone is bound only by their own feelings, their own scruples. But this order of the Prophet is considered especially sacred, and only the absolute worst individuals fail to follow through. Such charitable contributions are also never discussed, on the principle that the left shall not know what the right hand doeth. Neither father, mother, nor child may know what I have negotiated with my benevolent God. With scrupulous care, every effort is made to comply with this tithing duty down to the smallest detail in all aspects, to avoid being tormented by pangs of conscience later.

Under these circumstances, a large number of people who feign poverty, if I may say so, appears to be an indispensable part of every Islamic state. How else could this duty of self-taxation be fulfilled? These poor people are not to be compared with the pitiable, truly poor people we have here. Perhaps about half of the ones over there possess more than they actually need. Begging is their business, it has become second nature to them, and without begging they no longer feel happy. Often this trade is directly inherited, and that can lead to the following appeal: "Do you not recognize me? I am of course the daughter, son, in-law, etc. of this or that person, to whom you used to give so much while they were still alive. Now I am taking their place, and if you have alms to give, please send them to me at such and such address."

As far as religious vows, which we had opportunities to fulfill multiple times a year, hundreds of poor people would come to us from all directions to participate in the usual distribution of alms. If someone lay very ill in bed, poor people, who are quite skilled in scouting out these opportunities, would stand under the sick person's window, taking turns all day long, to be richly bestowed with gifts known as *sadka*. No Muslim would turn such a beggar away, even if it meant giving up his last coin. Perhaps this is pure altruism, perhaps it exemplifies a hope to win the Almighty's favor and obtain more of His grace, but it is, in any case, a beautiful custom.

Quite a few beggars are covered in wounds and ulcers. Some run around without noses and are horribly disfigured. They are victims of a serious disease we call *belas,* which attacks mostly the hands and feet, and the affected body parts turn white. No one wants anything to do with these sick people. They are shunned everywhere because their affliction is considered contagious. Whether this is leprosy, I cannot say. But even these lamentable poor always find ample alms, which somewhat alleviates their difficult existence.

There are no further religious celebrations in the nine or ten months that follow the small and big festivals. Life returns to its routine and is interrupted only now and again for special festivities, one of which I intend to describe in the next chapter.

We do not celebrate birthdays.

Shore scene in Zanzibar by Rosa Troemer

CHAPTER TWENTY-THREE

An Offering Festival at Chem Chem Spring

When I was fifteen, I once wore a new damask dress made of red silk for the first time. I became ill, and the next day a kind of inflammation had spread across my whole body. The older, experienced folk immediately knew with certainty that I had been bewitched, or had at least fallen victim to some jealous person's evil eye on my pretty fabric. Always somewhat skeptical of these things, I chose not to give up my new dress and wore it again at the next opportunity, despite all these notions. Whether the color contained a toxic substance, or perhaps another natural cause was at work, I became sick again and had to take to my bed. The situation was now clear. I could no longer wear the dress and, for some peace of mind, gave it to a dauntless common woman who believed in witchcraft as little as I did. Under prevailing custom, I should have subjected it to a spoken cure, or better yet burnt it, to thoroughly eradicate its bad influence.

This is just a small example of the superstitions that are so extraordinarily rampant in the Orient. I have already discussed this in previous pages, so I will present only a few additional details here, in connection with the description of a festival of sacrifice, which is entirely based on superstition.

Some springs are believed to possess especially magical powers—not the water, but the reigning spirit that resides within. If the spirit is properly handled, he will do everything for his devout follower. He can heal the sick, return missing people to their homes, bring lonely singles together in marriage, grant a baby to childless parents, cause enraged parents, spouses, and friends to reconcile and restore peace, recover missing items like gold, slaves, and cattle, or make the poor as wealthy as Croesus. This spirit is considered capable of everything.

The most popular spring on the island of Zanzibar is called Chem Chem. It lies several hours outside the city. A visit to this magical place gives the impression that its spirit is rather modest and easily satisfied even with minor offerings. A small strip about two-inches wide that waves in the wind, or even a mere eggshell, can be found there as objects left by poor and destitute believers. The spirit especially likes any kind of sweets (called *halve)*, smelling powder, or incense. However, anyone who wants to be totally assured of success must offer up a blood tribute.

Many troubled souls head to Chem Chem, to bring such sacrifices, as promised in explicit vows. It is customary to apply a clever precaution to these vows by setting a specific time period within which the spirit is to fill the pending wish, for which the sacrifice would be made. If the spirit does not fulfill the wish within the stated period, then the promised vow no longer applies. So the spirit better watch out. On the other hand, people keep their word. If someone dies before fulfilling a sacred vow (*nadra*), then that person's relatives take it upon themselves to fulfill it.

As a small child, I was often taken along to such a holy spring, and those were always lovely, enjoyable days. After I was no longer called *kibibi* (little mistress), but *bibi* (mistress), which is to say at an age when I was able to observe more astutely and think more clearly, I attended only one more, indeed a very spectacular festival of sacrifice.

My unfortunately now deceased sister Chadudj was struck by a grave illness. Her concerned caretakers made a sacred vow that if this suffering could be overcome and the illness fully cured, Chadudj herself would go to Chem Chem to make an offering for her regained health. She recovered and was thus obligated to follow through on this promise that had been made on her behalf.

Festival invitations from her friends and acquaintances went out to some of her favorite sisters a full four weeks before the appointed day. Extensive preparations began at the same time. Each of us not only had to make arrangements for ourselves and perhaps a few hopeful daughters, but logistics also involved a whole regiment of slaves, both men and women, that had to be outfitted in clothing and jewelry befitting the wealth of their mistress, in addition to arranging a great number of transport animals. For such an event, where hundreds of people would be coming together, the ladies themselves were also intent on presenting their full splendor, each wishing to be marveled at and ideally outshine all the others, a desire that likely recurs for people everywhere in both hemispheres. No wonder the artists and artisans had their hands full handling all the many orders. Jewelers, who never keep a stock of finished products, but always produce on demand, were the most besieged and overburdened. On top of which, they were also tasked with inspecting and cleaning all the gold and silver ornamented harnesses, as well as all the slaves' ornate weapons adorned with precious metals. Especially the riding gear had to beam and gleam, since pilgrimages like this always travel as pageantry. Everything was mobilized, and no costs were spared, even though some of the jewelry was priced ten times the usual because of the massive demand. We paid for our vanity with all these high costs and no fewer drops of sweat. In spite of the hot and burning African sun, we wore Lyonnais velvet and other heavy, exquisitely embroidered fabrics. Pride must suffer duress!

On the day of our outing, I rode out early at five thirty to pick up my sister. It was no easy task to reach her through the huge throng of people. Once everyone was seated on their richly adorned animals, we got the sign to commence, and the shining procession rode out chatting and laughing in pairs. The ride was long and brisk, but very pleasant in the fresh morning air. We finally arrived at the enchantingly situated spring.

All the necessary preparations had been completed in advance. Today this otherwise secluded and desolate place was a magical haven that defied description. Over the past several days, a large number of slaves had busily lugged in everything and anything that might be needed from the city; plus they had cut the high grass, laid carpets for us to rest under the mighty trees, nailed mirrors to the mango trunks, placed backrest cushions against the same trunks, and set out a full assortment of useful utensils. The day before had also been spent slaughtering, cooking, and roasting for the joyful feast.

Soon after we arrived, the food was put out, and we sat down to breakfast in the shade of the trees, whose broad foliage let the deep blue sky shine through here and there. This picture imprinted itself deeply in my memory: the beautiful, brightly colored, glittering clothes and precious jewels of this radiant gathering, set in the wild, rich, and romantic vegetation of a tropical forest, alongside a lively, rippling spring in the midst of the most elemental profusion of nature. It was truly a picture that no painter's imagination could conjure, and yet, just like the fairytale descriptions in *The Arabian Nights*.

The large Omani donkeys were immediately unsaddled after the riders had dismounted, which they did by either hopping off in high spirits in one fell swoop or gingerly descending onto the backs of bent-over eunuchs to step off. The front legs of each donkey were then tied up with a short rope to impede any get-away, and all were driven out to the meadow. There they stayed all day without supervision and were led back only in the afternoon.

About two hours after arrival, we got ready for the offering that had brought us to this place. Today the spirit of the spring would drink and enjoy the blood of a specially selected steer, not to mention the many sweets and vast amounts of raw eggs that had been smashed at the water's edge. We also dedicated two flags to the spirit, one in blood red, our house flag, and one in white, as a sign of peace. —

Our picnic grounds were located a few minutes from where the spring bubbled up. The entire group made its way there to witness the ceremony. One of my sister's older female slaves stepped up to the spring and gave a small speech to the spirit. She described the grave illness of her mistress and how they had had to proclaim the sacred vow as a last resort. She thanked the merciful spirit for ultimately returning her mistress back to health, so that the mistress could now personally deliver the avowed sacrifice in gratitude.

The steer was brought forward and slaughtered. The blood was carefully collected and sprinkled onto the spring and the surrounding area. Rose water was richly dispersed as well. Musk and amber were thrown onto glowing coals in silver incense burners, perfuming the air with a pleasant scent. A few prayers were said while standing in the round to conclude the ceremony.

Of the sacrificed animal, the invisible spirit got only the blood and its noble organs, heart, liver, and so on, which were cut up into small pieces and scattered around the spring. The remaining meat, according to custom, was to be distributed to the poor, and neither the person making the sacrifice, nor that person's relatives were to enjoy any of it. However, because the Chem Chem spring was so far from the city, and there were no poor people to be found anywhere nearby, a silent pact was agreed with the spirit at the time the vow was made that, in light of the distances involved, the sacrificial steer could be directly consumed, which meant the meat became part of our meal that afternoon.

During our stay at the site, we had frequent cause to note that this or that member of our group would disappear for short periods and then evade any queries about their absence. We in turn refrained from probing too much. They had sought a tranquil moment at the miracle spring to complain to the mighty, but discreet, spirit about their troubles, their physical and spiritual suffering, perhaps an unhappy love, and beseech his help. Naturally, they preferred to meet with the spirit alone, and it was always quite embarrassing when two similarly despondent individuals unexpectedly encountered each other at this peaceful place. —

155

Not all sacred vows were well-suited to be trumpeted out loud, if the idea was not to subject one's innermost thoughts to the reckless tongues of her dear compatriots. In cases where a strictly-held secret wish had been fulfilled, it was possible to deliver the promised sacrifice to the spring through a confidential proxy, without drawing attention, but, of course, only if this had been expressly included in the originally sworn vow. On the other hand, when it came time to thank for being cured of a serious illness, or to ask the spirit to help find a beloved someone who had gone missing—in other words, when there was nothing to hide from the world—then the sacrifice was, as a rule, celebrated as a grandiose festival with all manner of pomp.

We passed the time until four in the afternoon with food and drinks of sharbet, coconut water, and lemonade, and with walks, games, rest, and prayer. Then the horses and donkeys were brought over from the meadow to be saddled. And so another lively scene unfolded. The process of saddling the animals, specifically with women's saddles, is a special skill that perhaps only one in twenty slaves has mastered. I have often enough seen both a lady and her saddle slide under the belly of her mount within minutes and be subjected to the worst laughter. Whenever a lady has brought such a skilled person as part of her retinue, he is eagerly besieged from all sides and hard-pressed to satisfy all the enthusiastic and impatient ladies desiring his assistance.

Patience is put to the test on other fronts as well. Among their faults, Africans commonly misplace and forget the most basic things. It can take an inordinate amount of time for everything to get pulled together. Now and again, a donkey may also manage to slip out of its rope and take off, leaving its mistress in the greatest quandary. In short, there are always new grounds for anger or cause for more drama. It can easily take an hour before we are all seated in our saddles.

Mounted at last, we would settle smartly into our high saddles (woe to anyone who rode poorly, she would be mercilessly mocked and ridiculed) and shoot out towards the city in a joyful gallop, amidst the clatter and rattle of slaves and the loud cheers of a hundred voices. I have already mentioned how fast Africans can run. It was on precisely such occasions, when less familiar women joined us with their entourages, that they would really flaunt their abilities. Were I to suggest pausing for just a moment to wait for a sister or friend, so I could chat with them during the ride, my sweat-dripping speed runners would let me know their displeasure. It was a matter of honor for them to reach the goal first. As unlikely as it sounds, prior to such runs, these otherwise careless people managed for once to control their food intake and keep from overloading themselves.

We stopped for prayers again in Mnazi Mmoja or Ngambo, and then, after nightfall, rode together into the city to the door of my sister's house. Once again, there was a spirited mess. People dismounted to say good-bye to Chadudj, but could hardly wind their way through all the donkeys, horses, and other people to reach her. We, on the other hand, as sisters and close relatives, did not have to step down as a matter of etiquette. Once the crowd had dissipated, and we no longer feared trampling anyone with our donkeys, we simply rode over to Chadudj and also said our farewells. Thus ended a most splendid festival that remained the main topic of conversation for weeks thereafter.

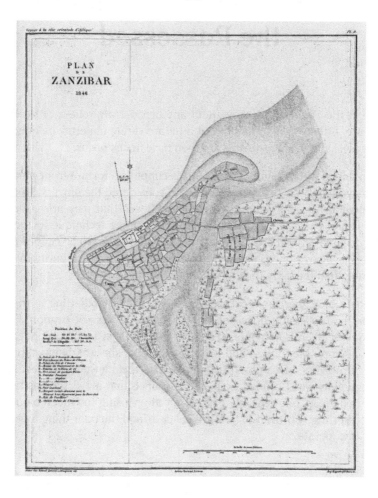

CHAPTER TWENTY-FOUR

Diseases and Medical Care; the Possessed

People in the Orient grow up without any broader awareness of health and body care. Efforts to help nature out a bit are rarely undertaken, only in the worst cases, and those measures are then pure hocus pocus.

A vile practice with a leading role in this is cupping, a torture from which only the very youngest children are spared. It is considered the universal response to all manner of aches and pains, for any illness that may arise, including smallpox and cholera. It is also used as a preventive technique for perfectly healthy people without any issues, who allow themselves to be cupped at least once a year, as was once customary in Europe. The idea is to purify the blood and strengthen the body to fight future diseases.

For people of higher rank, cupping is replaced by bloodletting in the same manner. Its application does not suffer from an excess of caution. Even to this day, I vividly recall the horrid sight of one of my sisters in a dark corridor in Bet il Mtoni. Motionless and pale as a corpse, she was being carried off by her caretakers. I let out a terrifying scream and alerted the entire house. Only gradually was I calmed by the reassurance that my sister was not, as I had feared, dead, but had only passed out after losing too much blood from the bloodletting. It proved to be a critical case, and the poor thing took a long time to recuperate.

Whether such bloodletting can occasionally be healing for the body in hot climes is something I cannot judge. Regardless, the way the technique is applied invites great danger.

Very pleasant and surely beneficial is getting one's limbs kneaded. I have already mentioned that gentle massaging is well-suited to both encouraging and ending sleep. I have also described the great skill that our female slaves display in this practice. Massaging is also a very common and popular way to relieve all sorts of ailments, especially all "body pains."

Another approach is the ugly act of vomiting. This method features a dreadful array of herbs, which are boiled together into an abhorrent brew that is supposed to be drunk. As a rule, however, the mere smell is enough to bring on the desired effect. —

When it comes to severe sickness, people turn to their faith, and as such, verses from the Koran are considered healing. A person who is widely acknowledged to be especially devout writes fitting verses on a white plate with a saffron solution. The writing is then dissolved with some water (usually rose water), and the mixture is fed to the patient. This procedure is repeated three times a day, mornings, midday, and evenings, taking extra care not to let any of this holy liquid drip onto the floor. I personally had to endure this method for a long time, as I lay in bed more than six weeks with an intense fever.

For a seriously sick female that benefited from the father's special attention, an exception might now and again be made to allow a male person, be he a real doctor or a sorcerer, to attend the patient at her bedside. I recall how my sister Chole suffered from persistent ear pain, which did not improve despite all the usual quackery, and for whom they then sent for a very famous Persian doctor (Arabic *hakim*). I was a small child back then and allowed to watch the consultation ceremony. Chole was first wrapped beyond the point of recognition in a *shele*, with only the one sick ear left visible. In this mummified state, she took her place on the *medde* that was described earlier. With her back leaning against the precious *tekje*, she sat flanked on the right by the father and on the left by my brother Chalid. My other younger brothers formed a closed circle around her, all dressed in their street outfits and loaded with weapons. The doctor was brought to the patient's room under the escort of a host of eunuchs, while other eunuchs were stationed as guards at various points around the house to signal for female inhabitants to retreat before the Persian passed through. —Naturally, the *hakim* could not speak directly to the patient, but posed his questions to the father through the brothers, who then also relayed back the responses. —

When I was later ill with typhoid and lay for several days in a delirium, and none of the Arab or Swahili treatments had done anything to help, my Aunt Aashe, the sister of my father, decided to enlist the assistance of a European doctor. Because our father was no longer alive, and I had essentially become my own master, I no longer needed the kind of ceremony Chole had received. The relevant doctor was familiar with Arab customs, but nonetheless insisted on being allowed to feel my pulse, which my concerned aunt, despite her strong misgivings, permitted. For this, a group of eunuchs was brought in after all, and I was wrapped in my *shele*, just as they had done with Chole. Since I was incoherent at the time, the incident was only later recounted to me by my aunt. When the doctor then additionally insisted on checking my tongue, he was so vociferously attacked by the chief eunuch Djohar, who refused to tolerate such an impudent request, that this disciple of Aesculapius, feeling professionally insulted, stomped out of our house in anger without completing his exam.

The underlying problem revealed by such attempted one-size-fits-all cures is, of course, always an inadequate, or indeed absent, understanding of the human body, its regular functions and related disruptions. Arabs know nothing of all this, and therefore also cannot classify sicknesses. They simply divide all internal ailments into one of two categories: body pains and head pains. Regardless of whether the stomach, liver, spleen, or abdomen is affected, it is all generally labelled "body pain." Anything affecting the head, from cerebral softening to sun stroke, is referred to as head pain. The actual cause, the basis for the affliction, cannot be ascertained. When all home remedies have failed, a eunuch is sent to a European consulate doctor to request medication. It is obvious that this doctor, who is not allowed to see the patient and receives only the vaguest description, is in a tough spot. It is equally obvious that most female patients end up with the wrong, or at best harmless, medication.

Diet likewise is not a topic. If someone with typhoid, cholera, or smallpox wants to eat something, they can freely eat anything the kitchen can deliver. Whatever nature wants is assumed to be beneficial. The strong belief in divine destiny plays into everything. This also makes Muslims blind in most cases to the possibility of contagion. No one is thinking, for example, of keeping someone with smallpox strictly quarantined from others. This deeply rooted perspective also undercuts precautionary hygiene rules. The Persian bath mentioned above, between Bet il Sahel and Bet il Tani underneath the bridge that connected the two houses, had deteriorated and become a total garbage dump. Nevertheless, as demand for living space continued to grow, these half ruins became the site of new housing, whose occupants ended up, so to speak, living on top of rubbish. It is well-known how deeply this belief in predestination obstructs all efforts toward progress and makes the *cordons sanitaires* for cholera and stricter supervision of pilgrimages appear superfluous.

I would like to highlight just a few more details about some specific diseases. Smallpox unfortunately resides permanently in Zanzibar and claims thousands of lives. The entire body of a smallpox-infected person is covered with a cream made with *djiso* (turmeric) and placed in the sun. Or the bumps are spread with coconut milk, which is always preferred to the burning *djiso*. When a body is so extensively covered with lesions that a sick person can no longer tolerate the warmth of a bed, that person is laid on a soft straw mat or a large, newly-picked banana leaf from which the hard, central rib has been carefully removed. This is all the relief provided; internal measures are not applied. Contact with water is avoided, but not with anything else.

Consumption, unfortunately another frequent guest, especially the galloping kind,[18] is left completely untreated, as we have no remedy whatsoever. And yet, this sickness is feared more than any other. It is considered contagious, and correctly so, according to European doctors. People keep their distance from anyone who has consumption, which makes that individual suffer even more. No one wants to take a seat where the poor person was sitting. No one wants to extend this person a hand or drink from a cup that has touched their lips. A very beautiful, young stepmother of mine suffered terribly from this disease. Even so, she was able to leave her bed every morning and visit the other residents in the house, until the very end. My eyes of a child did not miss how unwelcome she was to everyone. I felt incredibly sorry for her, and when she finally lay confined to her bed, I often snuck over to express one or the other kindness, in complete secrecy of course. She had only a young son, and no daughter who could have cared for her.

More than a few of my loved ones succumbed to this insidious disease, most of them in the prime of life! Their belongings are handled with the greatest caution, even after death. Clothing and bedding are washed some distance from the house on the beach. Gold and silver are heated to bring out any contagious materials.

---

18 An especially acute form of tuberculosis that almost always ended in death.

Children are afflicted by the dreaded whooping cough there as much as here. They are served large amounts of "dew water" that is gathered every morning from the giant banana leaves. A superstitious remedy is applied as well. A number of round discs the size of a one mark coin are cut from the dried rind of a type of gourd called *hawaschi*, which are then strung with thick twine into a salutary necklace to be hung around the child's neck. —

A painful type of abscess is also very common. These abscesses are pasted over with the dried, brown skin of an onion, which also serves as an English-style bandage. Warm flour dough is used to get them to open and drain.

It is evident: Everywhere there are only the most basic home remedies, no medical treatment, no doctors at all. People never really know what to do. Is it any wonder that folks reach for miracle solutions or like to turn to soothsayers? These *basarin*, as they are called, are very sought after and do quite well. When someone around us got sick, we usually called on a one-eyed woman from Hadhramaut, a *shihrie*, about fifty years old. She kept her tools of the trade in a very dirty old sack, which featured quite a collection: small shells, all sorts of sea pebbles, round, bleached bones from some dead animal, various shards of porcelain and glass, rusty iron nails, crooked copper and silver coins, and more of the same. When asked in a particular case, she would pray to God that he might let her see and speak only the truth, would then untie her sack and stir the contents around before emptying them all out in front of her. Depending on where they landed, she would give her answer, whether the patient would recover and so on. Chance tended to favor this particular *basara* more than most. Of all her prophesizing that I saw, her pronouncements often came to pass, and she made a good business of it. Upfront she would get only a small amount, but if her forecast proved true, she always got a larger bonus as well.

External injuries are naturally easier to heal than internal ailments. They often respond to normal home remedies, a piece of tinder fungus to calm the blood from open wounds and the like. Broken bones are more challenging, as I discovered myself. I was still very young and not yet ready to join everyone at the table. My father had once again sent me a plate full of goodies, and I rushed down the stairs to show them all to my mother. In my happy haste, I missed a step, tumbled a long way down, and broke my forearm. My aunt, the sister of my father, and my brother Barghash bandaged my arm, but unfortunately without really straightening the bone, so that it remains somewhat crooked to this day, a reminder of my fall and the plight of my country in having no doctors.

I have yet to address a very important topic: that Mister Devil! It is well-known that practically everyone in the Orient believes in the devil incarnate, but maybe less known that he especially likes to take up residence inside humans. There is hardly a child among us that has not at some point or another been possessed by the devil. As soon as a newborn cries too much or becomes somewhat restless, no matter the reason, then it must surely be possessed, and immediate steps are taken to exorcise the evil spirit. Tiny onions and garlic cloves are strung like pearls on a string and hung in a strand around the neck and arms of the child. The technique is simple and not as foolish as it might appear. If the devil really had an olfactory organ, he could hardly withstand this attack.

Adults, too, are often possessed. Men only seldom, but many women and notably about half of the Abyssinians. The external signs are frequent bouts of cramping, lack of appetite and general apathy, a preference for solitary stints in dark rooms, and similar signs of sickness. A woman who is rumored to be possessed carries a special aura and is exceptionally respected—or feared.

To be sure, whether she is in fact possessed by a spirit requires some confirmation, and so she must undergo a special examination for this purpose. She or her family members invite only individuals who are recognized as possessed to this ceremony. These poor people form a type of secret society amongst themselves and prefer to keep all they do hidden from the eyes of the world.

They take the patient and place her in a dark room, wrapped in her *shele*, so that not even the slightest ray of light can penetrate through to her. She is then smoked, in the truest sense of the word, by putting the incense holder under her shawl directly below her nose. The group launches into strange chanting, while constantly shaking their heads back and forth. They cannot make do without an Abyssinian brew, a mixture of wheat and dates that is brought to the brink of fermentation, and not bad as far as drinks go. Subjected to all these influences, the victim begins to lapse into a kind of clairvoyance and, as reported to me, speak in very incoherent terms. Finally, she reaches full ecstasy, rampages about with a foaming mouth, and rants scattered exclamations of muddled words. Now the spirit is in her. Those present start to speak with him to ask about his intentions. This matters because there are not only evil spirits that come to afflict individuals, but also good ones that attach themselves out of love and affection because they want to safeguard and protect their hosts for life. And often two spirits, both a good one and a bad one, fight each other to possess the person, as becomes apparent when they reveal themselves during the conjuration ceremony. This can lead to horrendous scenes, and only a few valiant souls are able to witness such events all the way through. Once the ceremony concludes, the experts determine whether the subject of the examination is possessed of a good or bad spirit.

Experienced female masters of these ceremonies often succeed in exorcising an evil spirit. By contrast, a good spirit gets bound into a firm contract. Under the usual terms, the spirit may visit the victim only at prescribed times, although it can always count on a festive welcome, and it must give its darling advance notice of all that awaits him and his family members, be it good or bad.

This wicked superstitious activity is unfortunately accompanied by various other forms of crudeness. Many of the possessed do not tolerate the advance slaughter of the animals (chickens and goats) that they have selected for their secret feasts because they drink their warm blood. They also wolf down raw meat and use raw eggs by the dozen. The ones who are tested to see if a spirit really lives in them are, poor things, laid low for many days thereafter.

Here, too, I could observe how the worst examples seem to have the greatest impact on people. Although all Muslims have a strong propensity for superstition, those from Oman are far from believing such nonsense. When they visit Africa, they initially find that our conditions are heavily affected by native culture and would rather return home again immediately. And yet, in no time, they can become the most susceptible of all, internalizing exactly what they had put down. I personally knew such an Arab woman who was at first dismissive, but soon became entirely convinced that an evil spirit inside her kept making her sick, and she would need a feast to appease him.

But enough of these lamentable things!

CHAPTER TWENTY-FIVE

Slavery[19]

The subject of this chapter is controversial. I realize I will not make many friends with my views, but consider it my duty to share them. I have come across too much unawareness everywhere on this question. Even the more informed people too often overlook that this is about more than genuine humane efforts by Europeans, considering that they take place against a backdrop of hidden political interests.

I was still a child when, on the date agreed between my father and England, all resident English subjects, the Hindus and Banyans, were to release their slaves in Zanzibar. It was a very difficult time for the affected owners. There was no end to their crying and complaining. The highest-ranking ones sent their wives and daughters to us and begged for our intercession, even though this was, of course, entirely out of our hands. Some of them owned a hundred and more slaves to run their plantations. From one day to the next, all were free, and the masters ruined. Their workers were gone. Unable to cultivate their crops, they lost the whole harvest. And our lovely island had suddenly acquired the dubious good fortune of harboring several thousand loafers, vagabonds, and thieves. The freed older children took freedom to mean they no longer needed to work. They thought only of celebrating their freedom, completely unfazed that they could no longer expect lodging and upkeep from their masters. Meanwhile, the humane emissaries of the anti-slavery associations went silent. They had accomplished their goal and freed the poor victims from slavery, a

19 This chapter is a product of the author's time and place. It reflects a racist perspective and acceptance of slavery that is not acceptable today, as more fully considered in "On Controversy" on pages 243–51.

status unworthy of any human being. What was now to become of these slaves was no longer their concern. Or at most, their ladies, to complete the nonsense, knit wool socks for the residents of the hot South. Let the rulers of the relevant countries figure out for themselves how to deal with these unindustrious people. As anyone who has lived for even a short time in Africa, Brazil, North America, or wherever there are Africans can attest: In addition to all their advantages, such people have a great reluctance to work and require constant supervision.

Only the English subjects, I repeat, were no longer allowed to hold slaves. England could not impose any rules directly on my father for his country. One must, however, guard against judging slavery in the Orient based on what one hears about slavery in North America or Brazil. The slaves of Muslims find themselves in an entirely different, incomparably better position.

The worst part of this institution is the slave trade, the displacement of these poor people from the interior of the continent to the coast. Countless numbers perish on these long marches from the hardships, hunger, and thirst, all conditions that, however, also affect the leader. Under these harsh conditions, it makes no sense to ascribe a special malice to the slave handlers, who often have their whole fortunes invested in such caravans. It is naturally in their own interest to get people out in the best possible condition.

Once the end destination is successfully attained, the slaves are well taken care of in every respect. They admittedly have to work without pay for their masters, but they are also free of all concerns and have the assurance of continuous upkeep, with owners that take their well-being to heart. Or should one believe that every non-Christian is totally heartless?

Africans above all love to take it easy and work only when they must. It takes strong management to get them to perform to the local standard, which constitutes a rather small workload compared to here. They are certainly not exemplary, with thieves, drunks, runaways, and arsonists among them. What to do with these? It is of course unacceptable to let them go unpunished; that would soon lead to a nice case of anarchy. Imprisonment is also no deterrent. To the contrary, they would very happily spend a few days in a cool place, interrupted only by meals, and otherwise free to daydream and sleep, in order to then resume their bad ways with new vigor. No doubt the majority of African slaves would soon be maneuvering to get such pleasant accommodations.

Under these circumstances, that leaves but one effective solution: corporal punishment. As usual, this provokes an outcry here, naturally from certain circles that are always pushing their claims while spurning any attempt to study the practical conditions. Clearly, beating is inhumane, but what alternative is there? For that matter, would it not be better for some of the thousands of inmates here to receive a beating now and again, rather than subject everyone to the same false humane treatment that lumps everyone together? —

Tyranny is rightly decried everywhere, whether it affects the poor natives of Africa or, indeed, civilized people languishing in the Siberian mines. But one must take a fair and fitting approach, as not every system is just or unjust everywhere. Slavery is an ancient institution in Oriental society. Whether it can be entirely eliminated is doubtful, and it is in any case folly to want to overthrow such longstanding customs all at once. Everything takes time, and it would help to set a good example for Orientals. In my time in Zanzibar, rather many Europeans kept their own slaves and bought them when it suited their interests. Of course, this is not reported back home. Whether Arabs use slaves to work the land or in the house, or civilized Europeans use them as baggage carriers, whose workload is usually much harder and harsher, it matters not, the morality is the same. And these European slave owners are certainly not always humane enough to later free their purchased slaves, as Arabs so often do. Instead, when the slaves are no longer useful for their European master, they are simply sold again. Considerable resentment was felt among the Muslim population in Zanzibar when it became known that an Englishman, whose very government had scorned slavery with such imperious morality, had not only purchased a female slave himself, but upon leaving the island to return home, had even resold her to an Arab official, instead of freeing her. Another case was no less offensive to all Arabs. This involved the arrogant interference by a European in an Arab's domestic chastisement of an insubordinate slave. Everyone would do well to sweep in front of their own doors, and whoever keeps their own slaves should not be playing themselves up to judge the treatment by others.

It should come as no surprise, after such experiences, that Arabs harbor the greatest distrust toward Europeans. They yearn for a return to happy times when things were still stable, before the upheaval wrought by European ideas. The abolition of slavery, they reason, is intended merely to ruin them, so as to harm Islam. First and foremost, they suspect England of having all sorts of underhanded plans in store.

Some may say that I am biased, that I am unable to free myself from these views after having been raised with them, that I cannot evaluate the matter objectively. Therefore allow me to cite from a few authoritative accounts by full-blooded Europeans on the subject.

The explorer of Africa, Paul Reichard, reported in 1881 from Gonda (from *Mittheilungen der afrikanischen Gesellschaft in Deutschland*, Volume III, Folio 3, pages 171-172, Berlin 1882):

In the night of October 12, I was woken by the screams of a woman in tears, seeking to be let in. I sought information from *askari*[20] and learned that the woman had fought with her husband and wanted to enter so she could break something of value, which would then have made her our slave according to local custom. A locally resident Arab had recently experienced three similar cases, but had accepted compensation for the damage. It is not at all uncommon for a free person who is dissatisfied with his current situation to let himself be made a slave in this manner. This is clear evidence of the exaggeration and one-sidedness of many derogatory reports about slavery that are specifically stirred up by missionaries, especially the English....

As far as slavery, it is indeed the case that slaves are mistreated during transport and nearly die of starvation. When the latter fate occurs, however, we have been able to confirm that it almost always affects the relevant owner as well, since provisions easily run out at the end of longer trips.

A sudden and forced end to slavery can result only in the ruin and complete upheaval of the affected countries, unless other replacement measures are immediately assured, for which the current condition of the once so prosperous island of Zanzibar may be an apt testament to my view.

Once a slave is in firm hands, his lot is by no means worse, but the same or even better than in his homeland. For example, slaves brought here from under the rule of particularly cruel sultans south of [Lake] Tanganyika are loathe to return at any price.

Slaves kept by Arabs are not at all overburdened with work, and only criminals are subjected to corporal punishment, since excessive strictness would require overly costly oversight. Moreover, Arabs usually free their slaves after ten to fifteen years of loyal service.

---

20 A native African soldier in the service of a European power, especially in the African Great Lakes region.

Slaves that have children while in slavery are considered family members with their own free will. No one speaks of punishing them, but rather the opposite, since it is not unusual for violent acts of defiance against their masters to have no consequences. Others run off to the coast without their masters' permission and then return as *pagasi* (porters).

An Englishman, Mr. Joseph Thomson, assesses in his book *Expedition to the Lakes of Central Africa* (page 22) as follows:

All social classes exemplify a cheerfulness and contentment that would seem unusual anywhere else. But here life is ideal, where 4 to 6 pence a day allows for an ample lifestyle. There are no hungry or mistreated slaves to be seen anywhere. When any such cases of inhumane treatment are reported to the Sultan (of Zanzibar), he immediately frees the sufferers and protects them from abuse. This class, in fact, is in a strangely agreeable position and enjoys ten times more freedom than thousands of our servants and shop girls.

More concisely, another Englishman, who lived in the Orient many years and knows the conditions well, recently told me the anti-slavery movement with its countless meetings was simply "humbug."

To conclude, I would like to recall one more thing. This Gordon,[21] who at the time had presented himself as the most determined opponent of slavery and slave trading, commenced his second, very short-lived rule in Sudan by removing his earlier laws. He may not have been convinced of the need for slavery in Africa, but he surely understood that such a deeply rooted institution should not be eliminated all in one fell stroke, but rather only eased out gradually toward subsequent elimination.

---

21 British Major-General Charles George Gordon, 1833–1885.

CHAPTER TWENTY-SIX

My Mother's Death;
a Palace Revolution

Following the death of the father, I lived, as previously described, in Bet il Tani with my mother and Chole in wonderful love and friendship. About three years had gone by when a horrific cholera epidemic spread across the city and the whole island of Zanzibar, also ravaging our house with another life expired practically every day. It was the hottest time of the year. One night, in the oppressive heat, I struggled to find sleep in my elevated bed and therefore asked my female slave to spread a soft mat on the floor, where there was just enough coolness for me to eventually doze off.

Who can describe my surprise when I awoke towards dawn to find my most cherished mother lying at my feet, writhing in pain. Shocked, I asked if her moaning meant she was sick, to which she replied only that she had been lying there since the middle of the night, fearing that cholera had taken hold of her, and wanting, if it was time, to at least die in my presence. It was a hard torment for me to watch my dearly beloved mother undergo such suffering from this vicious disease, without being able to help. She resisted its attack for all of two days before being torn from me forever.

My pain knew no bounds. I clung to the precious corpse against all admonitions, defying all warnings to protect myself from this epidemic. I wanted nothing more than for God to call me to Him and let me join my mother! And yet, the epidemic spared me. It was the will of the All-Merciful and All-Knowing; I had to yield.

Barely fifteen, I now stood without a father or mother in this world, like a rudderless ship flailing about on a stormy sea. My mother had always guided me so adeptly and wisely, and cared for me so thoughtfully and empathetically, but now, all of a sudden, I needed to step up to adult responsibilities, both for my own well-being and that of my people. Fortunately, God knows to match new responsibilities with the strength to meet them. I was eventually able to get a handle on my situation and attend to my own affairs without requiring outside help.

But new trials came my way, and I succumbed to them. Before realizing what had happened, I suddenly found myself deep in a conspiracy against my own noble brother Madjid!

Indeed, it was as though the death of our father was meant to usher in complete discord among us, rather than have us all come together, one for all and all for one, as it should have been. Granted, it is rare to achieve complete consensus among thirty-six siblings, and so we gravitated to various groupings of three to four, drawn close by the bonds of love. To outsiders, our relationships were completely indecipherable. Even our close friends could not always penetrate our alliances, which resulted in no shortage of challenges for them and us. A loyal friend of my brother, a devoted friend of my sister, if they fell outside my inner circle, were necessarily my bitter enemies, no matter how they felt about me personally. Any neutral observer could see that no good would come from such disunity and disarray. But our eyes were clouded with passion, and we pursued each other with blind hate for basically no good reason.

Interaction among us soon stopped altogether. A great many spies, since all of us had them, served to widen the chasm as they tipped us off about every word and every intention of our opponents. Night after night, these honorable folks would show up and receive their rewards in relation to the importance or ugliness of the news they brought in. The Louis d'ors and guineas never flowed so freely. Often we did not even count the pieces, but just grabbed blindly into the linen *kis* (sack or purse), pulling out round handfuls of coins to compensate their efforts. Sometimes we were woken in the middle of the night because a mysteriously draped shape was seeking entry from the doorman, demanding to speak to us personally. Such nights were especially good for lightening our *kis*, while also making further sleep impossible and firing up the mood by another several degrees for the next while.

We were all struck by a kind of delirium. Everyone sought to outdo the others. If one of us showed interest in buying a nice horse, house, or plantation, the opponents would drive up the price four and six times higher, to the great joy of the sellers, but of course only to play tricks on the buyer. If a sister wore a new piece of jewelry, the jeweler would immediately receive orders from all sides for the same thing or, if possible, an even nicer one. The people were quick to comprehend our great weakness, and both merchants and artisans knew how to reap rich benefit from our discord.

Madjid and Chole had the best relationship at the time, which meant a great deal to me, as I loved them both dearly. They each treated me as their own child after I lost my mother. But this pleasant situation soured over time for my brother Barghash's sake, and eventually resulted in a formal rupture between Madjid and Chole. As close as I was to Chole, I still have to admit, in all honesty, that she, and not Madjid, was to blame for this break. But far be it from me to detail every circumstance that devolved into such ugly relations. We were all as if bewitched and deluded.

On a personal level, this was a time of great inner struggle. I lived with Chole in the same house, we ate and drank together and were inseparable the whole day. And then she started shunning my equally beloved Madjid more and more, for no reason, in the end even wishing him ill on everything. Initially, I hoped to stay neutral, yes, I even dared to defend my irreproachable brother, whose only fault lay in him being the reigning Sultan, not Barghash. But man knows no justice in his passion, and Chole did not let up on her resentment.

For months, I stood between two fires. I wanted the best, but could do nothing. I wavered back and forth between two beloved people, until I could no longer avoid taking a stance, and then decided for Chole. She was in the wrong, but closer to my heart, with more and more influence over me. What in this whole world do we not ultimately sacrifice for our loved ones, even if we have to fight against ourselves? In the face of their pleas and appeals, our opinions, our principles, yes, even our most sacred convictions fall like withered autumn leaves from the tree, while the healthy trunk stands helpless by.

Madjid, a truly noble man, enjoyed the heartfelt love of the people. But he was in poor health and could not engage everywhere, thus leaving much of his business to his ministers. One of these, Sleman bin Ali, knew only too well how to make himself indispensable to his master. A clever, selfish sort of man, he ultimately succeeded in making his voice the word of the land, against which the other ministers counted for practically nothing. He was presumptuous enough to act like he was the top man in charge whenever it suited. And yet, he did not even have the respected maturity of old age to justify this stature, but was instead, as we like to say here, still very green, not to mention the model of a dandy that would do anything to further his noble passions. In his vanity and savvy, he courted one of my stepmothers, who for her age could well have been his mother. Fatme, a Circassian, did not reject his overtures. That proved a shortsighted move, for which she paid dearly later. Sleman had been interested only in her sizeable fortune.

This evil spirit influenced Madjid in every way and surreptitiously riled the siblings against each other, all to leverage their dissonance into his personal power. He succeeded in stoking trouble everywhere. Friction begot friction in our family, many individuals of rank were put down and damaged, and the situation became so fractious that people began to grumble out loud.

What a blessing that we had at least one minister holding out against him, a competent, diligent man, who always tried to soften or fix Sleman's mistakes. This was Mhamed bin Abd Allah il Shaksi, a man born into great wealth, with a generous, noble character, who was anything but self-seeking. Clearly, there could be no good relations between him and his colleague.

Meanwhile, my brother Barghash sought to take advantage of the tensions among the siblings and the discontent of the population. Because Madjid had only a daughter and no son, Barghash was next in line for the throne and generally considered Madjid's successor after our father's death. The fact that two older brothers, Muhammed and Turki, lived in Oman was not a factor; Oman lay so far away.

Unfortunately, in the Orient, successors to the throne are always in a rush to claim the reins of power. They are unaffected by assertions that others may have greater rights to the throne. They do whatever it takes and pay no heed to law and order to achieve their goals.

And so it was with Barghash. Although he had failed to become Sultan upon the death of the father, he had never given up on his plan. Ever since moving from Bet il Mtoni to the city with his proper sister Meje, he had been thinking more seriously about its implementation. The two siblings took up residence in the house directly across from Chole and me that had previously served as a secondary cavalier house for the father's second official wife, Princess Shesade (of Persia).

Thus began a most agitated time for us. Sisterly piety keeps me from sharing every minute detail, while certain activities truly do not merit much consideration. Even the great harshness with which I am still treated to this day cannot provoke me to lift the veil. Our Arab saying sticks too deeply in my mind: "All the oceans of the world are not enough to wash away my blood relations."

The brother and sister had barely moved into the area when a great friendship emerged between Barghash and Chole, and the former soon spent whole days at our place. Meje in turn felt neglected, and as she started expressing her resentment to others, a major rift developed with Chole. It got to the point that they would not even greet each other when they crossed paths. Relations continued to go downhill, and the peace in our formerly tranquil homes began to disappear forever. I was glad to have no part in the new fracture between Chole and Meje. But the two deathly enraged sisters always poured their hearts out to me in their rancor to each other, so I also got drawn in.

Sultan Barghash bin Said

Chole was in the wrong with respect to Meje. In general, she was hardly recognizable during this terrible time. Barghash was her idol, for whom she recklessly gave up everything, and I, who paid as much homage to her, followed her again and again in all she did. Privately, I truly regretted the deeply distressed Meje, who, despite her proud nature, had so much insight and measured understanding that one had to sympathize with her. She alone among us saw clearly that no good could come from these anti-Madjid partisan activities, and she constantly warned us: "You will see! You will see!"

My friendship with my two nieces, Shembua and Farshu, soon carried over to Barghash, and they joined our band. They also lived across from us, and only a small alley separated their quarters from those of Barghash. Our three houses thus constituted a very dangerous focal point for a plot.

Barghash now worked especially hard to recruit a number of chieftains and other high-ranking individuals to his side. Arabs subdivide into countless larger and smaller tribes, each with its own leader, whom they strictly obey. Every prince, therefore, has a great interest in maintaining a close friendship with one or more of such chiefs, openly or preferably in secret, to be assured of their support when the time comes. Of course, promises of influential positions and other advantages play a major role in this arena. No tribe would ever fail to support its leader, given the strong feelings of affiliation and solidarity. How far this goes is best demonstrated by the fact that anyone who has learned to write invariably adds the tribe's name to their own name. We, for example, belong to the *Lebu Saidi*, a small but courageous tribe, and my full signature must always include that reference.

Barghash entered into closer relations with these chieftains and eventually pulled together a small court, which prompted much talk on our island. The greatest scandal arose from the fact that these people, who came and went day and night, were mostly of ill-repute, quarrelsome, and looking for trouble, the kind from whom he should have decidedly kept his distance. But of course, it had to be this way. Well-disposed, law-abiding individuals simply would not have subscribed to his overthrow plans.

The more Barghash added dubious elements to his engagements, and the more his subversive plot became apparent, the more those who cared about the well-being of our family and were not enamored of adventure pulled back. Stepping into their place were the kinds of people of whom Zanzibar, indeed the world, has its share: jealous individuals that have been jilted and self-important individuals that have been slighted, who would do anything to quench their thirst for revenge against their perceived mistreatments. Dozens of these malcontents could already picture themselves as Barghash's ministers or in other higher posts. Hundreds surely counted on property and honor beyond anything they previously could have imagined. Such creatures came from far and wide to join the conspiracy, to serve Barghash, yes, but really to serve themselves. It was obvious that even the most deplorable among them would be embraced with open arms.

As the number of Barghash's adherents rapidly grew, detailed plans for the uprising became more concrete. The plan envisioned taking Madjid unawares and immediately proclaiming Barghash as Sultan. But we also had to consider the real possibility of an open fight. Meeting upon meeting was held to win over this or that additional chieftain, always in the dead of night, sometimes at eight, sometimes at four, depending on when the moon came and went, and Barghash personally presided over them all. How often we cursed the bright light of the moon that kept us from convening, while we sought to stay completely under wraps. Feverish excitement and the deepest mistrust took hold of us all. We constantly suspected being observed and overheard, and often did the work of our servants just to keep them distant and from divining our evil deeds. Among the ladies, we stopped all our visits to others and very rarely received any guests.

Barghash was increasingly on edge. Having previously participated regularly in the formal audiences under Madjid's leadership just like all the other princes, Barghash started to neglect them, showing up only once or twice a week and ultimately missing them altogether. By our standards, that signals great discontent, and such ostentatious insubordination is simply punished. Now no one could doubt Barghash's hostile plans any longer, although many had not wanted to believe them. And Barghash himself acted very unwisely in the heat of things. He tipped off his adversaries, and it became hard to see how a surprise attack could possibly succeed.

Madjid tried once more, in private, to pull me back from my misguided ways before it was too late. As he was no longer able to come to Bet il Tani under the prevailing conditions, and I similarly had avoided his house for a long time, he asked an especially beloved stepmother of mine to seek me out and convey his request that I please separate myself from the partisan activities of his enemies and not simply allow them to tow me along; I could never expect any thanks from that side or be spared the remorse of having remained loyal to this evil affair. And I would also have to accept the consequences of my actions. If it came to bombardment of my neighbor's house, he would no longer be able to make an exception for me.

My venerable brother's warning came too late. I had already pledged my word to Chole and Barghash and now considered it my sacred duty to follow through on my promise. My stepmother left me deeply distressed and crying bitter tears. She had meant so well! Later she had the sad satisfaction of reminding me of Madjid's prediction, which proved so very correct.

So as not to stir any distrust, nor incur the ugly label of "mother of two faces" for perceived double dealings, I decided to strictly avoid any connection to Madjid and his associates and instead devoted myself entirely to the conspiracy.

At this point, with such increasingly compelling suspicions, Madjid could still have easily detained this errant brother and his followers, sticking them in a fortress and locking them up long enough to return to their senses. But such decisiveness was beyond him; he was not a forceful man by nature. To the last, he continued to hope for a voluntary reversal on the part of his brother and hesitated to go after him prematurely. Indeed, nothing had yet happened between him and Barghash to justify such hostility. Above all, he hoped at all costs to spare us four women, who were so deeply enmeshed in the affair.

Madjid's forbearance lasted a long time. Only when whole throngs of figures completely covered in their *barnus* converged at Barghash's door did the government consider it advisable to monitor our three houses. But this step offered only limited success, since the guards were all Baluchi soldiers recruited from Baluchistan, who in their touching devotion to our dynasty would rather have put themselves at risk than allow any of us family members to be compromised. My skilled and savvy siblings soon figured this out and used it to their advantage. The more dangerous operations were always carried out by us directly, heedless of our customs. No one dared bother us, even as others were trailed and investigated every step of the way. Now and again some careless participant would be arrested, but that did no real harm to our party.

Our houses were like an ant colony. No one sat around, everyone worked hard to make our project a success. Our spies brought news that the government had finally decided to bring our conduct to an end, either to lock up all the suspects or expel them from the island. Our preparations were far from complete when this news came, so we had to work twice as hard. We baked great quantities of a kind of long-duration cake and brought them under cover of night to Marseille, our nieces' plantation, which was the chosen base for the insurrection.

177

I, the youngest female member of the conspiracy, became what was effectively the general secretary of the alliance because I was able to write and thus expected to handle all correspondence with the chieftains. To be sure, I was old enough to be tormented by bitter pangs of conscience. That the bullets, the powder, the guns I had to order were destined to kill totally innocent people weighed heavily on my soul. What should I do? Break my word and abandon my beloved sister, now of all times, with danger increasing every day? Never! I would sooner have walked through fire for her. My closeness to Chole bound me tightly to the conspiracy, far more than any devotion to my brother Barghash.

Barghash, the son of an Abyssinian, was extraordinarily gifted and exceeded us with his far superior insights and clever calculations. Proud and regal in his manner, he knew how to impress everyone. But what little love he had won was evidenced by the fact that no one in our sizeable family took his side, except us four women and one brother, twelve-year-old Abd il Aziz, and then only because he was Chole's foster child. Ever since Barghash had buried our father's corpse in secret, bereft of all ceremony, no one wanted anything to do with him. As he took the final steps to organize his coup, people all drew back from him. I recall one evening when I ran into two of my sisters on one of my rare outings, how they walked with me until about five hundred steps from my house and then hastily turned back, so as not to get near Barghash's house.

Even under extremely strict oversight, we kept up our zealous efforts. Meetings were still held despite very challenging circumstances. The date for the overthrow was set when, suddenly, several hundred soldiers surrounded Barghash's house. The soldiers had astutely waited for a time when Barghash was sure to be home. They had orders to cut off complete contact with the outside world until all the residents surrendered peacefully. Our shock was indescribable, but soon prompted a redoubling of our efforts.

Of course, we awaited the same fate for our house, and then the whole cause would have been lost. As we later learned, the ministers and other dignitaries had indeed argued in favor of simultaneously blocking all three dangerous houses. But Madjid could not be persuaded, as he wanted to spare us women from any consequences.

Within minutes of the soldiers' deployment, the six of us conspirators, two in each house, stood at our windows and consulted across the small alley about what to do. We were in a frenzied state, and Barghash refused any talk of submission or surrender.

But our plight was severe. Virtually no house in Zanzibar has a private well, so that everyone, regardless of rank, gets their water from public wells. As a precaution over the past few days, some water had been put in reserve in Barghash's house, but with the heat, this water was no longer potable and could at most be used for washing and cooking. There was plenty of food, enough to last the besieged for several weeks, but it was water they lacked, the one thing needed most in the tropics. Under the circumstances, there was no chance of lasting more than a few days.

While the men were at a loss and devolved into talk, one woman with an inventive bent devised a fortunate solution that saved them from quick defeat. She suggested sewing a hose out of sailcloth to run water from our roof over to Barghash's roof. Someone got the cloth, several dozen hands sewed a hose in half an hour, and by the time it got dark, the captives were enjoying a deliciously cooling drink. Of course, we had to be extremely careful to avoid detection. Fortunately, the guards focused on Barghash's one seaside door, perhaps they even *preferred* not to see our rescue efforts.

With the women having already helped substantially, very substantially, it was now also up to us to keep everything going. Only our intermediation through the window enabled Barghash to maintain contact with his party. Some of the leaders were locked up with him and found themselves in a very tough position. With my sister Meje in the house, they had very limited ability to move around and were basically stuck in the gathering room on the ground floor. But the influential, hard-charging leader of the *Hurt* tribe was still free and able to recruit the soldiers.

Our whole plan had to be revised. It was decided to gather all party members at Marseille, my nieces' beautiful estate, and entrench them there. The idea was not bad. Marseille rather resembled a small fortress and could comfortably hold several hundred men. To serve as a base from which to roil the whole island, we had the arsenal and ammunition brought there and the assembled troops quartered in the area. With everyone pitching in, everything fell into place very quickly. There was no general battle kitty, but we took turns contributing what we could from our private pockets, in addition to each contributing a number of well-armed slaves.

Once we had secretly gotten everything over to Marseille, we started to consider a major maneuver. The plan was nothing less than having us women free Barghash from his house to return his leadership to the conspiracy and have him personally direct everything from Marseille. That we were undertaking a very dangerous venture was clear, but danger was no deterrent. We were determined to take the risk.

Up to this point, we had made no effort to visit our captive siblings. We had wished to avoid any spectacle that could have harmed our venture, and we feared a blow to our pride in being rebuffed by the guards. But well begun is half won! We no longer had any second thoughts and instead resolved to proceed with the removal that evening, the only way to save ourselves.

After darkness had descended on this weighty day, Chole and I left our house with a large, handpicked entourage to meet up with our nieces' retinue that had set out at the same time, and together we walked to Barghash's door. Our vanguard was held up at the sentry, without the soldiers really knowing who was in the procession. Fearless action was the only way our expedition could succeed. "Chole," I said, "let the two of us advance to the top guard and reveal ourselves, they will certainly respect us."

This suggestion transgressed all customs and norms, but in so dangerous a situation, we could not afford to be caught up in the usual concerns. Were we not already on the cusp of achieving extraordinary things? Was the whole conspiracy not already crossing all boundaries? We forgot everything in our passion.

Chole and I stepped out of the procession, walked up to the unsuspecting officers, and started to berate them forcefully. It is easy to picture their astonishment. They could never have imagined such an ambush. For quite some time, these poor men were at a loss for words, but after somewhat collecting themselves, they gave us such profuse apologies that I felt deeply ashamed in the knowledge of our bad intentions. Not a single guard could have thought us capable of such a plan, and we presented ourselves so indignantly that no hesitation betrayed us.

We had achieved our goal. We were even given an allotted time to visit our captured siblings. After entering so successfully, we hoped to exit just as successfully, together with our brother.

We found Meje and Barghash in an understandable uproar. They had watched our whole scene with the guards from above, all the while growing increasingly anxious and uneasy that we would be turned back and leave them to their fate. And now Barghash was causing new trouble. In a fit of machismo, he refused to hide under the coverings of some female attire. But we had to hurry. We could not know if the sentry had notified our visit and sought instructions on how to proceed. And the way Barghash now stood before us, no one was going to let him out of the house. The guards had strict instructions to shoot down any suspicious person on the spot, a clear indication that they could not have dreamt of our audacity, or they would have handled our situation quite differently. It felt like we were standing on a crater that was liable to crack open at any moment and swallow us whole.

Barghash finally let us dress him in a *shele*, after loading himself to the teeth with weapons, so that only his eyes were free, and Abd il Aziz was disguised the same way. Only these two brothers were to leave the palace with us. We selected the tallest women in our group to walk right beside us and shield Barghash. Before setting out, we all thought again of the Almighty and said a quiet prayer that could well have been our last.

So as not to raise any suspicion, we again had to practice the art of deceit and, despite all our excitement and racing heartbeats, had to move slowly and evenly, while appearing to chat nonchalantly. Too quick a step and that would have betrayed us. But lo and behold! The guards respectfully let us pass, allowing us to proceed undetected with our prize. Anyone who has ever found themselves in such an anxiety-ridden situation will surely understand that I will never forget this evening as long as I live, not even the smallest detail.

We had previously informed a few chieftains in writing of our plans and agreed that they should gather with their followers at a certain hour outside the city. If we did not arrive within the agreed time, that would mean our mission had failed, and they should disperse to await further news. The meeting place lay far outside the city, deep in the greenery.

After passing through the populated part of the city at our customary pace, we began to run in order to reach the gathering in time. Like a fleeing column, we raced across the field with our normally dainty feet, rushing over sticks and stones, not caring a wit for our beautiful, gold-embroidered slippers. Our servants' quiet, whispered warnings to please run more carefully, we were entering a field of thorns, fell on deaf ears. And meanwhile the night all around was dark, and we had had our lanterns extinguished as soon as we had left the city.

Dripping with sweat and completely out of breath, we finally got word from our front runner that the gathering was up ahead. This was our cue as women to act more reserved. We moved more slowly and soon heard quiet coughing and throat clearing, marks of nearby sentinels, but could not make out any individual forms in the dark of night. A muted voice inquired carefully: "Your

Highness, is that you?" and the affirmative answer evoked a broad, hushed: "Praised be the Lord!" We had made it.

Barghash, who had shown great agitation but barely spoke a word on the way, now hastily threw off his covering, called out a clipped farewell, grabbed the twelve-year-old Abd il Aziz by the hand, and immediately disappeared from view. He still had to reach Marseille by foot before the night's end.

For some time, we stood there exhausted and speechless, peering in vain at fleeting profiles vanished in the night. Meanwhile, the late-night hour pressed us to return home, and so we walked noiselessly, with trepidation, the long way back. To avoid any kind of scene, we split up as we neared the silent city and headed in small groups by detours to our homes.

Back at last, we felt utter exhaustion. We were in a pitiful state. The intense excitement of the day and the highly unusual, certainly for Arab women, long and fast march were not without consequence. There was no chance of getting any sleep, nor any sort of peace this night. Everyone was moaning and groaning. Some fainted, others convulsed into fits of crying, first here, then there. It was no surprise that the group was coming undone. The experiences of the past hours had been too much and taken too great a toll on our strength. Twice we had had to pass through rows of soldiers bearing sharply loaded guns and brandished bayonets. The slightest misstep would have sufficed to bring us down. No one could have known upfront that the rescue would be such a success, and setting out, we had had to anticipate either outcome: a completed mission or death.

Throughout the rest of the night, we fearfully registered every little noise. Weighed down by our consciences, we kept hearing horse hooves or gun shots. At any moment, we expected our enemies to close in and dole out our well-deserved punishments after discovering our role.

And yet, to our considerable astonishment, all stayed still. Looking down from above, we could see the guards the same as before, calmly pacing back and forth in front of the house where Barghash had been hostage only a few hours earlier. Finally, dawn was starting to show, and as usual, the slaves signaled the time for prayer. Normally, Chole and I prayed separately. Today, when it was as yet unclear what lay ahead, we found ourselves in the same room praying to the Highest together. And then we raised the joyful hope that at this time, about five in the morning, Barghash and his followers would have reached Marseille.

Soon, however, we received shocking news. Around seven o'clock, we found out that our opponents knew exactly what had transpired the night before. As we had walked directly past the guards the previous evening, a Baluchi had recognized Barghash, despite his coverings. The guard chose not to sound an immediate alarm out of devotion to our late father, whom he had long and loyally served, thinking Barghash would use his freedom only to flee the country. And the guard could not bear the thought of openly compromising us women.

When the early shift of market vendors described seeing many Arabs hurrying to the area around Marseille, suspicions arose that this had to do with the conspiracy; but only this Baluchi knew what had really transpired. At this point, he realized his duty lay in sharing his discovery with the regime, rather than keeping it to himself. At the hearing, he excused himself solely by saying he would rather have given his life than put us women in a compromised position. I never found out what became of this noble man, whom we had thrown into such a deep conflict of conscience with our escapade.

The government had no choice now but to put an end to this open rebellion with open violence. Several thousand soldiers were sent to Marseille with cannons. Our partisan friends had counted on a successful overthrow and limited battle. An open fight was beyond their means. The cannon balls shattered the once charming palace of Marseille and overwhelmed the rebels, who, after putting up a brief and dogged fight, then scattered to the wind, but not without the loss of hundreds of innocent lives. —

The reader will surely wonder what happened to us women as a result of our crucial role in the insurrection, what punishment was imposed upon us. We got none! Clearly, had not the noble Madjid been at the helm, we never would have come away so easily. Our engagement had certainly deserved the strongest retribution.

We had not yet heard the outcome of the battle when we were surprised to learn one morning that Barghash, whom we assumed to be in Marseille, had arrived in his house the night before, a totally defeated fugitive. Meje filled us in on all that had happened, while Barghash, who hoped to remain undiscovered, kept away from the window. Even then, he insisted on resisting to the end, with nary a thought to surrender.

Beyond Barghash and little Abd il Aziz, who despite his youth had proved absolutely unflappable with no hint of fright or fear, a number of dignitaries and many servants had dribbled in, making the house, primarily the downstairs rooms, overcrowded once again. Barghash still hoped to implement his plan using these forces, although he had already failed once before with much more support. We, too, despite having lost so much of our assets, sacrificed such a great number of recruited soldiers and slaves on the battlefield, and forfeited the sympathies of all our siblings and relatives, we had not yet come to our senses. We were far too blinded by our passion to have registered the wretched shipwreck.

That same day, word spread throughout the entire city about Barghash's return. Everyone assumed he had come only to give himself up to his brother. Madjid himself wanted to make the surrender easy for him. Instead of soldiers, he sent his nephew, Suud bin Hilal, with the message that he was prepared to forget the past if Barghash would agree to renounce his plans forever. Suud, an extraordinarily mild and benevolent man, was to undertake this mission alone, as a sign of his peaceful intent.

At first, Barghash would not allow his significantly older nephew into the house, and instead insisted that he announce his affair from the street. Naturally, Suud firmly refused to do so. After a long wait, the front door was finally opened just enough to ensure that no one else could slip in, and he was then allowed, in the truest sense of the word, to climb the heavily barricaded stairs. Measures had been taken everywhere to make an easy target of any intruder. The top of the stairs had also been closed off with a massive, sturdy trapdoor, a mechanism that dated back to the days of our stepmother Shesade, and which had been loaded up with additional heavy chests. Madjid's envoy thus encountered a rather humiliating entry, and no less mortifying was the outcome of his mission. He left again without having accomplished anything after Barghash categorically refused to make any kind of concession.

In the face of such stubbornness, Madjid again had no option but to resort to violence, despite his great reluctance. The English Consul, with whom he consulted, finally persuaded him of the need to bring an end to the enduring offense and offered his assistance. An English cannon ship, which happened to be in the harbor and whose shallower draft was better suited than our large warships, was to anchor directly in front of Barghash's house and set up a boat blockade with its dispersed marines. If even this demonstration failed to impress, the enemy palace and all its inhabitants were to be bombarded to bits.

One morning I left my room, which faced the narrow street without an ocean view, and headed to Chole, to show the usual respect befitting an older sister and wish her a good morning. I found her visibly distressed, wringing her hands and striding back and forth in her room. "Salme, oh my dear, where have you been all this time?" she wailed, pointing to the ship and English soldiers and explaining in broken sentences what had happened.

My reproof that it never would have come to this if she and Barghash had brought things to a timely end was met with the old song that I showed so little interest in the cause. But my God, what more was I to do? Had I not compromised myself just as much as she and the others? Had I not sacrificed everything without hesitation? Had I ever spared myself whenever it mattered to serve the alliance? All of this seemed forgotten now, simply because I had called things as they were. We are never so deeply and painfully wounded by an undeserved reproach as when it comes from those we love the most and to whom we have given our whole soul!

Soon the marine soldiers started shooting at Barghash's house, at first only with guns. Several bullets broke through the windows, and one whizzed right past my brother before flattening into the massive wall behind him. The seriousness of the situation was now clear; these were no empty threats. Barghash, Meje, and Abd il Aziz, along with the other occupants, had to flee to the back of the house or face being struck by whistling bullets flying everywhere.

At the first shot, Chole broke down in wrenching tears, cursed all of Madjid, the government, and the English in a jumble of accusations, and decried them for their injustices towards us! As the shooting increased, our own house went into a panic. We lived directly behind Barghash's palace and were also at great risk. Everyone, high and low, young and old, ran aimlessly around. Here some were saying good-bye forever; there they were asking mutual forgiveness for injustices committed during happier days gone by; the steelier ones grabbed their valuables to bring them along when fleeing; others clung together crying and deploring, unable to think or act; many prayed as and where they were, in the corridors, on the stairs, in the courtyard, on the palisade-protected roof. More of us began to follow their example, so that in place of the intensive agitation a wonderfully calming awareness set in, that it is the will of God, not man, that comes to pass, that our fate is decided since the dawn of time by the All-Merciful and Almighty. Everyone had now dropped to their knees in prayer and was touching their foreheads to the ground, to show their deepest humility toward the Lord. Some in enlightened Europe may call this fanaticism, or whatever the label, but such faith certainly brings unfathomable peace to its adherents, saving them from despair in times of need, and letting the most impassable paths of our lives appear less fraught than they really are.

All the hundreds that so fervently turned to the Lord after the first shock could just as easily have fled. Our front door stood wide open, and everyone could have secured their safety. Under the circumstances, not a soul would have held it against us if we had sought refuge in broad daylight in Bet il Sahel. But no one even gave it a thought.

In the face of such danger, Chole finally got her stubborn brother to offer up his surrender. Against all rules of etiquette, she herself ran to the English consulate to relay the message and ask for hostilities to cease. One might ask, why did she not go to Madjid to arrange everything? And that was the question a great majority of Zanzibari residents also asked themselves. They could not believe that Barghash's and Chole's hatred for Madjid was so bitter that they refused to meet him under any circumstances. The two probably also felt too ashamed. It was still better to take on the humiliation (indeed a great humiliation in the eyes of all true Arabs) of turning to a foreigner for help and intervention. Back then, the English were still far from the great power in eastern Africa that they are today. They had as little place to meddle in Zanzibari domestic affairs as, say, the Turks in the German Republic. Not until 1875, thanks to English slavery politics, did relations change significantly to their benefit—and the gradual ruin of our people.

Chole did not encounter the English Consul. However, since calls of *amn! amn!* (peace, peace!) were also being shouted from Barghash's house to the soldiers, they immediately stopped firing, and doom was averted just in time. For if the cannon ship had in fact started its bombardment, then Barghash would have never become Madjid's successor, and instead, he with us women would have become victims of our reckless enterprise. By the same token, we all surely would have emerged less intact if a man less noble than Madjid had had our prospects in his hands.

To preclude the return of any such insurrection, it was decided to send Barghash to British East India, namely, to banish him to Bombay. This followed the advice of the English Consul. The English probably sought to keep him under their control, as the lawful successor to Madjid, to groom him in their interest for their later intentions. That evening we gathered at the home of Barghash and Meje to bid farewell to the departing brothers (for Abd il Aziz had volunteered to join Barghash's exile). Already the next morning they received orders to board ship. An English warship brought them to Bombay. Barghash lived there for two years, then returned peacefully to Zanzibar, and finally, in the year 1870 following Madjid's death, succeeded him to the long-coveted throne.

Thus ended our enterprise, having begun with such high hopes. It came at a great cost to us, especially my two nieces, although they were wealthy enough to readily absorb the loss. Many of our best slaves had fallen, and others reminded us daily as disfigured invalids of the catastrophe we had created. But that was not all to come of our terrible adventure. Chole, Meje, our nieces, and I took a much heavier toll from the way all our law-abiding siblings and relatives demonstratively shunned and ignored us. I, in my heart of hearts, knew there was no begrudging their accusations.

And yet, Madjid remained a most benevolent brother all throughout. He was often criticized for letting us off so easily, since everyone knew that without our collaboration Barghash would have landed in jail long ago, and many consequences, yes, including the bloody, public fight, could have been avoided. He always responded that, yes indeed, it was all true, but that he could not bring himself to see us women punished, or even degraded, thereby showing such mercy and generosity that we did not deserve, even as some around us pegged this as weakness. To me, of course, it was incomprehensible how someone could call it weakness when a brother and uncle shows exemplary mildness to his sisters and nieces and forgives them to prevent further humiliation. Nevertheless, with all the vilifying against us, we stuck to our stance that all we had done had been right and proper. Our pride kept our heads from sinking lower; but only to the outside. On the inside, we suffered that much more.

Many people who wished us ill, or hoped to use denunciations against us to gain advantage with the government, went to great lengths to keep us in their sights. But we had nothing to fear. Our venture had failed so thoroughly that there was no rebuilding even if we had wanted. Nonetheless, the spying hurt us by dissuading any loyal friends we might have had left from engaging with us in public. Even the greedy Banyans kept their distance from us for a long time, only gradually daring under cover of darkness to slink their way back to us again to peddle their Indian treasures with their usual unscrupulousness. Our houses, which were previously like pigeon lofts and always full of guests, now stood desolate, abandoned by the outside world.

This ultimately became unbearable for me. Why stay in the city, where I encountered only hate and hostility? The litany of complaints I had to endure all day long could not improve my quality of life. And so, I finally decided to move, for an extended time, to one of my plantations.

Natives picking Cloves, Zanzibar

Zanzibar, Cloves plantation

CHAPTER TWENTY-SEVEN

Kizimbani and Bububu

Only days later, the rising sun saw me hurrying out on my little white donkey towards my plantation Kizimbani. Here I hoped to tide over the next period in peace, until the intense waves of hate and hostility toned down. Not long after, Chole, Meje, and my two nieces followed my example of forgoing the city and also retreated to the countryside.

After the death of my mother, I had seldom visited my three plantations, and then at most for one or two days. Now I appreciated the quiet country life all the more, after the restless churn of the city, compounded by my inner churn from our discord. My mother had loved to spend time in Kizimbani, and I found traces of her everywhere. I took pleasure in revisiting all the places she had gone to walk or rest. Everything reminded me of her watchful care, after she had been torn from me so early in life. All that she had handled so deftly was now mine, including all the business challenges that single Oriental women are condemned to bear in a society that excludes them from the world of men.

Under the tyranny of our customs, women are not even allowed to speak directly to our regular officials when they are free men. Orders and accounts with them must be arranged through our slaves, as virtually no high-ranking women know how to write. There are plenty of single women who have never in their lives received a written statement of accounts from their managers. If these managers fund only what the household needs and then hand over however many thousands of Maria Theresa thalers from the sale of the annual harvest, that is enough to take full care of these women. Cloves and coconuts bring in the large sums. We are too proud to sell the potatoes, yams, and other produce that come from the soil, but just use them for the household and leave the rest for the manager's own use. That explains why these individuals, who mostly come from Oman as very poor immigrants, are able to return home after but a few years with respectable gains.

During my time in the city, my Kizimbani manager, Hassun, would come to my house every week or two to report on the land and receive my instructions, all as conveyed through my slaves. Single women always set up separate rooms on the ground floor of their homes, so that their male visitors can get some rest after their long rides, with a chance to eat and drink, before heading homewards on their donkeys.

Now that I was planning a longer stay in Kizimbani, the good Hassun became a challenge. The poor man no longer knew what to do. At every moment he was having to slip in here or rush out there, just to make sure that he, as a free man, did not intentionally see us women. I therefore decided to send him to a different plantation, which had also been under his charge, and gave his original position to an Abyssinian slave named Murdjan (coral), who was very educated for his status in that he could read and write. He was also full of energy, an essential quality for someone charged with the oversight and management of several hundred plantation slaves. Abyssinians are generally very capable, and we always preferred to purchase them, instead of Africans.

Now I could walk and ride about to my heart's delight, without coming across poor Hassun bin Ali at every step. My ever-increasing number of pets gave me much joy, and I spent several hours a day tending to them. I also found great pleasure in seeking out old and sick people in their small, low-build huts and sharing the overflow from my kitchen with them through my servants. I had all the young slave children—a kind of "dividend" for their masters—come to me every morning to be washed at the draw well, using dried leaves from the Asian *rassel* tree that foam up like soap when dropped into water, and then made sure they were amply fed. These children would stay in a part of the courtyard and play under the watchful eye of a female slave until their parents returned from the fields around four in the afternoon. This way the little squirmers were in much better shape than if they had had to spend the whole day tied to the backs of their mothers in the blazing sun.

This free and unconstrained life in the countryside suited me tremendously, and my whole soul was elated to have escaped the commotions of the city for this comfort. Mothers and daughters of high-ranking families within a two-mile radius called upon me to welcome my arrival, as was proper, and soon guests were coming to the house for weeks, indeed, months.

Even complete strangers would stop by during their excursions to rest and relax in my men's room. This is completely in keeping with custom. Kizimbani lies at the intersection of two lively thoroughfares, which meant we got many such visitors.

My closest plantation neighbors were two of my sisters and a nephew. The latter was the good Fesal, Hilal's son, who, as noted, had been orphaned early on and was very kindhearted, but widely misjudged. In me, he found someone that, for the first time, understood him. He latched onto me with almost childish trust and rode over to me daily.

I similarly kept up with the city. Two alternating messengers had to set out daily, leaving early in the morning and returning with all the news in the evening. I also sent my chamber maid to my siblings and friends two or three times a week to be informed of what there was to know. And the reverse, messengers arrived daily from various others who wanted to check in on me.

This way I remained in constant contact with the city, and it was my great joy to receive only harmless visits and be rid of those evil spies.

The outrage caused by our so pathetically conducted plot eventually calmed down, but the hate and disharmony among the siblings remained. It was just one more reason to resist thoughts of returning to the city any time soon. Even a short visit was best avoided, despite needing only two or so hours to get there. On the other hand, the siblings that stuck by me came to see me quite often.

And so I was happy and content, except for one thing: I missed the sublime sea, the view of which had greeted me every day, with only very short interruptions, for as long as I had lived. All three of my plantations were in the interior of the island, but I was not used to having any unfulfilled desires, and I was still resolved to stay away from the city, so I decided to acquire a waterfront plantation. And yet, to my chagrin, that proved quite difficult, since all the desirable locations were already owned by others who had purchased with the same consideration, more for pleasure than profit. The *dellal* (broker) whom I entrusted through my slaves to undertake the search swore up and down that he would not rest until he had found a suitable plantation, but in the end had to concede that not a single one was for sale.

He had just come to Kizimbani and conveyed this unpleasant news through one of the servants when a friend stopped in for a visit and told me of a country estate that belonged to one of her cousins, complete with a lovely villa and directly by the sea. This cousin lived permanently in the city, hardly ever used the property, and might allow me to purchase or rent.

191

For some, my dilemma will appear incomprehensible, as most people in Germany seem to believe the whole country is the personal property of the Sultan and his family and that his subjects have neither rights nor ownership. It is presumed that if we want something, we can simply take it, without needing consent of the affected owner. But conditions in Zanzibar were not that primitive in my time. Private property was just as untouchable as here. The best example is how hard it was for me to get what I wanted, even though I was offering good money. Regrettably, however, during my recent visit to Zanzibar, I learned that the legal situation has changed considerably of late. Among other things, I was told that the English Consul's estate was a present from the Sultan, who is said to have taken it from the prior owner without any compensation.

The next morning, we rode early to Bububu, the name of the estate, to take an initial look. We found the house locked, and it was a long time before someone finally let us in. The overall estate gave the impression that no one had spent much money or effort on it, as opposed to relying only on nature's care. The villa was large, massively built, and stood on its own, connected on only one side to a spacious courtyard with a kitchen and servants' quarters off in a corner. Streaming through the courtyard was a creek, such a priceless advantage in our climate, which reminded me vividly of the beloved Mtoni. The most enchanting feature, however, was the lovely view from the second floor of the house. Countless large and small palm trees flanked the sides, and there, straight ahead, lay the wide-open sea, sending waves that frequently sprayed the walls of the villa.

I decided on the spot that I would either buy or rent Bububu. The next morning, my friend rushed back to the city to tell her cousin. After a few days, she let me know that he was not willing to sell the estate, but had gladly offered to let me live in his villa. I, of course, did not accept this offer, but instead managed after long negotiations to enter into a rental arrangement for a fixed annual sum of Maria Theresa thalers.

About a week later, after the contract was signed—for this, too, is not unknown in Zanzibar—I moved to Bububu, where I could once again behold the splendid sea, my special love my whole life long, directly in front of me.

My joy was dampened only by the farewell to my nephew Fesal. He took our separation very much to heart and complained that he would now have no one other than his aged stepmother to whom he could speak freely and openly.

All my spoiled pets had to come along. They were rather surprised to have been driven off, or packed into cages and baskets, only to re-encounter each other in a completely different courtyard in Bububu. But apparently, they were as pleased with the change as I was. They drank with delight from the creek or, in the case of the parrots, ducks, and doves, cheerfully walked right in. Meanwhile, I happily sat and watched, or ambled along the beautiful beach and observed the various ships that had to pass this way, traveling from north to south towards the city, as well as the many small fishing boats that sped past with their singing crews. Often the sea looked just like a lively street.

I had now also moved much closer to the city and could reach it easily by both land and sea. Three of my brothers, Abd il Wehab (servant of the Lord), Hamdan, and Djemshid, took great pleasure in giving me surprise visits almost every day, traveling by either horse or boat, whatever happened to be most convenient. They were just a bit older than me and always funny and merry. Our favorite pastime was to head to the beach, where we talked, ate, drank, played cards, or burned off whole baskets of fireworks, all in harmless happiness and high spirits. In the evening, when Djemshid, with his "cat eyes," rode off alone in his boat, he saluted us for a good distance with many *fetak* (fireworks). We returned his farewell gesture no less lavishly.

I had much more of a social life here than in Kizimbani. No day passed without my hosting at least one or two, and often up to ten, ladies, some of them stopping over in Bububu to rest for a few hours on their way to another destination, some staying with me for one or more days. It was a totally cheerful and carefree time.

When I think back to those lovely days of my youth, a time when I knew only the good and wonderful sides of the world, as yet unaware of the many thorns that would later threaten to block my life at every pass, I get a heavy heart. In my hours of sorrow, however, it is these sacred memories of my youth, memories of parents and siblings, of my homeland, that give me renewed vigor again and again, and I bask myself in them almost daily. I acknowledge with thanks that the good hand of the Lord is everywhere, as he, in his infinite wisdom, measures out the good and bad fortunes and always gives at least some joy to comfort the unfortunate.

As it was, my time in Bububu ended soon after. One day around noon, I peered out onto the sea as usual through the large telescope on the second floor of the house, expecting to spot one of my brothers coming up from afar. Indeed, a single boat was soon headed toward us. Abd il Wehab came alone this time, and his face betrayed immediately that he was bringing an unpleasant message.

"Abd il Wehab, what's new, my brother?" I called as he came toward the house. "Oh sister, oh Salme," he answered, "I was sent to you today with a request that I do not like at all. But guess from whom!" On my insistence, he finally began: "You know that a new English Consul recently arrived." "What do I care about this Englishman? Is he the one who sent you here?" "No!" "Then answer, tell me everything, and do not torment me any longer." "But please, don't be upset with me, oh Salme." "No! No! Just be quick and tell me!" "I am coming on behalf of—Madjid, who is sincerely imploring you, if you still care about him, to give up Bububu. The new English Consul sent him the request yesterday, asking if he could have Bububu as his residence."

This request from Madjid hit me extraordinarily hard. Anyone else, I would have bluntly turned them down. But Madjid, against whose government and perhaps even against whose life I had so wantonly conspired, how could I leave him hanging? Until then, I had not sought a rapprochement and was even convinced that he had long ago forgotten the affair. But now that the offended and aggrieved person himself was making the request, I believed I could also unload a small portion of my heavy guilt by giving him what he asked. I shared this decision with Abd il Wehab.

Madjid had included the message that he knew I would not be inclined to return to Bet il Tani, and could instead arrange a suitable place for me in the city through Abd il Wehab. I was not ready to make a quick decision about this. I asked for time to reflect.

For possibly the first time in my life, I felt deep grief about something tangible. I had been so happy in Bububu that I could not have wished for anything else. Abd il Wehab left after having eaten, but not before once again emphatically discouraging me from returning to Kizimbani. And then I was left counting down a tearful farewell in my mind to all my favorite spots. I vacillated a long time about whether to really throw myself back into the clamor of the city. I had a dark premonition that new and inevitable misunderstandings awaited me there.

The next morning, I wrote to Abd il Wehab that I would vacate Bububu within the week and leave it entirely to Madjid's disposal. I arranged everything for my return to Kizimbani, my final decision. That same afternoon, the three dear brothers appeared and called to me as they walked in the door: "Salme, drop that Kizimbani idea! If you love us, then you have to come back to the city. "Or," added our jokester Djemshid, "if you decide to hide out on your plantation, then we will ambush you in the dead of night and set your house on fire!" They also conveyed the kind requests from their mothers (all three were Circassian) that I should please again make my home in the city. It was the last time all four of us were together in wonderful Bububu. When we separated, my brothers left in triumph, as I had promised to give up the move to Kizimbani.

The author's residence in Stone Town

CHAPTER TWENTY-EIGHT

My Last Stay in Zanzibar

A few days later, I found myself on the roof of my new city home that Abd il Wehab had arranged for me. It was a moonlit night around eight o'clock, as I chatted with an earlier acquaintance who was now my neighbor, when Selim came and announced a visit from Chole.

"Oh Salme, I expected better of you!" were the first words out of her mouth. "Good evening, Chole, how have I wronged you?" I asked in surprise, while leading her to the *tekje*, the seat of honor. "What? You really think you have not wronged me? Is it nothing that you relinquished Bububu to benefit Madjid and his godless *kafer* (Englishman)? "But dear sister," I replied, perhaps somewhat offended, "that is of course my own business, and moreover, I recently explained the matter to you in my letter." "Well, you apparently wanted to curry favor with the wretch (by whom she meant Madjid), isn't that true?" "No, you are completely wrong. I have no need to curry favor with anyone, you of all people know that well." "Yes, but then why did you gratify him this way?" she persisted more vehemently. "From what I heard, he is also to blame that you chose this house rather than Bet il Tani. Is that so?" "No, he was not responsible for that, it was Abd il Wehab, Hamdan, and Djemshid who urged me to come here." "Well, well, I see now that you are against us; so be it," she exclaimed as she rose to leave and waved off the refreshments offered by the servant. "From now on, you will have to choose between Barghash and me or the vassal of the English. Adieu!" And with that, she disappeared.

After that day, I never saw Chole again, even though we lived in one and the same city for several more years. Only after my departure did she start to become more conciliatory. Time and again, I asked myself if I had not in fact intended to offend her, but I always came to the reassuring conclusion that I never knowingly gave offense, that I had no purpose in leaving Bububu other than some slight relief to my guilty conscience. But this idea that I had wanted to ingratiate myself, what an absurd accusation! Chole was so overwrought that evening as she aired her grudge that she seemed absolutely incapable of any calm consideration.

Up to that point, I had not seen either Madjid or Chadudj again and was now even more determined to avoid them at all costs, so Chole's suspicions would not appear justified after all. And yet, that is not how it went. I had been in my new apartment barely two weeks when—Madjid himself, plus a large entourage, came to visit. "Good morning, Salme," he called to me, "you see, even though I am older than you, I am still coming to you first to express my thanks for not wanting to disgrace me to the Englishman." "Oh brother, that was nothing, nothing at all," I stammered, since no one was more surprised by the visit than I. Gentle and noble as always, Madjid made no mention of the past, not a word, but instead tried to alleviate my insurmountable embarrassment with all sorts of stories.

"Of course, you'll come soon to visit Chadudj?" "Yes, of course, I'll come," was my totally natural answer. "Our Aunt Aashe as well, who is so very fond of you, now lives with us and would be happy to see you again."

Madjid lingered for about an hour, and we had reconciled by the time he left. That very same day, news of the visit became general knowledge and was reported to Chole as well.

With the much older Madjid having come to visit me first, something I had thought impossible, I had no choice—even if I had been truly unforgiving towards him, this good soul—but to return the visit to him, Chadudj, and our Aunt Aashe, the father's only sister. That this simple act of reciprocity would come at such a steep price was something I could not have surmised at the time. Even to this day, this one step is held against me as the ultimate transgression, while my participation in the fateful alliance, and everything I accomplished and suffered for it, was completely discounted in no time. Though this jealousy might appear unseemly, I came to realize, too late, that it was built into our family relations at the time. As they would have it, I was not allowed to show any kindness to my brother, much less visit my brother, sister, and aunt, and even less have any close interactions with them, without immediately being forever spurned by these other siblings!

The two parties persisted, and the intrigues continued, although more as an undercurrent, less overtly than before. It was not uncommon for an unpleasant encounter at some location to cause the oncoming guests to immediately pull back or the guests already there to leave as quickly as possible, so as not to get caught under the same roof as the enemy. And meanwhile the hostess always found herself in a most uncomfortable position, having to maintain complete neutrality and refrain from any kind of interference. What use was there that I swore never again to be drawn into politics? The calamity had occurred and could never be undone. With everyone being so public in their attitudes, the enmity between the parties was that much harder to bear.

Orientals are by nature very candid and totally incapable of dissembling in certain situations, the way people so masterfully do here. There people make no secret of an avowed enemy and adversary and do not hesitate to heap on slights with cutting looks, gestures, and words. They simply have no sense for behaving other than how they really think and feel. The conventional courtesies, consistent with polite society, are just not in their repertoire. Indeed, efforts to dissemble, which rarely succeed with our hot-blooded natures anyhow, are considered cowardly. So often since that day did I hear these words: "Why should I not express myself the way I feel? Are not all my thoughts and feelings open and apparent to the Lord, my God? Why should I make any pretense toward these lowly children of the Lord or even be afraid?" —

To the delight of many, the engagements and weddings of two sisters to two cousins brought a happy distraction into our lives, and the eternal brawling and wrangling in our family circle seemed to die down for a few months. Even though the two sisters married two brothers, they drew entirely different lots, as so often happens in life. One ended up very happy, although she did not have any children; the other experienced joyful motherhood, but was not happy in the marriage. Who does not see in this a kind of compensating higher power that so wisely and mercifully cares for every individual?

Times were hard in Oman, and our family circle was augmented by a large number of immigrating relatives. That allowed me the renewed pleasure of experiencing the full comfort of being with family.

There is one friend, in particular, that remains unforgettable to me. I may not say her name or offer any details of our relationship and separation. But I can say that this friend was loyal to the end, even as I was on the cusp of leaving my homeland forever and at great risk. She knew all my household affairs, so I could not hide my plans from her. She stuck with me nonetheless, until I finally, in the last half hour before my departure, removed her with gentle force, for her own safety. "My honor," she said at the farewell, "may the Lord of this Universe protect you. I know I will have to give up my life within the next twelve hours, but for you, that is never too much!" Her words are still ringing in my ears at this very moment, and I can exclaim with complete conviction: "Blessed are those who can rely on good and true friends!"

Anyone who wants to experience a genuine and truly selfless friendship must go to the Orient. Not that this exists only in the Orient among Orientals, but it is a fact that Arabs, once they love someone, attach themselves with such tenacity and self-sacrifice that they necessarily lose sight of every other consideration. Even though the social classes are nowhere as pronounced as in the Orient, these status distinctions have no bearing on true friendships. A prince engages as dearly with a beloved son of a poor stable master as with another friend of noble lineage, without even a trace of difference between the two. And a princess gives herself in friendship to the wives and daughters of a simple plantation manager as much as to a higher-ranking Arab woman. My sister Meje, for example, had grown very close to just such a manager's daughter and eventually invited her to move into her palace. The two of them, this poor, modest, but very bright being and my sister, shared an extraordinarily intimate connection that only death could part.

It is not uncommon for a woman of status to forge a close friendship with a slave kept by someone else, naturally not with an African, but a Circassian or Abyssinian. That can prove especially fortunate for the slave, in that she may then be purchased for five or ten times the usual price or the slave may be gifted in order to be freed by her benefactress. This release is always legalized, so that no third party can ever harm the freed friend.

If someone is thrown into jail, his friend will ask to be locked up with him for several hours every day. If someone is sent into exile, his loyalists will follow wherever his steps take him. If someone has an accident or is impoverished, his faithful friends will rally with all their resources to his side, so there is never any need to resort to public charity and the collection lists. We grow up this way and learn these attitudes from our childhood onward, so this is all commonplace and just the way we are.

199

Rudolph Heinrich Ruete, the author's husband

CHAPTER TWENTY-NINE

Great Transformations

In this sad and dismal time, when disagreements and discord pervaded our family, I felt fortunate to receive the attentions of a young German, who was staying in Zanzibar as the representative of a Hamburg trading company and later became my husband.[22] There have been such frequent, public mischaracterizations of the ensuing events that were of such great consequence to me that I feel the need to provide a brief overview of what happened. Under the rule of my brother Madjid, Europeans enjoyed a very privileged status. They were welcome guests in his house and on his properties and always received the most attentive hospitality. Both my sister Chole and I were also on friendly terms with the Europeans in Zanzibar, which were manifested in various small gestures, as allowed by the customs of the land. European ladies that were present in Zanzibar usually visited only Chole and me.

I got to know my husband not long after my move from Bububu. My house stood directly next to his. The flat roof of his lay just below mine, and from a window on my top floor, I was often witness to merry gatherings of men, which he had arranged to introduce me to the art of European dining. Our friendship, which in time became a deep love, soon became known in the city, and the news also traveled to my brother Madjid. Despite all the rumors, I never experienced any animosity on his part, much less imprisonment because of this.

---

22 Rudolph Heinrich Ruete, born March 10, 1839, went by the name Heinrich. He arrived in Zanzibar in 1855 as an agent for the trading company Hansing & Co. out of Hamburg, Germany, later switching to Koll & Ruete as a partner and then his own Ruete & Co.

A union with my beloved would have been impossible in my homeland, so I naturally harbored the wish to leave the island quietly. A first attempt in this direction failed. Soon, however, a better opportunity presented itself. Through the assistance of Mrs. S, a befriended wife of the English doctor and Consular representative at the time, the commander of the English warship *Highflyer*, a Mr. P, picked me up one night in a boat. Once I was on deck, the ship immediately released steam and headed north. We reached our destination, Aden, in good shape. Here I was taken in by a Spanish couple that I had gotten to know in Zanzibar, and then waited patiently while my fiancé wrapped up his affairs on the island over several months until he could join me.

My baptism took place in the English chapel in Aden, where I was given the name Emily in recognition of the English friend mentioned above. Immediately after that, our wedding took place according to English rituals. And when the ceremony was over, we started our travels through Marseille to Hamburg, my husband's hometown, where we received a loving reception from his parents and relatives.

I soon adjusted to this strange setting and eagerly learned everything I needed for my new life. My unforgettable husband followed the different steps of my development with lively interest. He took special delight in observing my first impressions of European life and customs of the civilized world. I have written up these impressions in reverent memory and may find a subsequent opportunity to report on them as well.[23]

Our happy, contented, and unburdened life together was not to last. Barely three years had passed since our arrival in Hamburg when my beloved husband had the misfortune to fall as he jumped off a horse tram and was run over. After three days of intense suffering, he took his last breath. I now stood alone in this great and strange world, with three small children, of which the youngest was but three months old. For a while I considered returning to my homeland, but as fate would have it, two months after this tragedy, my unforgettable brother Madjid, who had always been so good to me, passed away as well. When I left the island, he had not laid a finger on my fiancé, but instead let him settle his affairs in Zanzibar freely. He also never held my clandestine escape against me. As a devout Muslim, he believed in divine predestination and was convinced that this alone had led me to Germany. He gave me touching proof of his enduring brotherly sentiments shortly before he died when he sent a steamship loaded

---

23 This refers to the "letters home" that the author wrote but never published during her lifetime. These *Briefe nach der Heimat* (Letters Home) will appear in my own translated edition to follow this one.

with a range of gifts to me in Hamburg. The ship was still on the way when this generous benefactor suddenly passed away. The items he sent never made it to me. I did not even know about Madjid's gallant act until much later when I learned that his intentions had been thwarted, and I had been cheated. At the time, the rumor had been spread that the ship was docked in Hamburg only for repairs. Nine years later I learned from a German friend, who had inspected Madjid's ship in Gibraltar and spoken with the captain, who was also German, that the ship had contained cargo destined for me! Notwithstanding the cover-up, the dark-skinned crew of this vessel was able to locate me in my house in Hamburg. The poor fellows were overjoyed when they succeeded, and they charmed me with their most endearing affection.

I lasted in Hamburg two more years, during which time misfortune continued to pursue me. I lost a significant portion of my assets through no fault of my own and was then forced to think about taking affairs into my own hands. The prospect of staying at the site of my earlier family joy had been thoroughly spoiled, especially after failing to receive as much courtesy in some circles of this maritime city as I might have expected.

I moved to Dresden, where I experienced the warmest welcome from all circles. From there, I took a trip to London, about which I will report in some detail in the next chapter. When I later found myself wishing for a calmer setting, I withdrew to idyllic Rudolfstadt for several years. Here, too, I encountered much love and friendship from the local society, including especially from the local nobility. This place also let me readily restore my health, which opened the possibility of moving to Berlin, where my children could get a good education. Here, too, I found dear friends that sought to lighten my stay. Even the very highest nobility engaged with me most graciously, which I will forever recall with love.

Sultan Barghash and his entourage

CHAPTER THIRTY

Sayyid Barghash in London

All this time, I continued to correspond with my homeland and never gave up hope of seeing it again someday. The rigid attitude of my brother Barghash had, however, made any such rapprochement impossible. His intransigence, as it were, has nothing to do with religious fanaticism, but instead came from his obstinate and hateful resentment. He simply could not forgive me for resuming friendly relations with his former enemy Madjid! The longing for my loved ones in my distant homeland, however, never abated, and I still held a silent hope that I might one day reconcile with them.

Then word spread in all the newspapers—it was the spring of 1875—with news that moved me to my core: My brother Barghash, the ruler of Zanzibar after Madjid's death, was planning a visit to London!

At first, I took no action in response to these rumors and kept any uneasiness to myself. I had already suffered far too many disappointments to be able to take courage again. Only the most insistent eloquence of my faithful friends persuaded me to take action. I finally decided to travel to London, and the foreign minister at the time, von Bülow, assured me of diplomatic support from the Ambassador, Count Münster, which unfortunately proved of little help.[24]

I used the short time before my departure to learn English, in an attempt to mitigate my significant state of helplessness at least a bit. During these six to

---

24 German Foreign Minister Bernhard Ernst von Bülow (1815–1879) and German Ambassador to the United Kingdom Georg Herbert zu Münster von Derneburg (1873–1885).

eight weeks, I consistently pored over books into the wee hours of the night, reciting one English dialog after another or learning vocabulary. Added to this was the ever-increasing concern for my three small children, from whom I would be, for the first time, separated for an unforeseeable duration.

These and similar thoughts addled my already exhausted brain, as I traveled through Ostende on my way to the giant city. Totally spent and feverishly excited, I was relieved to reach my destination, where I checked into a hotel room that had been reserved by friends of my husband. I knew no mortal soul in all of London except this couple, and even then, I had met them only once for all of an hour when they visited us, or more precisely my blessed husband, as they passed through on their honeymoon. Turning to them in my time of need proved an excellent step, as they both went to great lengths to take care of me.

I arrived in London about a week before my brother's arrival and used the time to settle into this complex, new setting. Most importantly, I paid a visit to Count Münster, who again assured me of his support.

On the fifth day after my arrival, as I sat in the hotel salon deep in dreary thoughts, my room number was suddenly called out, a sign that someone was looking for me. I was presented with the business card of Dr. P., Member of Parliament, the brother of a dear friend of mine.

Standing before him and his now deceased wife as a complete stranger, I came to know the most noble being, who did everything possible to ease my life there. They had come to lend their support and offer the very welcome suggestion that I take up residency in their home. I had to join them immediately for a leisurely ride and dinner, and then moved in completely the following day. And with that, London took a happier turn for me, and I summoned up fresh hope.

My friends in Germany had given me no peace until I made a firm promise to be as careful as I could and, in particular, engage the support of the English government for my cause. Having experienced so much heartbreak over time, and with the addition of indescribably difficult hardships because of my unfamiliarity with European languages, traditions, and customs, I had gladly concluded that one could do no better than rely on God and oneself in all challenges. I had therefore originally intended to tackle this endeavor on my own, before ultimately giving in to the urgings of my friends. As it turned out, my original fears that I would be put off with diplomatic courtesies and empty talk, and then simply have my matter relegated to the files, were way under the mark. I would find out soon enough that I had landed in a world where seeming and being completely diverged.

Not long after I had taken up residence in the heartwarming P. household, I received a visit from Sir Bartle Frere, whom I as yet knew only by name and who later became High Commissioner of South Africa. If ever my instinct was true, then on this day, on which my most fervent hopes and the future of my children were dashed and buried. I was overwhelmed with an ineffable foreboding the moment I laid eyes on this great diplomat, a man who, so to speak, had Zanzibar and my brother in his pocket.

After the usual introductory formalities, Sir Bartle began to inquire about my business and specifically the reason for my visit to London. Although he appeared fully informed about the exact details, I shared with him my full purpose. There was not much to tell, as there was but one thought: reconciliation with my family.

Who can describe my astonishment when Sir Bartle simply lobbed me a cool question in response: What did I care about most, reconciling with my family or—assuring the future of my children! Even today I feel far too weak to describe my emotions at the time. I was ready for anything but such a question. Surely no one would accuse me of lack of fortitude or consistency if I wavered at that critical moment. For me, the well-being of my children had to prevail over my personal wishes.

After overcoming my initial bewilderment at this absolutely unexpected diplomatic chess move, I asked my counterpart to clarify and explain the motivations behind his question. Sir Bartle responded decisively that, above all, the English government had no interest whatsoever in serving as an intermediary between me and my brother; they viewed him solely as a guest and did not wish to see him burdened by any inconvenience. (It is, of course, doubtful what the Sultan would have found more inconvenient, signing the slave treaties effectively under the duress of a pointed gun, thereby indirectly recognizing the English protectorate, or extending a hand to a remorseful sister.)

Elaborating positively on his proposal, he added that if I promised to refrain from any contact with my brother during his London visit, whether in writing or in person, then the English government would provide material support for the future of my children.

Sick at heart and deeply disappointed, I felt like that depleted soul who has marched for endless miles and craves a cool spring where he can take a refreshing drink as recompense for all the trials and tribulations along the way, and indeed finally comes upon such a coveted well, only to find its opening shut by a mighty hand. The choice lay before me, either operate on my own without any assistance from the English government, knowing full well they would put all manner of insurmountable obstacles in my way, for which my weak abilities would be no match, or accept the offer of the English government in the interest of my children. Mindful of the promise I had made to my motherly friend, the unforgettable Baroness von T. in Dresden, not to see my brother alone and unprepared, even though I never doubted my brother would stringently respect English law everywhere, especially in England, and even though I would have had no qualms to suddenly face him, I accepted the offer of the English government.

Even then, England's behavior engendered a degree of mistrust. When a friend of mine squarely asked Sir Bartle Frere how it was that the English government was suddenly so interested in taking care of me, this skilled diplomat presented no less than three reasons: 1. This lets us do the Sultan a favor. 2. We keep the princess at bay for a while. And 3. We preempt any subsequent ability of the Chancellor Prince of Bismarck to somehow meddle in the matter. That all sounded very plausible and reassuring.

In order to avoid a knowing encounter with my brother, whether in public buildings with paid access, or in Hyde Park and on the streets, I carefully studied the precise details of his scheduled outings in the papers every day, so I could plan accordingly. I asked my kind hostess to stop taking me on her local drives, as I preferred to stay at home and make sure I could not possibly break my promise. She responded quite firmly that I must continue to go out with her for health reasons, and she would be sure to follow only suitable routes. So we drove east when the Sultan was in the west, and the reverse. Unfortunately, this extra caution on my part was absolutely necessary. If a sudden encounter were to occur, I doubted I could control my emotions and keep my word in that critical moment. On the other hand, there was practically no risk that he might recognize me. Even my own dear mother, were she still alive, would hardly have known me in my current outfit, even less so one of my brothers, who seldom had the chance to see us without our masks on.

I would have preferred to leave the city immediately and return to my children in Germany, now that I saw my hopes and desires crushed. But I was not even afforded this relief. So distant from my children and always anxious and concerned about them, I still had to spend week after week of unspeakable torment in the very place that brought me only grief and disappointment. That is how Sir Bartle Frere wanted it, by insisting that a detailed pro memoria still needed to be prepared and submitted.

Completely unfamiliar with such business affairs and mentally so downtrodden that I was more of an automaton than a thinking person, I gladly allowed my devoted friends to prepare the note for me and had total confidence that this would surely turn out well. It was almost seven weeks before I could finally end my tortuous stay and leave England at long last to return to my children and Germany. My feelings and state of mind at that moment should not be hard to guess.

Because Zanzibar back then was already considered a certain prospect for becoming an English colony, my submission had to be routed to the Indian government, so to East India. This took a few months until one day, I was painfully surprised by a letter that arrived from London. It contained the duplicate of a document the English government had sent to Count Münster for transmission to me, and presented nothing more than a short rejection of the pro memoria Sir Bartle Frere had so insistently urged upon me. The letter gave the reason for the rejection: I had married a German, I was resident in Germany, and the German government would accordingly have a much greater interest in supporting me.

This tasteless turn of events was all the more ludicrous for my never having asked either one or the other government for any charity; I had in fact sought only moral backing, both here and there. Sir Bartle Frere himself was the father of the pro memoria, the same diplomat who had moments before elicited my promise to stay away from my brother in exchange for an assurance of my children's well-being! At the time, I had taken the need to prepare a written document as a mere formality, firmly believing that if I kept my end of the bargain, the other party would, too. Inexperienced as I was, it never occurred to me that even a helpless widow could be treated so outrageously and deceitfully in robbing her of all her hopes.

Whether such treatment of a dejected woman is worthy of such a power as England, I leave to all fair-minded people to judge. There is but one more question I would ask: Did the English government, did Sir Bartle Frere, as they approached me with their offer, not know that my husband was a German, that I accordingly also had German citizenship?[25] Was this even considered as they extracted my promise? And did I not hold to the agreement and fulfill my promise as exactingly as if I had resided in London and been called Mrs.

---

25 There would have been no mystery here, as the author became a certified citizen of the newly proclaimed German Reich when the State of Hamburg formally recognized her status in 1872 as a German widow (*Bürgerswitwe*). Emeri van Donzel, *An Arabian Princess Between Two Worlds*, plate XIX (1993).

Brown? Yes, clearly, as long as I was in a position to reach out to my brother, in whatever manner, I was not a German woman, but rather the sister of the Sultan, who could have damaged English interests. And now, long after my brother was back in our homeland and I was no longer to be feared, now it was time to play the card they had intentionally held in reserve, in order to finish me off forever. It was but a pretense to get out of an agreement that was entered into grudgingly to begin with!

Later, I came to better understand why my deeply desired reconciliation with my brother would have been especially unwelcome in London at that very moment. Since the Sultan neither speaks a European language, nor understands the subtleties of European diplomacy, the English wanted to keep him in a complete state of ignorance to ensure no last-minute trouble in getting specific treaties signed. Had I in fact made peace with him, they assumed I would have used my somewhat broader knowledge of European affairs to share various bits of information that would have benefited him and Zanzibar, but been all the more contrary to English government interests. Without suspecting a thing, I had simply become a victim of these "humane" politics.

It would, however, be a great lack of gratitude on my part if I did not sharply distinguish the English government from English society. Although I thank the former for my misery, indeed, through whose insidiousness I lost my true faith and trust in humanity, the latter showed me only kindness and caring. Empathetic interest in my fate was manifest all the way up to the highest echelons in England, and I remain immensely obliged for the rest of my life to very many people for their kindness.

The author and her children

CHAPTER THIRTY-ONE

Returning to the Homeland After Nineteen Years

When I wrote the previous chapter several years ago, I still could hardly have believed in the possibility of fulfilling a wish that had pervaded all my thoughts and feelings, indeed my whole being. The eventful period since I had last seen my beloved homeland had been filled with more storm and stress than I could have imagined. My life had undergone the most astonishing changes in that time. I had had experiences that not even the cruelest person would have wished upon his enemies. For a good while, my relatively hardy constitution had enabled me to endure the challenging life and raw climate of the North, but even that was becoming harder and harder.

One evening exactly two years ago, I said to my two daughters: "Children, I have spent some time contemplating whether now is not finally the moment to think about returning to Zanzibar." I explained my views to them in some detail. The one reminded me of the unlucky star that was always hovering over us and all our past failures, claiming that this time, too, would merely cause pointless excitement and disappointment. But the other chimed in enthusiastically: "No, Mama, you must not leave any avenue unexplored; you would blame yourself later for missing that one right moment to go." She said exactly what I was thinking.

I took the preliminary steps in confidence and was met with encouraging reactions from the relevant authorities. Even so, the matter failed to progress for a long time. After repeated disappointments, by which time it seemed the longing for my homeland would never be fulfilled, I received a request one day from the Foreign Ministry to keep myself ready to leave for Zanzibar shortly. The news moved me so profoundly that I initially failed to register my full joy at having reached this long-awaited good fortune. Beyond praise and glory for God's wonderful guidance, I first and foremost felt a deep appreciation toward our beloved, venerated Emperor William I[26] and his senior Ministries, for whom I and my children will forever retain undiminished gratitude.

This is not the place to belabor all the minute details of what took place, and I can more readily bypass them because the daily newspapers reported more than enough of the concurrent political happenings.

I was to be in Port Said on July 12, 1885. On July 1, I left Berlin with my children and traveled through Breslau and Vienna to Trieste, where we arrived in good shape on July 3. My children were delighted with all the new and beautiful things they saw. I was still too drained to share in their enthusiasm.

Not until we had boarded the Lloyd steamer *Venus*, which set off to sea at one o'clock the same day, did I again find the calm that I had been so sorely missing these past weeks, and the ability to enjoy what was around us. The weather was so lovely that we were able to stay on deck practically the whole time.

The morning of July 5, we docked in Corfu. We rode around for several hours and got to know the main attractions of this charming island. Fully satisfied, we were back at the steamer by afternoon and then continued aboard past the barren island of Ithaca at the southern tip of Greece and the towering island of Kantia for an arrival in Alexandria on Wednesday, July 8.

Upon entering this city, with its palms and minarets, I was overcome with the most blissful sense of my homeland, a feeling that can only be felt and not described, sentiments that can be understood and appreciated only by those who likewise had been long separated from whence they came. For nineteen years, I had never again set foot in the actual South, and winter after winter, I had passed my time by a heated stove in Germany. Even though I resided in the North and carried the many obligations of a German housewife, my thoughts were always far, far away. There was no better entertainment or distraction for me than sitting alone and undisturbed while burrowing into a book about the South. No wonder then, when I set eyes upon Alexandria, that I was deeply moved, as in a dream, watching the throngs of people in the port!

---

26 Kaiser Wilhelm I, German emperor from 1871 to 1888, the first to lead a united Germany.

At the customs house, we were stopped to present our papers. Determined to identify myself only if absolutely necessary, I asked my travel escort to try her luck with her calling card, which thankfully proved sufficient. Boxed in by boisterous crowds, we struggled mightily to find a coach with which to escape to a hotel. With some twenty people gathered around us, all simultaneously offering their services, it took the interference of a policeman to get them to disperse. Only then could the coach make its way, and even so, someone still managed to jump up on the back to extol his skills as a translator on our drive. That I spoke Arabic myself and therefore had no need for his assistance took a while for him to comprehend.

The two days we spent in the expensive and dirty hotel flew by way too quickly for me. My favorite activity was to head to the Arabic quarter, where I did not tire of watching the colorful commotion for hours on end. Folks appeared wary at first, but as soon as I spoke Arabic with them, their faces brightened, and their eyes glowed with joy. "Mother," (meant in the general sense) they would call from all sides, "where did you learn our language so well? You have surely been in Baghdad; how long did you live there?"

Our Arab coach driver, named Muhammed, became so attached to us that he ended up begging me to take him along as a servant. He would, he assured me, remain loyal to us until the end of his days—and never touch our bottles of wine. The next morning, when his coach arrived perfectly on time to take us back to the harbor, he was visibly despondent, and I had quite a time trying to console the poor man.

And thus our very enjoyable time in Alexandria flew by. It took eighteen hours from there to reach Port Said, where the tender vessel *Adler* of the East African squadron lay docked. We boarded that same evening. Port Said is a small port town, but it offers practically everything. The shops contain a great abundance of anything one could ever want.

Here is where the sand desert begins, through which the canal also runs, where the Mediterranean Sea connects with the Red Sea and so also the Atlantic Ocean with the Indian Ocean. The travel lane is so narrow that two ships cannot pass, which is why passing locations have been inserted at several spots with signs on shore that say *Gare Limite Sud* and *Gare Limite Nord*. Ships frequently have to wait for hours until the oncoming ship has passed through. Every steamer brings a canal pilot on board at either Port Said or Suez to successfully navigate the obstacles. These pilots bring a thorough understanding of the signal language that uses buoys hoisted on halyards, whose numbers and placements indicate if it is safe to proceed or how many ships are still in the queue ahead. Ships

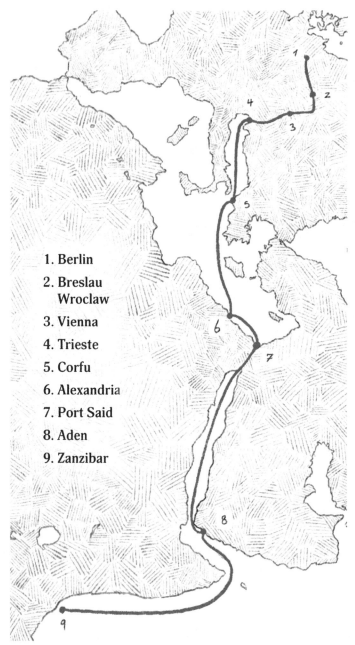

1. Berlin
2. Breslau
   Wroclaw
3. Vienna
4. Trieste
5. Corfu
6. Alexandria
7. Port Said
8. Aden
9. Zanzibar

The author's trip from Berlin to Zanzibar

are not allowed to traverse the canal at full power because the large waves can damage the loose sands at the shoreline. Ships also must anchor at night. The trip is nonetheless quite entertaining, especially when individual ships get into a "race," as often happens when they enter the Great Bitter Lake. All ships naturally want to be the first to enter the narrow ship lane up ahead.

Approaching the Suez, the canal widens, and there we could finally plow "full speed ahead" into the Red Sea. The heat in the Suez Canal is very intense, but it becomes almost unbearable in this arm of the Red Sea with tall cliffs bearing in on both sides. We were dripping wet both day and night. I felt better in this familiar temperature than all the years I was away, but my children had a hard time of it and became sluggish, even sullen. Because the sea rode high, we were unable to open the side windows of our cabins. The air became increasingly oppressive until one very hot night we abandoned our cabins to sit on deck chairs in search of some refreshing slumber.

The trip to Aden took seven days, and then we kept anchor in the same heat for another five days before the *Adler* was given the command to continue its travels. Who could have been happier than me? In a week, at last, after a long separation, I would see my homeland again.

Up to Aden, the sea had been easy on us, but the rocky city was barely behind us when we found ourselves in a horrific southwest monsoon. Our ship was entering the same dangerous regions where the SMS *Augusta* had gone under a few weeks before. One morning at eight o' clock, just as we were having breakfast on deck with the officers, the first wave careened across the deck and scattered the gathered company in all directions. So much for our peaceful, comfortable times, as suddenly the worst storm I had ever experienced let loose. Day and night the sea played our ship like a pinball. Spumes of mighty waves pounded so incessantly on both smokestacks that after the storm, once all the saltwater had evaporated, they looked completely white instead of black. Anyone who has not experienced such a sea cannot really imagine what it is like. Our situation was quite dire. After suffering greatly the first day from sea sickness caused by the terrible pitching and rolling, the next days were miserable because of the agitation and sleepless nights. Water was coming into all the rooms. The berths were so wet that we could not lie in them. The situation was so dangerous that we stayed dressed for three nights and slept in a small salon near the men, often with open umbrellas to catch water dripping through the deck. The hatches and skylight had been tightly closed, and the latter was even covered with a tarred sailcloth as a tarp. It does not take much to imagine how bad the air was. We women looked utterly pathetic all this time, as we could not really wash or coif ourselves. All our clothes in the drawers had gotten wet, so we could not change our completely soaked outfits into anything dry. Our shoes were totally ruined, and with no other dry shoes on hand, I had to borrow slippers from the commanding officer, Mr. von D.

After three days, the storm finally calmed down. Even though waves still frequently crested the deck, we were able to spend a few hours in an elevated space where the commanding officer had pitched a tent for us.

Although I had been quite fearful in the beginning, the awareness that we are always in God's hands and that I was with my three children, who meant more to me than anything, allowed me to soon become calmer.

On August 2, the island of Pemba came into view. Oh! what a word that was for me. Namely, the distance from Pemba to Zanzibar is only thirty nautical miles, a trip that easily takes a mere three hours. With encroaching darkness, however, we sailed only to the northern tip of Zanzibar to avoid the multiple sandbanks that make a nighttime port entry too dangerous.

It was a wondrous convergence for me that I would see my homeland again in the same month that I had left it nineteen years ago, and on the same day in the same hour that my husband had been taken from me exactly fifteen years before. I hardly need to describe what my heart felt on this day. I turned in earlier than usual, but then slept barely a wink the whole night. I was like a volcano inside, and only the most fervently hopeful prayer now and again gave me a passing moment of calm.

During the night, our ship drifted slowly close to the lighthouse. As I walked out onto the deck the next morning, the palms of my homeland were already greeting me from afar! What else could I do upon seeing this magical sight but run quickly back into my cabin and thank the Almighty for his great goodness! The events of my life are all too varied, and they in turn have shaped my feelings and perspectives. People are in large part no more than what their lives, experiences, and given circumstances make of them: I left my homeland as a complete Arab and a good Muslim, and what am I today?

But in this moment, it seemed as if my entire youth came back to me, as if to make up for the many years of strain and sorrow. Everything, everything appeared vividly before my soul, and the cheerful pictures of my past strode forth, one after another, before my inner eye.

This first impression also appears to have had a sobering effect on my otherwise so cheerful and lively children. All three could not hug me enough on this day, and they kept gazing at me with still and earnest eyes. Deep inside, I could not thank the Lord enough for such rich recompense for all the loss.

As we neared the city, we were disappointed to discover that the German squadron had not yet arrived. Since the *Adler* was supposed to be part of the ensemble, we had no choice but to backtrack and stay adrift on the east side of the island until the squadron came in. And so, we waited an additional eleven days. Then, on August 11, shortly before four o'clock, the sailor posted on the yard announced: "Ship in sight!" We figured it was just a passenger ship and barely registered the call. Soon, however, we noticed that the ship was headed directly for us. We therefore made steam, showed our flag, and signaled our name. A short time later came the countersignal, and minutes later, we recognized the tender vessel *Ehrenfels*. It soon lay broadside to ours and let us know through signals that it had been looking for us under instructions from the Commodore since the morning, to convey orders that we come to the harbor, where the squadron had already been docked for four days. We immediately set course for the harbor, but could not enter because of lacking steam power and impending nightfall, so we had to spend yet another night near the lighthouse at the northern tip.

The next morning, we were already up and about by six o'clock. On the horizon, we glimpsed the forest of masts in the harbor. For the second time, we rode close to shore, past marvelous palm groves in which little African villages lay scattered. Through steady signaling, the flagship directed us to a berth, only to have us switch locations again half an hour later. We saw four German warships: the SMS *Stosch, Gneisenau, Elisabeth*, and *Prinz Adalbert*; two English warships; five steamships belonging to the Sultan; and various sailing ships.

Commodore Paschen initially considered it necessary to treat me as "secret cargo," a description that garnered considerable amusement among the officers of the squadron. However, as soon as Admiral Knorr arrived with the SMS *Bismarck*, things changed, and I was able to go on land as I pleased. Beyond the feelings that had overwhelmed me upon seeing my homeland again, the fact that I now walked the streets in broad daylight in the company of men, whereas before I went out only veiled and at night, made a truly remarkable impression on me. One would think that, after living in Europe for nineteen years, I would simply take this aspect in stride. Indeed, I did, in spades. But now in Zanzibar, it was the first time after so many years that I became acutely aware of the transformations I had had to undergo over the course of time. I did not have these same sensations in Egypt, where I had been twice before, only on the ground of my homeland.

218

On our first foray into the city, I thought I saw unmistakable astonishment in the eyes of the crowds that gathered around us. People pressed in from all sides, calling to me in both Arabic and Swahili: "How are you, my Mistress?" Whenever we went into stores to make purchases, vast masses of people collected in the narrow streets, but then respectfully made room as we left. Day after day, our accompanying crowds grew larger, and the welcoming spirit of the public became more affectionate. That naturally annoyed the Sultan and his advisor, the English General Consul, more than a little. The former even had a number of those who followed us soundly whipped. He, as well as the English General Consul, moved to lodge a complaint with the squadron chief about these increasingly heartfelt demonstrations by the population towards me. Once I heard this, I felt I had to advise the people to stop flocking to us, but they answered that, no matter the punishment, they still wanted to show me their joy. Often slaves would push their way forward with utmost caution to convey greetings from their masters. They asked me not to doubt their loyalty and devotion; they wished fervently to be allowed to visit me on board, their houses were at my disposal at any time. Even letters, which slaves that had no pockets on their clothes carried under their little caps, were discreetly slipped my way. Sometimes, when walking past the houses, I would find ladies hiding behind a door, seemingly waiting for our arrival. As soon as I walked past, they would speak to me, at times just a short greeting: "God be with you and give you good health!" My siblings, relatives, and former friends sent repeated requests that I come visit them. But I never followed up on any of the invitations, not for personal reasons, as my feelings were too strong for any personal reservations to get in the way, but because the current circumstances forced me to this level of consideration.

Whenever our rowboats came in front of the palace, or passed under the windows of the harem house, we could always see the Sultan's women at the windows, greeting us kindly. Because all our outings were undertaken with the friendly escort of Marine officers, I had to ask the men, in the interests of the women, to please refrain from responding. I, too, avoided it, so the shortsighted beauties would not become unnecessarily ruined, as I had been informed that their ruler and master would often hide himself in the house where he could watch both the sea and the street and easily discover the unsuspecting culprits, followed by cruel punishments. That is not a mere assumption. It is well-known, and Europeans in Zanzibar know to tell the story, that hardly a year ago, as the Sultan was peering out of his hiding place, he noticed how a Portuguese man passed by on the water and greeted his favorite, a beautiful Circassian, who greeted back. This custom is nothing new. Already thirty years ago, when I was still a child, we were regularly greeted by Europeans, especially the English and French Marine officers that came over to our island rather frequently, as well as the local merchants, and we would return the courteous greeting. Our male society had always accepted this and thought nothing of it. Barghash, however, saw things differently and personally whipped his Circassian with such vehemence that she succumbed a few days later. He is said to have begged forgiveness at her death bed, but to no avail. Even today, he has someone say prayers regularly at her gravesite.

On our excursions to the interior, we often encountered people riding donkeys on the backroads. To show their respect, they always dismounted, led their animals past us, and then remounted. Despite all the punishments from the Sultan, the population did not let up on demonstrating its attachment, and the loud calls, *Kuaheri, Bibi! Kuaheri, Bibi!* (All good fortune, Mistress!), that resounded almost directly under the Sultan's own windows as we returned to our ships, could not have been comfortable for him. I was told that whenever our boats came into view, someone would use an empty cookie tin as a signaling drum to alert the population.

For obvious reasons, there was no shortage of spies lurking around us, mostly Hindus, who were very annoyed that we spoke only German amongst ourselves. Even on the last evening prior to our departure, two loyal friends, who had come on board under cover of night to bid me farewell, alerted me to a dark figure, who had already frequented our ship as a visiting salesman, but was actually just a skilled tool of the exceptionally influential, namely, the former lamp cleaner and court barber, the merchant Madoldji Pera-Daudji.

This Pera-Daudji, an exceedingly cunning Hindu, had elevated himself to the role of the Sultan's general factotum. He, this erstwhile lamp cleaner, serves the ruler of Zanzibar in all things high and low. All diplomatic negotiations go through his hands, and those same hands also wait on the tables of the Sultan's guests. For this, he receives a full thirty dollars every month. I was assured that everyone in Zanzibar takes great care not to get on the wrong side of Pera-Daudji; so very much depends on him. Naturally, thirty dollars are not enough to pay for his expensive outfits, so he needs other sources of revenue. The court jeweler of the Sultan, who declined to turn over a fixed percentage of his earnings from the Sultan's orders to the lamp cleaner, lost the entire business. Pera-Daudji blessed a more amenable rival with those orders.

It just so happened that my birthday took place during these few days. For the first time ever, I celebrated it in my homeland, where birthdays are not otherwise celebrated. The gentlemen of the squadron went out of their way to make this a truly joyful day for me, and they succeeded magnificently. I cannot be grateful enough for all their kindness. One thing, however, moved me especially oddly: The dear captain of the *Adler* arranged to have a pig slaughtered to honor me, a born Muslim, in my devout Islamic homeland. Had our most reliable local soothsayers prophesied this event to me nineteen years earlier, even as superstitious as we were, I would have laughed in their faces. What unintended humor can reveal itself in the most fateful challenges of our lives!

As seen from the sea, my impression of the city of Zanzibar was the same as before, perhaps even friendlier. There are many new houses, and the lighthouse rising in front of the palace looks quite stately with its electric lighting. The officers always called it the Sultan's "Christmas tree" because of the rings of lights wrapped around it. I was less pleased with the inner city.

With my extended time in Germany, I may well have lost touch with the conditions at home. In any event, I found the inner city in a truly sad state. From house to house, rubble was piled along the narrow, dirty streets. Ruins everywhere were filled with flourishing weeds and even hosted large trees that were growing unencumbered. No one was taking care of things. Everyone walked by with the most indifferent attitude in the world, sidestepping pools of water and piles of rocks. There were no separate depots for ash and trash, since that is apparently what the open street is for. The art of organizing a city administration must not be very easy, otherwise the Sultan—who has amply experienced the comforts of walking on clean streets in Bombay, England, and France—would have addressed this long ago. Indeed, he has introduced ice manufacturing, electric lights, a so-called railroad, and who knows what else in Zanzibar, not to mention French cooks and their cuisine.

The visible deterioration of the inner city filled me with indescribable melancholy. I could not yet know what conditions awaited me in my venerable Bet il Mtoni and the back-then barely completed Bet il Ras. The first time we went to the house where I first saw the light of day, I was utterly shocked. What a sight it was! Instead of a house, I saw a completely disintegrated ruin. No sound, no noise could pull me out of the distress that coursed through me at this wholly unexpected view. For a long time, I was unable to compose myself. One staircase was missing entirely, the other was so overgrown and decayed that it was dangerous to climb. More than half of the house lay in shambles, right where it had collapsed. Virtually all roofs were missing from the beloved baths that had once been so popular and teeming with happy people. A few were but heaps of rubble, and any parts left standing had been robbed of their roofs or floors. Everything either had fallen or was falling apart!

The whole courtyard was full of every kind of grass. Nothing remained to give the unknowing observer even the slightest hint of the former splendor of this palace.

How differently this sight impacted me than the others! My own children struck me in this moment as far too cheerful. Had I had any inkling of the devastation, I would have preferred to make my first visit here alone. From every door hanging askew and about to collapse, from the decaying masses of beams lying on top of each other, yes, from the mountain-high piles of rubble, I thought I saw figures of former residents stepping forward. For a brief period, my spirit escaped the dismal present back to the wonderful years of my youth. Only the friendly comments of the officers and the voices of my children, as they combed through various sections of the ruins with alarming dexterity, woke me from my gloomy contemplations.

I have occasionally encountered the mistaken view that Arabs show devotion to the dead by letting their former homes fall apart. That is wrong. This is not a matter of religious purpose, but rather the laissez-faire attitude of Orientals. Arabs rarely renovate their houses, and thus the weather, which is notably quick to destroy the bad limestone of the island, is left to do its damage undeterred. Once a house is run down, a new one is erected, and the old ruins are just ignored. The land itself has virtually no value.

One section of the house still contained relatively intact rooms, where my nephew Ali bin Suud, the son of Zuene, had lived until his death, out of pure attachment to the family's old homestead. He had passed away just two years earlier.

Upon entering this section, we were greeted by two Arab soldiers, who had come from Oman only a few months before. They had left their families behind in order to earn more in wealthier Zanzibar, but the situation was so bad that they sincerely regretted their trip and planned to return to Muscat as soon as possible. Both complained to me about their physical ailments and begged me to cure them. One had pain in his eyes, and the other had stomach trouble.

In response to my somewhat puzzled query, why they were even living in these ruins, I learned to my astonishment that they were not alone, but part of a troop that, unbelievable as it sounds, was charged with keeping a strict watch over the place. This measure could hardly have had a military purpose. More likely, it seemed to me, was a case of evil spirits. That said, since I have been distant from all these superstitions and their adherents for nineteen years now, I may be wrong.

I took a few grasses, some leaves, and a stone from the niche where my dear father used to say his prayers, as mementos of the place.

We were leaving the house when a well-dressed, very distinguished-looking Arab came towards us and presented himself as the first officer of the troop. He stayed with us a good while and then accompanied us to our boat. On this short stretch, however, we spotted a venerable old man, who stood in the Mtoni river to wash himself before praying. As we came closer, we realized he was totally blind. Since my arrival in Zanzibar, I had strictly avoided being the first to greet anyone, so as not to cause them any trouble. Here, for this blind person, reverence led me to make an exception. Going up to the old man, I wished him a good evening in Arabic. I hesitated to do even that small gesture. His prayer preparations were surely the least appropriate time for me, as a Christian, to bother him, and I expected at most a surly response to my greeting. He must have already realized from the foreign sounds of our distant conversation that we were European.

How astonished I was when he instead stretched out both hands, took my hand to his lips, and pressed it to his face for some time. I was extremely touched, but also embarrassed to think that he might be confusing me with someone else. I asked him, "Do you actually know me?" "As if I know you!" he responded, "Oh, you are my Mistress Salme, whom I so often held on my lap years ago when you were still a child. Oh, how happy we were to hear you had returned. God bless you and protect you, our precious dear!" With these and other words, this poor, helpless blind man said farewell from the fullness of his heart. The Arab officer, who was witness to this loyal devotion, reported to me that this long-bearded old man was the *muedden* (muezzin) of the Bet il Mtoni settlement and also had the Sultan's orders to pray at the gravesite of Ali bin Suud (to whom the Sultan had shown bitter hostility during all of his lifetime).

This last comment, in particular, caught my attention. I knew exactly how harshly and also immaturely Barghash had treated Ali bin Suud and my oldest sister Raje. Raje, the proper sister of Ali's mother, was already relatively old when she moved from Muscat to Zanzibar a number of years ago, at which time the Sultan gave her a house and an appanage. Later, as Ali bin Suud, whom Barghash hated bitterly for no good reason, lay dying in Bet il Mtoni, without any wife or children to take care of him and dependent on the mere kindness of his slaves, what would have been more natural than to have his proper Aunt Raje support him? But this approach got no support from Barghash, who had absolutely no sense for Samaritan assistance or the kind of compassion that moved Raje. To let her feel his wrath, Barghash not only withdrew her appanage, but alas! also chased her, his older sister, who could well have been his mother, ruthlessly out of her designated home. He did not show up to Ali's burial, a slight that no one bestows on even their worst enemy. And now he has someone praying at his nephew's gravesite! Stranger behavior would be hard to come by.

As long as I am commenting on the head of our family in Zanzibar, I am drawn to remove the veil from yet another story of his private life. It pains me greatly to share something bad about my own blood with the world. For even after all these years of separation from my loved ones, and despite all the heartlessness and harshness that Barghash has shown me even after I put my life and livelihood on the line for him, I still harbor the feeling of everlasting unity with my own family. Sayyid Barghash is, however, not a man to spare either his subjects or his own bloodline.

It is widely known in Zanzibar that Barghash, upon ascending to the throne in 1870, threw his next younger brother Chalife,[27] suddenly and wantonly, into the dungeon. The poor man had to languish three long years in prison in heavy iron foot rings and chains. And why? No one could say. It may well have been a fear that Chalife, as next in line for the throne, would plot treasonous plans against Barghash, just as Barghash himself had once done against Madjid.

Not until a sister, whom Barghash had also aggrieved, planned a pilgrimage to Mecca, did he feel any pangs of conscience and went to ask for her forgiveness. He feared the prospect of having a curse uttered against him directly in the holy city of the Prophet. But the sister refused to forgive him unless he set the innocent Chalife free.

And even then, Barghash continued to hound Chalife and his friends. He learned that Chalife had a loyal friend who was blessed with worldly riches. Barghash was reminded of the value he himself had placed in alliances with wealthy tribal chiefs and therefore decided to do anything necessary to cut off this support to his successor to the crown.

He had Chalife's friend summoned and spoke with him briefly along the following lines: "I have heard that you intend to sell your plantations; tell me, how much you would like for them, as I would like to buy them." "That must be a misunderstanding," came the response, "I have never intended to sell my property." "But it would be to your advantage to sell them to me; now go and consider the matter."

---

27 This half-brother, otherwise known as Khalifa bin Said, became Sultan when Sultan Barghash died, for a brief reign from 1888–1890.

A while later, this unhappy individual was again summoned and received with the following words from the Sultan: "Now tell me, how much are you charging for your plantations?" "Your Honor, I have never thought of selling them." "Well, what you think does not concern me. I will pay you 50,000 dollars for them. Here is the order for the designated amount; go and let them pay you."

Deeply dismayed, the poor soul slunk away from the man who thus serves as the "father of his people." But an even more painful surprise awaited him. When he went to claim the 50,000 dollars, he learned that the sum was payable over twenty years, and he would receive annual installments of only 2,500 dollars. And so the man was ruined, which is exactly what the Sultan had intended.

I will follow with an incident whose recounting makes my face red with shame and evokes my deepest commiseration. A malicious rumor had spread that one of my sisters was in love with someone Barghash did not want as a brother-in-law. When he heard the rumor, he confronted her directly. She protested that she knew nothing more than the next person, but in vain. The gentle brother then personally caned the blood-related sister fifty times. After this brutal treatment, the poor woman was bed-ridden for more than a month and continued to suffer from the consequences for a long time thereafter. I have no doubt he will also have someone pray at her gravesite after she dies, just like at the gravesites of his wife and Ali bin Suud.

Europeans are very frequently heard to praise the kindness of the ruler of Zanzibar. Let the reality be judged in light of the foregoing. It is in any case certain that, deep down in his heart, Barghash has never hated anything as much as the mere mention of a European.

It pains me greatly to touch on another issue here, but people would be apt to misinterpret its omission. Anyone who is aware of the situation in Zanzibar knows full well that the Sultan is the ruler only in small things, whereas the English General Consul rules everything. Even the enemies of the latter openly concede that he is one of the most adept diplomats there is. Were I still as inexperienced in the diplomatic arts and chess moves as I was ten years ago, and were I to take every friendly-sounding word at face value, then I surely would have been very happy to learn from one of the highest officers of the squadron that the English General Consul was very sorry he could do nothing to promote my interests, that he immensely regretted not having found an opportunity to meet up with the Sultan to urge my case.

It was indeed good that I did not put any stock into such assurances. I simply would have set myself up for yet another disappointment. Not long after, I heard that the good sir had just spent several days as a guest of the Sultan on one of his plantations two weeks prior, despite the isolation of harem life. I also learned of a much-used telephone line that directly connects the English General Consul with the palace of the Sultan.

From what I know, Germany has a law that subjects the unauthorized opening of private letters to harsh punishment. I do not know if England also has such a law, but if so, it would apply only to the motherland, while in the heat of Africa—the postal system in Zanzibar is English—one looks the other way. Indeed, some of my letters to Zanzibar never reached their destinations. In March of 1885, I happened to come across an article in the *Berliner Tageblatt* [28] titled "Germany, England, and Zanzibar," which clarified the matter for me:

> ...Long before the advent of German colonies, the Sultan was warned and shielded against any relations of this sort; long before the black cross on a white background [29] waved over Zanzibar, the English consulars and officers on the island—since even the Army has English instructors—always had the concern about whether letters from 'Germany' were in fact reaching the royal court....

The authorities leveraged everything they could to rile the population against me. A few officers asked me to help them select and procure jewelry for their loved ones back home, and so we made several trips to a goldsmith, who, without our knowledge, happened to do work for the Sultan as well.

As soon as the Sultan found out about this through his general factotum, Pera-Daudji, whose job it is to inform him of all news, he summoned the jeweler and dumped the full measure of his wrath on him for having dared to sell something to us. This normally meek businessman calmly answered this rage by saying he would have been ashamed to turn away the sister of his ruler from his store. The Sultan was not at all pleased by this response and threatened to withdraw his very substantial patronage. Even this did not phase the goldsmith. He retorted that he was already done with Zanzibar and would prefer, as soon as possible, to return to his homeland. To steer clear of any trouble, as he also wished not to appear unkind to me, he then closed up shop for the rest of his time on the island.

---

28 Major German language newspaper that published from 1872 to 1939.
29 The flag of German warships that carried the white-rimmed, black Iron Cross of the German Empire.

Similarly, it was thought that I would be harshly punished by a strict prohibition against donkey owners renting their animals to us. A few of my former slaves, who dared approach me out of long-standing devotion, were imprisoned for this demonstration of their loyalty.

These and similarly inane measures were not uncommon, but produced the exact opposite result. The verdict of the crowd came in their own words: *pija kana kasi ja watoto, Bibi,* meaning "he is behaving just like a little child, oh mistress!"

As I was approaching Zanzibar, I had been very unsure what reception would await me. That my brother would respect Germany's wishes, I had no doubt, and so it was. That he would hardly be kind towards me, at most putting on a good face in deference to Germany, for that I was also prepared. The ugly behavior he had shown my other siblings truly gave me no reason to expect any friendly outreach from him. But it was a different question as to how the population would react to my sudden appearance. To my greatest joy, I can simply repeat that I received the warmest reception. Arabs, Hindus, Banyans, and natives, they all pressed me over and over again to please stay in Zanzibar.

This fortified my belief anew that there was no way that religious hatred toward my person was at stake. One day, I encountered two Arabs, with whom I began to converse. When another person pointed out that they were relatives of mine—I had not recognized them—I told them, if I had known, I would never have engaged in conversation, being so unsure about how my relatives stood towards me under the current circumstances. They immediately responded that, to them, I was still my father's daughter. And when I touched upon my religion, one of them countered that this had been predestined as my fate from the beginning of time. "Yes, the God that has separated you and us from the homeland is the same God that all people praise and adore; it is through his mighty will that you returned to us, and we rejoice in it. Is that not so? Will you and your children now stay here forever?"

Such demonstrations of love and devotion have tided me over many a difficult hour, along with the blissful feeling of having seen my homeland once more. They have indeed made my trip a fount of delight for the rest of my life, and I can forever give thanks and praise to the Almighty for his goodness!

Not without great sadness in my heart did I say farewell to my homeland for a second time, and all my beloved, whom I had to leave again, felt the same.

There is no better ending for my book than to share such sentiments from my circle of friends as they appeared in an Arabic farewell letter that reached me in Europe, even if its literal translation loses much of its tenderness and originality of expression. It reads:

You left and did not let me know;
That tore my heart and filled me with all-consuming fire.
Oh, that I had wrapped my arms around your neck, inseparably, when
    you left us!
I would have let you sit on my head and walk on my eyes![30]

You live in my heart, and in leaving,
You have made my soul suffer like never before.
My body is emaciated, and my tears relentless;
One after another rolls down my cheeks like the waves of the sea.

Oh, Lord of the universe! Bring us together before we die,
If only for a single day.
Should we live, we will come together!
Should we die, the Immortal remains.

Oh, if I were a bird, I would longingly follow you;
But how can a bird fly, whose wings are clipped?

---

30   An Arabic expression for "I would do anything for you!"

In the foregoing pages I have endeavored to draw a picture of Oriental life and its customs, especially with regard to life at Court, and the position of woman in the East. Some of the subjects contained in this book may be thought to possess less general interest, but, as part of the whole, my description would have been incomplete without them. It must be remembered that I have not been writing a novel or a tale of fiction, but the faithful recollections connected with the life of my native land in all its phases.

I have naturally felt tempted to exalt such of our customs and institutions which, in my opinion, are deserving of commendation, I have, on the other hand, never endeavored to excuse or disguise others which, in the eyes of more highly-cultured nations at least, may justly be ridiculed or thought objectionable; and if, in drawing comparisons between foreign and Eastern customs, I have not shrunk from speaking my mind openly and candidly, and have sometimes sent home a shaft, I may aver, in justice to myself, that I have by no means spared myself, but have readily and rankly admitted the errors into which I fell.

Even in this century of railroads and rapid communication, so much ignorance still exists among European nations of the customs and institutions of their own immediate neighbors, that one can hardly wonder how little is actually known about those of races far removed. The ablest and most conscientious writer must always, to some degree, fall short of giving a perfectly precise and faithful picture of a foreign nation; and in the case of an Eastern nation, he will of course, find himself heavily handicapped out of all proportion when family and domestic life generally is so jealously guarded from the gaze of the outer world.

Having been born and bred in the East, I am in a position to set down the unvarnished reflection of my Oriental experiences—of its high life and its low life—to speak of many peculiarities, and lift the veil from things that are always hidden from profane eyes. This, I hope, will constitute the main value of my book, and my object will have been fully gained if I have been able to contribute my share, and above all, if I have succeeded in removing many misconceptions and distortions current about the East.

My task is done—and, in conclusion, it only remains for me to say farewell to my kind readers, who have followed me through these pages, and who, I trust, will always bear a friendly memory for one whose life has already gathered so rich a store of changes and vicissitudes.

᚛

---

31 Unedited English original added to the 1888 Ward and Downey London edition of the *Memoirs*.

ON CONTRIBUTIONS

Zanzibar is a small island, and Oman is a small country, but they shared a remarkable nineteenth-century history, including as recorded in Sayyida Salme's writings. She is not usually counted among the explorers of the time, but nonetheless stands with those who charted new territory. In so doing, she crossed boundaries, especially boundaries wrought by systems and institutions, in ways that still speak to us. We can hear her voice as an enduring contribution—ringing out to us, recounting, questioning, probing. We can see her light shining into the twenty-first century, encouraging us to stay centered and step forward.

Undertaking this translation expanded my own exploration of her legacy. Among those who supported this journey, my gratitude goes first to Professor Emeri van Donzel, who put the map in my hand. From his base at Leiden University, he spent decades researching Sayyida Salme's past and impact. His groundbreaking book, *An Arabian Princess Between Two Worlds* (1993), has been at my side and remains the seminal academic resource for anyone wanting to know more on the subject. In this connection, too, we are beholden to the Oriental Institute and the Netherlands Institute for the Near East (NINO) in Leiden, which over the decades safeguarded materials that were provided by the family to their good friend there, Professor Christiaan Snouck Hurgronje.

In that tradition of friendship, I was fortunate to discover Anita Keizers, subject librarian of the Ancient Near East at the NINO. For the past decade, she has been the custodian of much of the family's *Nachlass*, including the special Sayyida Salme bookcase. As a loving caretaker and our best resource, she has also become a kind of hub for Sayyida Salme inquiries. Through her, I met Freiburg-based researcher Godwin Kornes, who not only shared his scholarship, photos, and enthusiasm, but also led us to a branch of our extended family, the von Brands, descended from Sayyida Salme's daughter Antonie.[32] Small world, they live nearby, and Alexander has graciously shared his well-preserved family treasures with us, including some of the photos in this book. And that completed the trio along with Michael Bauer and his family, who are descended from Sayyida Salme's son Rudolph and reached out to us many years ago—all three branches having found their way to the United States, now reconnected here.

I also give great thanks for pre-release reviews of the full manuscript by Kathleen Ridolfo, the director of the Sultan Qaboos Cultural Center who has done so much to build Omani community in our area and across the United States, and by Eija Pehu, a former World Bank colleague and dear friend who has always been there for my books. In addition, I am grateful for feedback from Anita Keizers, Godwin Kornes, Andrea Nour, and Inga Harting, as I finalized these pages. I am also grateful to Torrence Royer, who has collected historical materials for decades and happily shared what he had.

My deep gratitude extends as well to the tried-and-true duo that has made self-publishing such a joy. While I was focused on bringing out Sayyida Salme's voice, they gave me the tools, and their professionalism and experience, to let me realize my own vision and voice. To my copy editor, the forever upbeat Lauri Scherer of LSF Editorial, and my graphic designer, the incomparable, indefatigable Joe Bernier of Bernier Graphics—thank you both for all your help in docking this ship.

As a family project, I have my family to thank, above all. My first mate on this journey has been my mother Ursula Stumpf, with whom this effort has been a shared joy. As a wonderful partner, she has been ever ready to help, ever diligent, ever thoughtful. Being able to create this book with her direct engagement has buoyed the project from inception to completion and made it all the more meaningful. I am also ever so grateful to Max, my wonderful son. He knows what

---

32 Antonie Brandeis is the subject of Godwin Kornes' current research project, which is based on her ethnographic Micronesia collection at the Museum Natur und Mensch in Freiburg, Germany, to be shared in a forthcoming book.

it took and always gave me full space and support. This marks his third book as my inhouse illustrator, now also mapmaker, and I have loved having him join in. Max does not need this translation to read his remarkable ancestor's story, but with Salme in his name, I now also give him this edition, much as she gave her original account to her children.

Credit also goes to my father Walter Stumpf, for putting the wind in my sails. His vision got us to Zanzibar in 1998, the trip from which all else followed. At a time when tourism was just beginning, we were the first of Sayyida Salme's descendants to set foot on the island in almost seventy years. Also noteworthy is my grandfather Erich Schwinge, who embraced the Arab side of the family and took up the mantle when his wife and her sister died so early in life. To keep the legacy alive, he put everything in place for republication of the *Memoirs* in the 1970s, but then refrained in full respect for the family's preferences.

This book is dedicated to my brother Martin, who promoted and pursued Sayyida Salme's memory more than anyone in my immediate family, including by working hard on a documentary film of her life. I still use his heavily notated copy of Professor van Donzel's book. One of my last memories of Martin was the two of us handing out little handcrafted packages—more than a hundred of them—with sunflower seeds wrapped in a paper as a gesture of peace and appreciation. One of my favorite experiences of all time, it was the summer of 2005, when the Smithsonian's Folklife Festival on the Washington Mall featured Oman. This book is in all ways indebted to Martin's inspiration.

In that same spirit of peace and appreciation, and recognizing the support and rapport of her worldwide audience, I hope Sayyida Salme herself would have considered this publication to be in her honor, as I have intended.

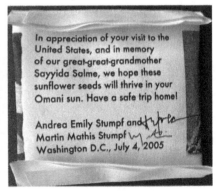

In appreciation of your visit to the United States, and in memory of our great-great-grandmother Sayyida Salme, we hope these sunflower seeds will thrive in your Omani sun. Have a safe trip home!

Andrea Emily Stumpf and
Martin Mathis Stumpf
Washington D.C., July 4, 2005

ON FAMILY

Sayyida Salme is my great-great-grandmother in a line that runs straight through the women: from her youngest daughter Rosa to Rosa's daughter Emily to Emily's daughter Ursula, who is my mother. The small percentage of Arab blood that links me to the historical Zanzibari Sultanate and the current Omani Sultanate may have limited biological significance, but is unambiguous. We are five generations over a century and a half.

Almost a dozen Omani Sultans later, the story remains interesting in part because my mother and both the late Omani Sultan Qaboos and the current Sultan Haitham are distant cousins on the extended Al Bu Said family tree. But when Sayyida Salme became Christian— taking a Christian name and a Christian husband on that memorable day in 1867 in Aden—she became an infidel. That was enough to banish her from the royal family, especially by her half-brother Sultan Barghash, who also found it politically and financially convenient to disown her.

In our particular case, the family ties were further attenuated during and after World War II. Rosa's immediate family remained in Germany, even though the Third Reich was no time to refer to non-Aryan ancestry.[33] Not long after the war, two generations of our family line passed away in less than two years, creating a generational gap. Rosa died in February 1948, preceded by her youngest daughter Berta in December 1946 and followed by her other daughter Emily in July 1948.[34] My mother was eleven at the time, too young to have learned much of the legacy. Her father preserved the special memory, some family contacts, and much-cherished original editions of the *Memoirs*, but beyond that, my mother grew up with little direct exposure to the family's unusual past.

Sayyida Salme
(1844–1924)

⋅ℳ⋅

Rosalie (Rosa)
(1870–1948)

⋅ℳ⋅

Emily
(1903–1948)

⋅ℳ⋅

Ursula
(1936–)

⋅ℳ⋅

Andrea
(1962–)

---

33 Rosa's brother Rudolph and his family, including his Jewish wife, had left Germany long before. Rosa's sister Antonie stayed in Germany, while one of her daughters moved to America with her husband in 1936. Antonie was tragically killed by the British bombing of Bad Oldesloe in 1945, near the end of the war.

34 With Antonie's death in 1945 and Rudolph's death in 1946, all the author's children died in these years.

As a result, some of our current connection to the family is more sentimental than personal. The link to Rosa's ancestry is perhaps most evident in the names. With us, the Christian Emily, as in Emily Ruete, abounds. It is also the first name of my mother's mother, my cousin, my niece, and the middle name of my mother and myself. Not until I had my own child did I appreciate the significance of naming. But rather than follow our tradition, I felt truly privileged to reach back to the original name, Salme, as a middle name for my child. To my knowledge, this has happened only once before, when Rudolph honored his mother by naming his daughter Olga Salme.[35] Perhaps more to the point, though, our current connection is also more deliberate. Like many others who have valued Sayyida Salme over the years, we too are circling back in history to get to know her.

On the subject of family, a few additional aspects are worth noting. For one, within the scope of Sayyida Salme's life, family was hard to come by. Although she grew up with dozens of half-brothers and half-sisters,[36] this was a family in the broadest sense, as she amply describes in her *Memoirs*. Telling, of course, is her reference to "the father" (*der Vater*),[37] a label that sounds more honorific than intimate. He was a father shared by scores of wives and children, not to mention the people of two countries.

More poignantly, though, Sayyida Salme went from being an orphan at age 15 to a widow at age 25. In between lay only three precious years of a partnered life with a happy, nuclear family, while the before and after were replete with challenge. Sayyida Salme not only faced the hurdles of making it on her own, especially as a girl and woman in a man's world, but did so in contexts that were unusually politicized; and, once in Germany, also completely foreign. In the time before she met her husband, she spent her teen years in the harem with no father or mother looking out for her, and with allegiances forming fast and furious around her. It has always made sense to me that she was still unmarried at the ripe old age of twenty-two, open to alternatives, possibly looking for a way out. And in the period after reaching Germany, she has given us enough clues[38] to know that her subsequent life took its toll beyond anything she could have anticipated.

---

35 In full, Olga Salme Mathilde Benvenuta Said-Ruete. Notably Rudolph's daughter was born in England outside the more restrictive German name approval process that might have disallowed Salme. Rudolph also honored his father when naming his son, Werner Heinrich Mathissen Said-Ruete.

36 Thirty-six sons and daughters were said to be living when Sayyid Said died in 1856, out of a purported hundred or so that were born from some seventy-five *sarari* (concubines).

37 *Vater* is capitalized in the original publication, as is the case with all German nouns, but potentially also in a titular fashion. For this translation, I debated whether to capitalize the word in English as well, but decided to stay neutral by keeping the "father" lowercased.

38 Many details appear in her *Briefe nach der Heimat* (Letters Home), which she wrote after the *Memoirs*, but which remained unpublished until the 1990s. I expect to publish a new English translation of this manuscript in 2023.

But we can also consider Djilfidan, Sayyida Salme's mother, the little we know of her from the *Memoirs*. She, too, was orphaned, although much younger and more tragically, bereft of her entire Circassian family by rampaging Russian mercenaries. The more I understand of her origins, the more I appreciate my own link to a people that no longer has its place on a map, of which Djilfidan's extinguished family is but one of a million and more stories. Circassian women were prized for their fair-skinned beauty, and Djilfidan was apparently just old enough to be trafficked. Or maybe there was another layer. Rather than purchased by the Sultan, perhaps she was gifted to him.[39] That seems plausible, since she joined the harem at an unusually young age, still a child herself, and grew up with children of the other *sarari*. The Sultan would have been a father figure to her before he made her a mother.

We can also recall that "family" among Arab royals (perhaps all royals) could be brutal. As a rule, governing was a male enterprise, and there was only one Sultan among the many sons (or two when they split Oman and Zanzibar). Sayyid Said himself had to eliminate his usurper cousin to become Sultan. After Sayyid Said died, his son Barghash had designs on his older brother Madjid. Madjid, in claiming Zanzibar, in turn defied his older brother Tueni in Oman. Even a century later, the young Qaboos had to sideline his father Said bin Taimur to take the crown. Although Sayyida Salme was born in a prosperous and stable period, the older she got, the more fragmented and fraught the family became. Loss of the beloved patriarch led to infighting right at the time that Sayyida Salme reached the age of agency and became a player herself.

That Sayyida Salme's Zanzibari family meant a lot to her goes almost without saying. Even so, we can note that in the *Memoirs*, her shortest chapter is about her marriage union and her longest is about the family rupture.[40] She does not dwell on what it was to fall in love with her husband, but gives us page after page on how the coup attempt unfolded. Memories seared in her mind, the saga was still deeply present a decade later when she wrote that account. She does not name her husband even once in the entire book, but Barghash is named a hundred times. Seemingly, the shadow cast over her life by her original family, not just politically and existentially, but also emotionally, was as long as the one cast by what became—and became of—her new family. We might say she freed

---

39 As suggested by our friend Dr. Abdallah Daar, who, in addition to providing great support on my first trip to Oman, had researched the question in relation to his own family.

40 Sayyida Salme would have preferred good relations with all, but ended up choosing sides in the power play and then later, having extended a hand to Madjid, being deemed by Chole and Barghash to have chosen. Such hard lines were clearly not conducive to family harmony, as such yet another example of that elusive middle ground: *In my opinion, the happy middle has not yet been found anywhere.* (Memoirs, *page 132*)

herself of the one to find the other, but there was no freeing herself from the memory of her original home and homeland.

On a more personal note, as far as family goes, where I see Sayyida Salme in the vanguard of feminism in her time, I see myself as a classic "sign of the times" in my own. Both of us single mothers, both shaped by our settings, we both wrote our own scripts. It was far easier for me than for her, which says something about society's progress. She chose to follow the love of her life and then had to deal with the rejection and isolation that followed. I chose a career path and still found my way into family, becoming a so-called—socially acceptable—single mother by choice. It is not lost on me that Sayyida Salme's grounding became her children, as for me with my child, despite the very different circumstances. To know my child is in her line of children, for whom she originally wrote her *Memoirs*, gives me a deeper connection to her and greater meaning to this family project.

ON FATE

I believe some readers may read the word "fate" and feel some pity towards me, or if nothing else, shrug their shoulders. But one must not forget that the author was a Muslim and raised this way. And I am of course telling the story of an Arab life, an Arab household, that is, a real Arab home, where two concepts in particular were as yet unfamiliar: the word "chance" and materialism. A Muslim not only recognizes his God as his creator and keeper, but also feels the presence of the Lord at all times. He is certain that it is not his will, but the will of the Lord that comes to pass, in all things, large and small. (Memoirs, page 14)

Fate weaves its way throughout Sayyida Salme's *Memoirs* like a red thread that appears and reappears at consequential moments. Predestined fate is at work when the tracks are shifted, as in German *die Weichen werden gestellt*, and thus becomes both the explanation and extrapolation of events. In her story, it was fate that determined their move to Bet il Watoro; fate that took father, mother, and many others, but spared her; fate that brought her to the city; but also fate that let others excuse her transgression, namely her apostasy, thus making it an act *of* the Almighty, not against Him.

Of course, in our multicultural society, fate belongs to the beholder, as does its corollary, faith. Sayyida Salme tells us that fate is part and parcel of being a Muslim, woven into everyday life. Being Ibadi, her form of Islam, meant deferring all power to Allah's omniscience and omnipotence. But even after the author becomes Christian, we continue to feel the imprint of fate on her life. It is a stark exercise to draw a line through Sayyida Salme's most fateful span of years: finding Bububu, losing Bububu, moving to the city, meeting a German merchant, falling in love, bearing a child, losing a child, bearing three more children, losing her husband, losing her assets and inheritance—incidents that laid down the tracks for what came next, with no way back. What is given and taken in each of these strokes hits high and low pitches that are octaves apart.

Fate in this story can feel not only fatalistic, but also quite fatal—especially where medicine is mystery, and fate is how people, as she says, come to grips with death. Even so, with her mother and father already gone, what a calamitous

239

tragedy it was that Sayyida Salme's first born died less than a month after her baptism and betrothal, while they were still on their journey to Germany! This little life that precipitated her escape from the island was now gone, less than a year later. How could Sayyida Salme not have taken this as a sign from God? She never writes about it, and that is comment enough.[41]

Fast forward just a few years. What are the chances that her beloved husband, to whom Sayyida Salme had hitched her entire destiny in an entirely new place, culture, language, family, religion, and all—no way back—would die so tragically at the prime age of thirty-one? What a crazy fluke of an accident! It was not the first time Sayyida Salme felt the helpless despair that beckons thoughts of fate. She lost both her mother and husband by watching them disintegrate, painfully, unfathomably in a matter of days, with nothing she could do, even told to stay away as they succumbed. By the time Sayyida Salme starts writing her *Memoirs* several years later, her three children have become her one and all. And yet, as she alludes in her Preface, and as she has learned all too well, nothing is assured, not even her chance to tell them her story unless she writes it while she can.

Indeed, Sayyida Salme describes an early incident that almost cost her her life, when she rode straight into a twisted, bent-over palm while horse racing her brother, but—as if by a miracle—threw herself backwards in the last seconds. Such fate! And then on the very next page, we read about her mother's story, how her mother's parents were murdered by marauding mercenaries, who then rode off with her brother and sister, never to be seen again, while she lived on. More fate! What let Djilfidan escape death at that perilous moment and live a long and comfortable life thereafter? Could one even say she had a better life for being forced into servitude as a child? The question may test our understanding of slavery and society, especially because we can never prove counterfactuals. We might more readily conclude that none of this, these *Memoirs*, your attention, and least of all me, would have happened if she and her daughter had not been spared by this hand of fate.

When fate determines life's events, and things are pre-ordained, then everything is what it is, beyond us. In this way, fate is the foil of free will. But this letting go to the Lord may also prompt believers to look for signs that validate their

---

41 Not until the death certificate of their infant Heinrich was discovered by Heinz Schneppen in a Hamburg archive (*Staatsarchiv*) did the puzzle piece fall into place. Schneppen served as German Ambassador to Tanzania from 1993 to 1996 and published the first German edition of Sayyida Salme's/Emily Ruete's *Briefe nach der Heimat* (Letters Home) in 1999. My new English translation of *Briefe nach der Heimat* is due to appear in 2023.

circumstances and choices. Like, perhaps, the very devout Djilfidan more readily accepting her lot as part of the harem—and accepting it all the more when bestowed with a free and royal child. Or like the intensely pious Barghash believing narcissistically in his own destiny as Sultan—and believing it all the more once he finally got there. It is etymologically significant that in the German phrase for "it is fate"—per the *Memoirs*, *es ist bestimmt*—the word *bestimmt* has a double meaning as "it is certain." And so, invoking fate lets us move forward with more certainty, indeed, more confidence, less confusion, less concern.

For Sayyida Salme, whether fate or free will, she also bore a free heart.[42] At first blush, this is an early multicultural tale of what we do for love, long before such crossovers were accepted, much less in vogue. But sometimes we are propelled by forces beyond our choosing. Perhaps it was just such a love that led Sayyida Salme to leave home, where, in her words, a union with her beloved was impossible. And then it became a love for her budding child and even love of self, to escape for their lives. But there are also early clues that Sayyida Salme was headstrong and independent. As a child, she learned gun shooting and cock fighting, becoming "half an Amazon." She was not much interested in needlework and lace making, and she was a prankster. And somewhere along the way, she probably pined for a life beyond the narrow and rigid confines of cloistered royalty and sequestered womanhood.

To me, the fact that she secretly taught herself to write is the most important clue. She was ambitious and capable and non-conformist. She knew writing for girls was taboo, but that did not stop her. "When word got out, I was denounced in the strongest terms, but not much bothered" is one of the most telling sentences in the *Memoirs*. And then come to find out, this special skill was in demand; it even elevated her to an indispensable role. For a young teen, it must have been quite the flattering headrush to become the scribe for such an important intrigue, whether she liked the plan or not.

One could say, though, that it all began with Sayyida Salme's birth into royalty. This quirk of fate was all the more significant with her coming from both royalty and slavery. Unlike the Americas, Arab society privileged this combination with full ranking, full royalty, full rights of inheritance (and even subsequent freedom for her mother). And so, she woke up in the harem household every day knowing she was at the top of the hierarchy, not for anything she did— just by fate—surrounded by second class eunuchs and supported by third class servers and slaves. But what did it all mean anyhow? Moving across extremes,

---

42 Notably, one of Sayyida Salme's themes is to let us "not forget the heart for the head." (*Memoirs*, page 60)

from lowest to highest, it is strange to see what fate wrought. Her mother, a slave, ultimately lived a life of comfort, but she, a princess, found a life of strain.

We start the story in a time and place of fairy tales—once upon a time long ago, there lived a princess. . . . Coming from such a world, Sayyida Salme can feel almost mystical to us today. But in confounding such a world, she becomes inspirational. It is a real life, whose fate, like history, may not repeat, but can give us rhymes. She, as author and narrator, primarily worked off of contrasts— East to West, Muslim to Christian, women to men—in other words, what is different? We, as readers, instinctively seek meaning in her life and writings. Coming many generations later, when differences are the default, we seek the parallels—what is the same? For all that has changed between then and now, it is surprisingly easy to find rhyming couplets between her time and ours.

It is perhaps my fate—the red thread that lets me connect the dots—that I am here, reaching back to give voice to her life through mine. Should these pages also resonate with rhyme for you, dear Reader, perhaps you feel your fate here, too.

ON CONTROVERSY

The subject of this chapter is controversial. I realize I will not make many friends with my views, but consider it my duty to share them. I have come across too much unawareness everywhere on this question. Even the more informed people too often overlook that this is about more than genuine humane efforts by Europeans, considering that they take place against a backdrop of hidden political interests. (Memoirs, *page 165)*

Sayyida Salme says it herself, in the opening words of her chapter on Slavery. She knows she is treading on fraught ground with her views, but is nonetheless compelled to add to the conversation, rather than stay silent. I believe that is to her credit. She knew she had an unusual, indeed unique, perspective. Writing to a European public, her lens and pen drew from the local slave society she had personally experienced. Clearly, that personal connection colored her views, for better or worse, but also came from a place of genuine concern about her community. And, in contrast to the prevalent, colonial, missionary, West-over-East attitudes of the time, that voice arguably deserved to be heard.

We can see Sayyida Salme and her *Memoirs* as part of a difficult contemporary conversation about societal transformation, while still today flatly rejecting some of her views. We can even call her racist, while still appreciating that she chose to use her voice. There is always more nuance to the matter, and Sayyida Salme was not afraid to go there. She prods her audience to become more aware. She makes us consider that multiple truths can co-exist.

This is not to excuse or defend Sayyida Salme's views, particularly on race and slaves, only to put them in context. Rather than cherry-pick controversial statements to discredit her wholesale—what some have done and what others may call cancel culture—I suggest that both she and her story are more complex and layered. Indeed, there is much to study here, as the flourishing scholarship that draws from the *Memoirs* would indicate.[43]

---

43 As one indicator, according to Google Scholar, citations of "Memoirs of an Arabian Princess" more than doubled each decade from 1971 to 2020 (2, 6, 29, 58, 128). A Google search at time of publication brought up over 12,000 results.

Exactly this position was taken by the expert opinion recently commissioned by the Free and Hanseatic City of Hamburg, where Sayyida Salme spent her first years in Germany. In 2019, the city elected to name one of its open spaces in honor of Emily Ruete, Sayyida Salme's Christian name. After the street sign went up, some individuals filed a complaint on account of her racist beliefs and writings. The sign was taken down, but an expert opinion was also sought to evaluate the complaint and give the matter a full and fair hearing. Hamburg has been exemplary in running this process openly and transparently, with the expert opinion readily and globally available online. Reading the opinion, city government may have realized that Sayyida Salme cannot be boxed into one category, and for now, the matter remains under consideration:

> In the Salme/Ruete biography, the categories of gender, class, and race overlap in various combinations. Her [cross-continental] migrations add to the other different, above-referenced roles of a woman, who, as a princess and migrant, author, single mother, and anti-black racist, that was cosmopolitan and excluded, exoticized and privileged, was also—as a self-determining subject of her own rights—a feminist.

> The description of Salme/Ruete is complicated by the effort to situate her in the international colonial (today North-South) relationships, the various contexts, and the racialized black-white hierarchy in which she lived.

> .... The censure cops of the global North that decide, rightly or wrongly, how people like Salme/Ruete should be remembered risk serving a Eurocentric point of view. A decision to rename [the location] is no invitation to dialogue and exchange, but rather an imposition of a final judgment that does not allow for nuance with respect to the forced category of race and instead reduces Salme/Ruete's identity to her racist statements.

> Salme/Ruete's works are, by contrast, the first documented non-white female voice from the global South that addresses Germany (Europe) and Zanzibar (Africa). She could be remembered as such, with all her ambiguities and ambivalences, in that her writings are read as a window into German colonialism, a display of racism, and a report of the challenging, even impossible, integration into nineteenth-century German society.[44]

---

44 „*Gutachten: Ambivalente Identitäten—Salme/Ruete, koloniales und kolonialisiertes Subjekt zugleich,*" pages 14, 22, by Tania Mancheno at the University of Hamburg (2021). At: Microsoft Word - Gutachten_SalmeRuete_2022_Text_ed.docx (hamburg.de)

Sayyida Salme was no stranger to controversy. She acted controversially and spoke on controversial subjects, even as what counts as "controversial" has shifted over time. Views that were mainstream then, in both East and West, like racial hierarchies, are unacceptable now. But other views that were unacceptable then, like choosing to reject Islam, are currently accepted, even validated as religious freedom. Clearly, society is not done working out complex topics.

Conversion to Christianity

For all her striking behavior, Sayyida Salme's most controversial act was her apostasy, when she became a Christian to marry her husband. The most severe and sustained consequences came from her Sultan brother Barghash. Despite Sayyida Salme's many efforts and entreaties, both directly and through others, he never forgave her infidelity and never allowed a reconciliation. Surely she was crestfallen when her brother Barghash replaced her Sultan brother Madjid, who died at age thirty-six shortly after her own husband, both deaths so early and untimely. It was another blow to her connections to home. Whereas Sultan Madjid had reached out with gifts (unbeknownst to her at the time), Sultan Barghash proved implacable.

Not only did Sultan Barghash reject Sayyida Salme out of hand, but his recalcitrance abnegated the unwavering loyalty she had shown him and his cause during the failed coup attempt. She had been an indispensable figure in his aggrandizing venture—as scribe, financier, plotter, rescuer, and more, putting her relations, reputation, even life at great risk. But Islam was both his conviction and cover. Sultan Barghash seemed so personally offended by her rapprochement with his archenemy Madjid, the Sultan he had sought to depose, that he could not get beyond his own emotions. Her reconciliation with Madjid seemed to offend Barghash as much as her conversion to Christianity. Later, Barghash's dogged piety was also in stark contrast to the overwhelmingly enthusiastic reception she received from the island population upon her return at long last after nineteen years. He could not stand the outpouring and instead cracked down on his people. And yet, as she reports, the throngs were not to be deterred, even at pain of punishment.

Sayyida Salme was perhaps her own harshest critic. Caught in her circumstances, she remained unsettled: "I left my homeland as a complete Arab and good Muslim, and what am I today?" With her heart on her sleeve, she started to answer—her famous answer: "A poor Christian and somewhat more than half a German!"—but then deleted it.[45] We can speculate about why she struck that response in her edits, but we can also feel the anguish in her conflicted soul.

Faith was no less important to her than it was to Barghash. Originally an unquestioning Muslim, and then persisting as a Christian despite encouragement and even financial inducements from her Zanzibari family and friends, she spent a lifetime close to her Lord, seeking Him as much after the conversion as she did before. She never lost her faith, no matter how much the circumstances changed.

But having transgressed, Sayyida Salme was no longer considered part of the family.[46] For some, it remains a point of sensitivity. For others, views may be softening. The Omani/Zanzibari Sultanate has historically shown great tolerance for different religions and is a strong proponent of religious freedom today.[47]

We can see that for someone like Sayyida Salme, religion was not an open, inconsequential choice at the time, nor was marriage. Clearly, Sayyida Salme broke two cardinal rules, knowingly and boldly, when she chose her husband and thus her religion. But just as clearly, today we can see that those rules deserve more criticism than her behavior.

Views on Slavery and Africans

In our present day, the greater controversy is about Sayyida Salme's racism. Today she is criticized for her acceptance of slavery and her denigration of black Africans. Both aspects merit a closer look.

In the years since Sayyida Salme left Zanzibar, the anti-slavery movement had continued to build in Europe. To a shocking degree, the interior of East Africa

---

45 The translated version in this book reflects her latest views by including all edits that appeared in her handmarked copy of the original German publication that was digitalized by the Leiden University Libraries and resides in the Netherlands Institute for the Near East at NINO SR 613 a-b.

46 Rudolph Said-Ruete tried to engage the British on behalf of his mother starting in 1914, but not until 1923, less than a year before she died, was she finally granted a small annuity by the Zanzibari Sultanate. In 1932, Sultan Khalifa also recognized Rudolph as the grandson of Sultan Said bin Sultan and a member of the royal family, conferring on him the title "Sayyid" at his request. Nevertheless, Sultan Khalifa later declined to invite him to the bicentennial of the Al Bu Said dynasty in 1941, explaining to the acting British resident that "the elopement of Mr. Ruete's mother was and still is regarded by the Arabs as a shameful affair and they prefer not to be reminded of it." Emeri van Donzel, *An Arabian Princess Between Two Worlds*, pages 105, 119, 125, 131 (1993).

47 The majority of Omanis and many Zanzibaris follow the Ibadi strain of Islam, which is distinct from Sunni and Shia Islam and is known to promote social harmony and tolerance. On a web page entitled "Religious Freedom," Oman's Foreign Ministry assures "the freedom of religious belief, worship and education" under the Basic Statute of the State, naming Christians among the protected citizens and referring to Oman's "long history as a multicultural society."

was being increasingly raided and ravaged. The East African slave trade, which Sayyida Salme rightly criticized, grew to horrifying dimensions. However, far from simply being "Arab" slavery, as some made it seem, it involved a wide network of players, in large measure by Africans upon Africans, and propelled by market forces that fed profiteering financiers, Zanzibari coffers, labor-needy plantations, and European appetites for grains, spices, ivory, and other commodities.[48]

Ironically, and tragically, British anti-slavery efforts appear to have spurred, not deterred, increased slave trade in Zanzibar. At first, as demand for labor increased, prices of slaves went up, which fueled more caravans into the hinterlands, which in turn fueled the export slave market. But when the British tamped down on slave exports with the treaty of 1845, under which Sayyid Said agreed to limit legal slave trade to routes between East Africa and Zanzibar,[49] the slave movement was concentrated and prices in Zanzibar fell. At the same time, to keep the Sultanate from complete demise, Britain pushed for the export slave trade to be replaced by "legitimate commerce," which included cloves, rubber, and copal, all export products that required extensive slave labor, and—helped by the cheap cost of slaves—the sale of slaves surged again. Trade in domestic slaves eventually exceeded export slave trade, as the rise of Africa-sourced farm commodities turned more Africans into commodities.[50]

Despite this broad web of complicity, it was easy, even trendy, for British, German, and other anti-slavery crusaders to criticize from West to East, enlightened to backward, and assume a certain superiority. Zanzibaris had grounds to look skeptically at European imperial agendas, and British anti-

---

48 To underscore how intertwined these forces were, 1834 was both the year the British Slavery Abolition Act ended slave trade in the Indian Ocean and the year Sayyid Said bin Sultan entered into a commercial treaty with the United States. To offset British pressure to end slavery in Zanzibar, the U.S. treaty brought in major quantities of cotton produced by African slaves in America, whose currency was used in East Africa to purchase more slaves. Clifford Pereira, "'Naturalists,' 'Explorers,' and Imperialists: German Ambitions in the Horn of Africa and the Anti-Slavery Movement," p. 9, on www.academia.edu; Steven Feierman, "A Century of Ironies in East Africa (c. 1780–1890)," in P. Curtin, S. Feierman, L. Thompson, and J. Vansina, *African History: From Earliest Times to Independence*, p. 357 (1995).

49 Given Zanzibar's pivotal role in the slave trade, some even recognized Sayyid Said as an exemplary figure in the anti-slavery crusade. "His stalwart and fearless personality prompted him, at great moral and practical inconvenience, and even danger to himself, to identify himself openly with Great Britain (who enjoyed no co-operation from other western powers at that time) in her determined efforts for the suppression of the African slave trade...." Foreword by Major-General Sir Percy Cox (p. ix) in Rudolph Said-Ruete's *Said bin Sultan (1791–1856)—Ruler of Oman and Zanzibar: His Place in the History of Arabia and East Africa* (1929).

50 Cosmo Rana-Iozzi, "Why did slave trading intensify in the nineteenth century, and with what consequences for East African society?," on www.academia.edu; Steven Feierman, see footnote 48, pp. 352–76.

slavery treaties, in particular. This vulnerability bore itself out over time, as Germany and Britain struck inland deals, and Zanzibar increasingly came under British debt and control. Indeed, there are those who cite a continuing history of British repression of Arab culture, who also think those forces were hard at work in efforts to tarnish Arabs, and antagonize Africans against them, leading up to the rampaging Zanzibar revolution in 1964 and its aftermath.[51]

Without the benefit of such hindsight, Sayyida Salme certainly had her own reasons to attribute ill will to colonial powers, starting with Great Britain. It was, admittedly, the British who originally helped her escape the island, but also the British who kept her from her Sultan brother, callously strung her along, and then pathetically reneged. Although she is full of praise for the very kind couple that hosted her during her interminable London nightmare, it is hard not to speculate that this was all calculated design. Out of the hotel and into their house for the entire time, she was conveniently under constant supervision, always directed away from her brother on daily outings, and ever so grateful that they were only too happy to draft Sir Bartle Frere's pro memoria for her. A bit too perfect, no?

More to the point, rightly or wrongly, Sayyida Salme was speaking up for Zanzibari society as a Zanzibari, whereas others sitting a continent away had no problem disaggregating slavery from the rest of society. We can more easily draw a bright line—zero tolerance—today than at a time when slave societies, like Zanzibar, still existed. Back then, when class and race defined every relationship in Zanzibari society, meaning the entire social strata, it was natural to consider the topic for its effects across all of society.[52] Without condoning her positions, can we blame her for flagging that an abrupt end to slavery would precipitate calamitous consequences for slaves and slavers alike in a society where an estimated two-thirds of the population were slaves?[53] Should one perhaps blame others for not having dealt with the question of transition

---

51 Nasser Abdulla Al-Riyami, *Zanzibar Personalities and Events (1828–1972)* (2014); Anne Chappel, "Zanzibar: A Question of History, a Question of Slavery" (July 2010), on www.afrikacalismalarimerkezi.com. As Chappel points out, Zanzibari slavery was weaponized in politics around independence and is now being commercialized for tourists. In her view, fabricated slave sites not only feed tourism but also perpetuate racial splits and stereotypes that continue to stoke island tensions today.

52 To bear this out, Zanzibar became a British protectorate in 1890, but slavery was not completely outlawed there until 1897, and even then concubinage, as a form of "privileged slavery," was still allowed until 1909. As we can see here, even the British, once they were in control, felt the need to transition slowly to maintain social stability. Elke Stockreiter, "British Perceptions of Concubinage and the Patriarchal Arab Household: The Reluctant Abolition of Slavery in Zanzibar, 1890s–1900s," p. 6, in *Slavery & Abolition* (2015).

53 Thomas Vernet, "East Africa: Slave Migrations", p. 3, in *The Encyclopedia of Global Human Migration*, ed. Immanuel Ness (2013).

more holistically? Zanzibar is not the only country where a precipitous end to a slave society created so much social upheaval that the turmoil is still being played out today. In any case, the end of slavery pushed Zanzibar straight into Western colonial hands, presumably according to plan.

And meanwhile, Europe was less inclined to look critically at itself and its own social and class dynamics, as Sayyida Salme was asking her readers to do. She challenged her audience to think about the condition of all lower classes, even suggesting—based on her direct empirical observations—that many Zanzibari slaves had better conditions than many Western workers who were subjected to the dehumanizing pressures of industrialization and capitalism. That is no doubt debatable, but in comparison to other slave states, she knew that Arab society in general, and Zanzibar in particular, had a more nuanced approach, one that rested on Islamic tenets, legal rights, and social conventions. Here slavery existed alongside a complex array of other forms of dependence and covered a spectrum of arrangements, including many slaves who were held primarily for prestige, where productivity was less important than total numbers and personal attachment.[54]

Lest we forget, even Sayyida Salme's mother had slave status as a concubine (*surie,* pl. *sarari*).[55] In another slave society, Sayyida Salme herself would have been born a slave. Instead, as a princess, she was given slaves as her own personal servants and surrounded by caretaking slaves from infancy onward. She even became the owner of her own retinue of slaves, with full responsibility, when she was declared of age at barely twelve. Sayyida Salme grew up amidst an extensive stratification of slaves—including eunuchs, *sarari*, house servants, and plantation workers—who were further stratified amongst themselves. This extreme juxtaposition of slavery and royalty,[56] numbering up to a thousand in the same household, and the intimacy of this day-to-day experience, necessarily gave Sayyida Salme a different view of slavery than the one presented to members of German or British anti-slavery societies or experienced by inland explorers, like the abolitionist crusader David Livingstone.

---

54 Ibid.
55 Abdul Sheriff, "*Suria*: Concubine or Secondary Slave Wife? The Case of Zanzibar in the Nineteenth Century," in G. Campbell and E. Elbourne, *Sex, Power, and Slavery* (2014). Sayyida Salme's mother Djilfidan was torn from her Circassian homeland as part of a century of Russian invasions that eliminated and dispersed up to 90 percent of the indigenous population. Stephen Shenfield, "The Circassians—A Forgotten Genocide?" from *The Massacre in History*, ed. Mark Leven and Penny Roberts (2006).
56 This tendency to separate classes and recognize noble status was hardly limited to Oman and Zanzibar. We can keep in mind that Europe also had its share of royalty at the time. Sayyida Salme was able to connect into this echelon of society through her own royal status.

The more intractable point is that most of this slavery, certainly the East African trade, rested on hierarchical concepts of race. Race—and especially blackness—was the salient marker of social status and human value. Sayyida Salme was hardly alone in taking this view. This was not a matter of West over East in a hierarchy of international relations—putting Arab and Zanzibari society down—but a matter of social relations, putting blacks and natives down. To say it clearly, the anti-slavery movement was not seeking to elevate the status of black Africans as equals to enlightened Europeans. Scholars have noted, for example, that foreign missionaries took slavery to be a "natural phenomenon for the African *Naturvölker*," which fed right into the colonial ideology of the time. Explorers were entering the "dark continent," and freed Africans were prized as candidates for evangelizing and enlightening, even to the point of keeping younger ones from their families.[57] Moreover, the British view, as documented explicitly, considered white slavery far more "revolting" than black slavery, indicating that even purported anti-slavers harbored racist views that debased Africans.[58]

The places in the *Memoirs* where Sayyida Salme treats Africans as less capable and less worthy were the most difficult to translate because they are so uncomfortable, so dismaying to take in. She was otherwise open to and appreciative of different races and origins, making it all the more striking how much she deprecated indigenous blacks. But she wrote about the behavior she saw around her, and to see her, and many others, jump from such observations to wholesale determinations of inferiority and a license to pre-judge challenges us to realize how blinkered we can be. How easy it is to confuse cause and effect, with no apparent awareness that the conditions of slavery, limited access to resources, and disparaging attitudes of society would give rise to such behavior, rather than reflect a natural state of being. In the same way that Sayyida Salme sought to open the eyes of the European public, our eyes have been opened through greater exposure and understanding over the decades. Sayyida Salme is, of course, not in a position to take her words back today, but I think she would if she could.

Today the international community understands human rights differently and rejects all human bondage and racist hierarchies. We would like to believe that we have a different understanding of humanity now, and that we also

---

57 Clifford Pereira, see footnote 48, p. 9.
58 Quoting British Consul Sir John Kirk, who began consular duties the year Sayyida Salme left Zanzibar, after five years accompanying explorer David Livingstone as his physician and naturalist, as cited in Jeremy Prestholdt, "Symbolic Subjection and Social Rebirth: Objectification in Urban Zanzibar," p. 129, in *Domesticating the World: African Consumerism and the Genealogies of Globalization* (2008).

would not have "othered" Sayyida Salme in the same way that she herself experienced at the time.[59] The *Memoirs* are part of a rich tapestry of complex, at times contradictory and counterintuitive, dynamics of history that deserve a nuanced, holistic, intersectional view of the world. As my friend SB Rawz says: "Acknowledging the complexity of humans, our history, and our institutions cannot erase their value, unless we trade one kind of oversimplification for another."[60] In this era of soundbites and stereotypes, cancel culture and caricatures, it is all the more important to listen fully, lest we miss some of what is really going on.

Certainly, the assessment is a personal one. Each of us can decide individually whether Sayyida Salme's racist statements overshadow the rest of her writing. If we take up the challenge, though, we can both reject some of what she had to say and recognize what she may have to teach us—about her life and times, but also what she reflects back to us about our own lives and times. And with that, I would let Sayyida Salme have the last word from the *Memoirs*, as she was the first to admit:

> *The events of my life are all too varied, and they in turn have shaped my feelings and perspectives. People are in large part no more than what their lives, experiences, and given circumstances make of them.* (Memoirs, *page 217*)

---

59 Sayyida Salme describes this stereotyping and caricaturing more fully in her *Briefe nach der Heimat* (Letters Home), which I expect to release as a new translation in 2023.
60 Rawzcoaching.com (June 28, 2021).

ON TRANSLATING

When I first embarked on this translation more than twenty years ago, it was me and my little Langenscheidt to take my German that extra mile. I got through one-third of the original *Memoirs*[61] and then set the project aside. A career, a child, a couple of professional books, and considerable time and events later, I found the neglected file deep in my storage drive and decided to pick up where I had left off, literally with the next paragraph. The pandemic was still rocking the world, and as we hunkered down, I was finding room for other things.

It began as a desire to get to know my esteemed ancestor better, to literally get inside her words. She had taken care to leave this record behind; I had the privilege to explore its import. As I delved in, I found real pleasure in revealing her meaning. To make sure I could find my voice in response to hers, I translated the first run cold, without any comparison to other texts.

When I used round two to cross-check against the two early English translations,[62] I was stunned by their sloppiness (what else to call it when whole words, sentences, paragraphs, even chapters, simply go missing?). One translation had some lovely renditions, but must have been done in haste. The other translation took such license that the translator's discretion at times seemed to morph into his own flights of fancy. Perhaps notions of authenticity have changed over the years,[63] but in neither case was I truly reading the author's own story. Seeing these reconstructed versions of her tale, I was no longer just intrigued for myself. I felt compelled to translate for others.

Also compelling was that I have had my mother as a partner. Although the translation is mine, she has given it her meticulous review and quality control, along with much sensitivity and thoughtfulness. What better way to continue the family legacy than by combining generational forces in the effort. It appears that mother and daughter had already collaborated once before

---

61 *Memoiren einer arabischen Prinzessin* made its German debut as two volumes in 1886, which are reproduced as a composite publication here. Public interest was so great that four editions were sold that same year.

62 The first English translation came out in London by Ward and Downey in 1888 as *Memoirs of an Arabian Princess* and also appeared in New York through D. Appleton and Co. that same year, with no translator named. A decade later, in 1907, a new—apparently unauthorized—translation was presented in New York by Lionel Strachey with Doubleday, Page and Co.

63 Almost ironically, the Lionel Strachey edition included a front section titled "Authenticity of these Memoirs," in which the translator informed his readers that his book, having to do with "the Black Continent and its peoples," presented "so romantic a supposal seeming to require confirmation," which he then delivered.

when Rosa, Sayyida Salme's youngest and my direct ancestor, helped hone the original manuscript. Perhaps this translation, too, will become part of the greater family story.

One need not look far in the marketplace of books and ideas to appreciate the mutable form that Sayyida Salme's legacy has taken and will continue to take, whether in the service of scholarship, social or political agendas, or commerce. This publication, too, is inevitably new and different, but sets itself apart from the readily available translations and other variations[64] by hewing as closely as possible to the original German.[65]

We are all born into our circumstances. For my great-great-grandmother, that meant a fantastical combination of royalty and slavery out of which her extraordinary life unfolded and to which she gave voice in her *Memoirs*. For me, born German and raised American, and for my mother, raised in Germany and then raising her children in the United States, we bring both languages from both sides of the ocean. It feels like we have been perfectly placed these generations later to restore and revive Sayyida Salme's voice. Rather than speak for her (as in the perfect German word *bevormunden*, to "put in front of the mouth"), our project strives to reinforce her story in her own words, as much as a translation can. This book is meant to free her voice, to have her speak directly from her time to ours by both rebooting back to the original and refreshing for today.

Our two watchwords have been *accuracy*, saying what she says, and *authenticity*, portraying what she presents. My mother and I have been mindful of Sayyida Salme's writing, word-for-word, along with her context, while staying attuned to her wit, irony, passion, nuance, and even silence, all of which emerge from her pages. I have kept her exact volume, chapter, and paragraph structure, even virtually all of the same sentence structure (although changing many semi-colons to periods), as well as the one-off dashes she so characteristically inserted. But the goal was also accessibility and readability for modern eyes and

---

64 In addition to the two original English translations, G.S.P. Freeman-Grenville published an annotated and somewhat corrected version of the 1888 London edition almost a century later, in 1981. Since then, with open season on copyright, both the 1888 and 1907 translations have become available in multiple guises, some more packaged than others. Of note as well, Annegret Nippa took the significant step of resurfacing the original German work in 1989, also a century later, with her lightly edited *Leben im Sultanspalast*.

65 One other more recent English translation also stands apart for its commitment to accuracy. Anyone interested in the full historical context will be grateful for Professor Emeri van Donzel's remarkably comprehensive and thoroughly researched book, *An Arabian Princess Between Two Worlds* (1993). Containing his own translations of the *Memoirs*, *Letters Home*, and other writings, this scholarly work has been an important resource for us and others seeking to learn more about Sayyida Salme's life and legacy.

ears, a matter of adjusting Victorian recounting to contemporary resonance—keeping her tone and style, while speaking plainly. For it must be said: The original *Memoirs* are quite fluid in their German narrative and deserve an easy, lucid reading in English, with some elegance as well.

It has felt like the right time and place for me to do this—perhaps you know the feeling. I am not a professional translator, but I am a trained wordsmith. I have played with words all my life. My early years as a transactional lawyer spilled into poetry to offset the rigors of legal memo writing. As I eased into my metier over time, I developed the deep conviction that you can always find some combination of words to make things work. I have practiced the written form as a skill; I have published about the power of shared articulation. The joy of words, both to convey understanding and ground common understandings, has given me much professional and personal fulfillment over the years. And so it has been a joy here, the ultimate word game. Like an extended crossword puzzle, I have sought that exact word, that exact turn of phrase, to match the meaning and suit the setting. Like a game of pick-up sticks, I have tried to take that layered, interwoven German and give the whole just enough daylight to flow into neatly unpacked English.

Along the way, I also had a choice to make.[66] To be true to Sayyida Salme's intentions, I opted to incorporate edits she had left behind.[67] In her additions and deletions, she brought forth helpful clarifications and better judgments several years after publication. With so much preparatory work already done, why was this edited version never published? Whatever the case, the decision to honor her subsequently annotated version became a further justification for an updated translation.

For my own process, what a difference two decades can make. The technology boost since my first foray in 2001 has been remarkable, something I envisioned little more at the turn of my century than Sayyida Salme could have anticipated at the turn of hers. Now, in the internet, smartphone, and app age, the

---

66 There were other choices to be made as well regarding the spelling of Arabic words and names in English. I am aligned with Professor van Donzel in mostly following the author's original spellings "for historical and linguistic reasons" (ibid. at p. x), with a few adjustments, like ungermanizing "sch" to "sh." I also appreciate the author's son's approach in the biography of his grandfather "to follow my own judgment in the matter," after noting five accepted English spellings of the capital of Oman. "In the circumstances I hope my arbitrary decision will be accepted with forbearance." From the Introduction to Rudolph Said-Ruete, *Said bin Sultan (1791–1856)—Ruler of Oman and Zanzibar: His Place in the History of Arabia and East Africa*, p. xviii (1929).

67 Her book with handwritten annotations is available digitally in the Leiden University Libraries Special Collections at NINO SR 613 a-b. Professor van Donzel also reflected Sayyida Salme's subsequent edits in his book (ibid.), in a rigorous presentation that clearly identifies deletions and additions for direct comparison.

translator's arsenal is remarkable: multiple tabs for various German-English dictionary sites (and immediate visibility of dozens of possible translations), tabs for searches in actual translated texts (turning phrases into scores of sample paragraphs), tabs for synonyms (and synonyms of synonyms), and, of course, general Google searches. Translating has always been a skill, but what used to be mostly in the head has acquired such abundant supporting resources that it is now more like a mix-and-match puzzle of invigorating proportions.

That brings me to our other watchword: *respect*. In this translation, I have sought to reflect Sayyida Salme's own words and style, but go no further. Within this safe harbor, I could provide a faithful reproduction without trying to tease out the unspoken, fill in the interstices, or add manufactured details. Unlike those who have fictionalized her tale, as more than a few have done, I dared not trespass and write the story for her. Instead, this translation let me work within my comfort zone, a chance to get closer—respectfully—without overstepping.

But even translators have a tremendous responsibility to the authors of the works they translate. Inserting myself in this role, I have felt that calling perhaps more than most. How interesting, on the one hand, that the original English translator for the London publication was not named—no accountability there. But equally interesting, on the other hand, is that the subsequent English translator in the United States named himself prominently on the title page, perhaps more accountable to his own work than her original. I have meant to position myself differently, both named and accountable, but as a conduit, a bridge, to Sayyida Salme herself.

May the spotlight on this story shine back on her, in her full intensity and complexity. It is with all due deference that I seek only to illuminate her own words for all of us, to turn her German into English with utmost fidelity, in both senses of the word.

LIST OF IMAGES

[iv] Indian Ocean showing the relationship between Oman and Zanzibar, two countries that were conveniently connected through monsoon trade winds that blew downward from the cool, dry northeast during December to March and then reversed to blow upward from the warm, wet southwest from May to October, while also connecting to India to complete the trade triangle; by Max S. Stumpf, © 2022.

[v] Map of the island of Zanzibar, showing select nineteenth-century destinations, most of which are mentioned in the *Memoirs*; by Max S. Stumpf, © 2022.

[xi] Book announcement pasted into a scrapbook that belonged to the author's son, Rudolph Said-Ruete, including the following text: "Sensational novelty! An important contribution to the cultural history of the Orient. The author is the sister of Sultan Said Barghash [sic] of Zanzibar. The first work of an Oriental woman about the Orient and its social and societal relationships. Fourth edition, September 18, 1886. Publishing company of Friedrich Luckhardt in Berlin;" located in the Leiden University Libraries at Or. 27.135 C1.

[xiii] Hard cover of an edition of Volume 1 of *Memoiren einer arabischen Prinzessin* from 1886; from the collection of Alexander von Brand, great-grandson of Antonie Brandeis, oldest daughter of the author; here rimmed in blue, as compared to the translator's family copy rimmed in brown.

[xiv & xv] End paper and title page of the third edition of Volume 1 of *Memoiren einer arabischen Prinzessin* from 1886; from the translator's family collection.

[xvi] Bookplate of Emily Troemer, granddaughter of the author through Rosa Troemer and grandmother of the translator; appearing in Emily Troemer's books in the translator's family collection.

[xviii] Studio portrait of the author taken by photographer H.F. Plate in Hamburg, Germany around 1868, not long after her arrival, and used as the frontispiece for her 1886 publication of the *Memoiren*.

[2] Drawing of Bet il Mtoni in Zanzibar of unknown origin; provided by Torrence Royer, curator of www.zanzibarhistory.com.

[4] "Vue de M'Tony, Résidence de Campagne du Sultan, prise de la pièce d'eau"; from C. Guillain, *Voyage á la Côte Orientale d'Afrique, exécuté pendant les*

années 1846, 1847, and 1848 (1856), in the Leiden University Libraries at NINO SR 190a-c.

[10] "Vue de M'Tony"; ibid.

[13] "Ruined Palace of Syed Saaid ben Sultan at Mtony," by Celia L. Weeks, who travelled with her American husband and captain to Zanzibar in 1869; also provided by Torrence Royer.

[28] A rare portrait of Sayyid Said bin Sultan, Sultan of Oman and ruler of Zanzibar from 1806 to 1856. It was used by Rudolph Said-Ruete, the author's son, as the frontispiece for the biography of his grandfather, with likely attribution to Lieutenant Henry Blosse Lynch, who was in Muscat in the early 1830s; presented to the Peabody Museum in Salem, Massachusetts, in 1906 by the wife of Michael W. Shepard, who traded in Zanzibar from 1837 to 1852. R. Said-Ruete, *Said bin Sultan (1791-1856): Ruler of Oman and Zanzibar—His Place in the History of Arabia and East Africa (1929).*

[29] A colored replica of the original portrait by Amy Clive Edwards and presented by the Peabody Essex Museum to Rudolph Said-Ruete, the author's son, in 1929; now in the Leiden University Libraries at Or. 27.135 D15.

[36] Top: The author's signature in tunghra-style calligraphic Arabic, translating roughly from bottom to top "Salme bint Said Sultan," as it appeared on the title page of her *Memoiren* in 1886. Bottom: Handwritten version of the author's signature. There may be some question about how to properly anglicize the author's name, as the Arabic shows variations, and spellings vary in the secondary literature. However, the author and her family consistently wrote "Salme" in both German and English contexts (see, for example, the great bookcase from her son and her own use in the original *Memoirs* (pages 232 and 9 here)), so there should be no doubt that this is the correct spelling.

[45] Coffee servers as part of the image captioned "Some Presents from Zanzibar" in *Three Journeys* by Viscountess Cave (Anne Estella Sarah Penford Matthews Cave) published in 1928; in the Leiden University Libraries at NINO SR 135.

[46] "Vue de la Ville de Zanzibar (Prise du Mouillage)"; also from C. Guillain's *Voyage á la Côte Orientale d'Afrique.*

[54] Painting of Stone Town's coastline signed and dated "Rosa Ruete 1886" by the author's youngest daughter; from the translator's family collection.

[65] Painting by Rosa Troemer with "Bet il Ras–Zanzibar 1888" written on the back, likely from her second trip to Zanzibar with her mother; from the translator's family collection. Construction of the palace was started by Rosa's grandfather, Sayyid Said bin Sultan, in 1847, but never completed.

[72] "Muscat from the Harbour," from R. Temple, *Sixteen Views of Places in the Persian Gulph, taken in the years 1809-1810* (1813); located in the Leiden University Libraries at Or. 27.135 J17.

[79] Top: "Muscat Harbour from the Fisher-men's Rock"; ibid. Bottom: "A View of Mutra from the East," ibid.

[83] "Altes arabisches Kriegschiff" (an old Arab warship) handwritten by Rudolph Said-Ruete, the author's son, under a photo in the album he gave as part of his collection to Professor Christiaan Snouck Hurgronje in 1929; now in the Leiden University Libraries at Or. 27.135 H5.

[88] Two images of Madjid bin Said, Sultan of Zanzibar from 1856 to 1870. Top: Colored lithograph; located in the Leiden University Libraries at Or. 27.135 D18. Bottom: Image provided by Torrence Royer, curator of www.zanzibarhistory.com.

[116 & 117] Two of four studio portraits of the author by photographer H.F. Plate, taken in Hamburg in 1868; from the Leiden University Libraries at Or. 27.135 D1.

[118 & 119] End paper and title page of the third edition of Volume 2 of *Memoiren einer arabischen Prinzessin* from 1886; from the translator's family collection.

[120] Bookplate of Rudolph Said-Ruete, the author's son, with calligraphy stating "Rudolph Said Ruete, son of Salima bint Said Sultan, ruler of Oman and Zanzibar"; appearing in various books in the special bookcase located in the Netherlands Institute of the Near East (NINO) in Leiden.

[122] Drawing of Stone Town viewed from the sea with the following handwritten notation at the bottom: " –sibar 18?: Handzeichnung v. Heinrich Ruete für seine Eltern in Hamburg" ([Zan]zibar 18– : Sketch by Heinrich Ruete for his parents in Hamburg); from the translator's family collection. Rudolph Heinrich Ruete, who went by Heinrich, was the author's husband.

[136] "Zanzibar from the Sea" included by Richard F. Burton in Volume 1 of his book *Zanzibar: City, Island, and Coast* (1872); located in the Leiden University Libraries at NINO SR 115a-b.

[151] A Zanzibari shore scene by Rosa Troemer, the author's youngest daughter, likely from 1888 during her second trip to Zanzibar with her mother; from the translator's family collection.

[157] "Plan de Zanzibar" from 1846 with a map of Stone Town before the lagoon was filled in, noting A through D on the coastline as buildings of the royal family; also from C. Guillain's *Voyage á la Côte Orientale d'Afrique*. Ngambo is the area east of the bridge.

[174] Image of Barghash bin Said, Sultan of Zanzibar from 1870 to 1888, taken during his visit to London in 1875, when the author had hoped to meet him; provided by Alexander von Brand from his family collection.

[188] Horizontal: "Zanzibar, Cloves plantation"; from Photo Artist A.R.P de Lord of Zanzibar, showing one of many clove plantations that were introduced during Sayyid Said bin Sultan's reign and helped the island prosper. Vertical: "Natives picking Cloves, Zanzibar"; from A.C. Gomes & Son of Zanzibar. Both part of the Torrence Royer and Pamela Washington Collection of Zanzibar Images and Archives at the Sultan Qaboos Cultural Center in Washington, DC.

[195] View of Stone Town with the following notation on the back: "Haus von Bibi Salme, Sansibar 1867" (House of Mistress Salme, Zanzibar 1867); provided by Alexander von Brand from his family collection. According to Professor van Donzel, "[T]he four lower barred windows belonged to the house. The upper storey was later added when the Hansing firm acquired the house." Emeri van Donzel, *An Arabian Princess Between Two Worlds*, page 15 (1993).

[200] Image of Heinrich Ruete, the author's husband, with the following notation on the back: "Für Tony" (referring to Antonie Brandeis, the author's oldest child) and "Mein Vater, geb. 1839, gest. 1870, Rudolph Heinrich Ruete" (My father, born 1839, died 1870, Rudolph Heinrich Ruete); provided by Alexander von Brand from his family collection.

[204] Image from a glass plate of Sultan Barghash, together with his traveling entourage in London in 1875; located in the Leiden University Libraries at Or. 27-135 D37-13.

[211] Image of the author with her children (from the left): Antonie (Tony, Thawka) Brandeis, Said Ruete (later Rudolph Said-Ruete), and Rosalie (Rosa, Ghuza) Troemer; from the translator's family collection.

[215] Itinerary of the author's travels from her hometown, Berlin, to the island of Zanzibar in 1885; by Max S. Stumpf, © 2022.

[230] Image of the author's husband, Heinrich Ruete, with an imprint of "E. Bieber, Hamburg" and handwritten "1863" on the back; from the family collection of Alexander von Brand.

[231] Image of the author in Germany; provided by Alexander von Brand from his family collection.

[232] Original bookcase with the golden header "Seyyidah Salme (Emily Ruete)," designed by the author's son Rudolph to house the "Said-Ruete Library," as the collection became known, that he presented to the Oriental Institute (Oosters Instituut) founded by family friend Professor Christiaan Snouck Hurgronje; currently located in the Netherlands Institute for the Near East (NINO) in Leiden.

[234] Front and back of one of more than a hundred small, handcrafted packets containing sunflower seeds that were handed out by the translator and her brother Martin to Omani participants and other visitors on the last day of the 2005 Smithsonian Folklife Festival on the National Mall in Washington, DC, which featured four programs: Oman, USDA Forest Service, Food Culture USA, and Latino Music.

[260] Seaside view of the port of Stone Town, Zanzibar, signed on the front side and dated "W. Rice. Ship River Krishna. 12.12.70"; located in the Leiden University Libraries at Or. 27.135 D16.

[Back cover] Top: One of four studio portraits of the author by photographer H.F. Plate, taken in Hamburg in 1868; with the Leiden University Libraries at Or. 27.135 D1. Bottom: The translator in front of the special "family" bookcase in the NINO on her first visit to Leiden in 2014.

View of Stone Town, Zanzibar

Made in the USA
Monee, IL
30 January 2023

26602327R00155